THE ALL-SUSTAINING AIR

The All-Sustaining Air

*Romantic Legacies and Renewals in
British, American, and Irish
Poetry since 1900*

MICHAEL O'NEILL

OXFORD
UNIVERSITY PRESS

Great Clarendon Street, Oxford OX2 6DP

Oxford University Press is a department of the University of Oxford.
It furthers the University's objective of excellence in research, scholarship,
and education by publishing worldwide in

Oxford New York

Auckland Cape Town Dar es Salaam Hong Kong Karachi
Kuala Lumpur Madrid Melbourne Mexico City Nairobi
New Delhi Shanghai Taipei Toronto

With offices in

Argentina Austria Brazil Chile Czech Republic France Greece
Guatemala Hungary Italy Japan Poland Portugal Singapore
South Korea Switzerland Thailand Turkey Ukraine Vietnam

Oxford is a registered trade mark of Oxford University Press
in the UK and in certain other countries

Published in the United States
by Oxford University Press Inc., New York

© Michael O'Neill 2007

The moral rights of the author have been asserted
Database right Oxford University Press (maker)

First published 2007

All rights reserved. No part of this publication may be reproduced,
stored in a retrieval system, or transmitted, in any form or by any means,
without the prior permission in writing of Oxford University Press,
or as expressly permitted by law, or under terms agreed with the appropriate
reprographics rights organization. Enquiries concerning reproduction
outside the scope of the above should be sent to the Rights Department,
Oxford University Press, at the address above

You must not circulate this book in any other binding or cover
and you must impose the same condition on any acquirer

British Library Cataloguing in Publication Data

Data available

Library of Congress Cataloging in Publication Data

Data available

Typeset by Laserwords Private Limited, Chennai, India
Printed in Great Britain
on acid-free paper by
Biddles Ltd., King's Lynn, Norfolk

ISBN 978–0–19–929928–7

1 3 5 7 9 10 8 6 4 2

In memory
of Jonathan Wordsworth (1932–2006)

Acknowledgements

The author has tried, in quoting copyright material, to abide by the conventions governing 'fair dealing'.

A number of chapters, or parts of them, have appeared in different forms in the following publications, to whose editors I am indebted: Chapter 1 in *Romantic Voices, Romantic Poetics: Selected Papers from the Regensburg Conference of the German Society for English Romanticism*, ed. Christoph Bode and Katharina Rennhak (Wissenschaftlicher Verlag Trier, 2005) and in *The Monstrous Debt*, ed. Damian Walford Davies and Richard Marggraf Turley (Wayne State University Press, 2006); Chapter 2 in the *Journal of Anglo-Italian Studies*, 8 (2006); Chapter 5 in *Romanticism and Religion from William Cowper to Wallace Stevens*, ed. Gavin Hopps and Jane Stabler (Ashgate Press, 2006); Chapter 6 in *The Wordsworth Circle*, 31 (2000), and *English Romanticism and the Celtic World*, ed. Gerard Carruthers and Alan Rawes (Cambridge University Press, 2003), and in *Representing Ireland: Past, Present and Future*, ed. Frank Beardow and Alison O'Malley-Younger (Sunderland University Press, 2005); Chapter 8 in *The Thing about Roy Fisher*, ed. John Kerrigan and Peter Robinson (Liverpool University Press, 2000).

Ideas for a number of chapters received their first public airing in a number of invited talks, and I am grateful to the relevant organizers and institutions: the organizers of the Regensburg Conference in 2003 of the German Society for English Romanticism; Monica Class and Felicity James for inviting me to speak at the 'Romantics Realignments' seminar in Oxford in 2003; Christoph Bode for inviting me to lecture in Munich in 2005; the University of Glasgow for an invitation to speak in 2002; the Scottish Universities International Summer School for invitations to lecture in 2004 and 2005; the Byron Conference in New York in 2001; Edward Larrissy for inviting me to speak at the 'Romanticism and Colonialism' conference at Leeds in 2005; Nicholas Roe for inviting me to deliver the George Jack Memorial Lecture at St Andrews in 2006; Peter Vassallo for inviting me to speak at the Anglo-Italian conference in Malta in 2005; Essaka Joshua for inviting me to speak at the Midlands Romantic Seminar in 2006; and the late Jonathan Wordsworth for inviting me to deliver the Pete Laver Memorial Lecture at the Wordsworth Summer Conference in 2000.

For encouragement, help, and stimulus, I am indebted to many people, especially Ash Amin, Bernard Beatty, Christoph Bode, Sean Burke, Richard Cronin, Patricia Ellul-Micallef, Marilyn Gaull, Gavin Hopps, John Kerrigan, Edward Larrissy, Jamie McKendrick, Alison O'Malley-Younger, Posy O'Neill, Catherine Paine, Seamus Perry, Alan Rawes, Gareth Reeves, Stephen Regan,

Nicholas Roe, Mark Sandy, Matthew Scott, Jane Stabler, Peter Vassallo, Pat Waugh, Timothy Webb, Sarah Wootton, and Jonathan Wordsworth. I owe a great debt to Andrew McNeillie at OUP for all his advice, and to Jean van Altena for her immensely attentive copy-editing. Anita O'Connell has been a splendid research assistant, helping, among other things, with preparing the bibliography. I am grateful to Durham University for the award of Research Leave, and to the British Academy for the award of Overseas Conference Grants in 2001 and 2005.

The book is dedicated to the memory of a remarkable critic, scholar, and teacher, who possessed and communicated a profound sense of Romantic poetry's continuing life.

Contents

Note on Texts	xi
Introduction: 'Original Response'	1
1. 'The All-Sustaining Air': Variations on a Romantic Metaphor	15
2. 'A Vision of Reality': Mid-to-Late Yeats	34
3. 'Dialectic Ways': T. S. Eliot and Counter-Romanticism	60
4. 'The Guts of the Living': Auden and Spender in the 1930s	83
5. 'The Death of Satan': Stevens's 'Esthétique du Mal', Evil, and the Romantic Imagination	105
6. 'Shining in Modest Glory': Post-Romantic Strains in Kavanagh, Heaney, Mahon, Carson, and Others	121
7. 'Just Another Twist in the Plot': Paul Muldoon's 'Madoc: A Mystery'	145
8. 'Deep Shocks of Recognition' and 'Gutted' Romanticism: Geoffrey Hill and Roy Fisher	165
Bibliography	192
Index	203

Note on Texts

The following texts have been used for major Romantic poets: unless indicated otherwise, quotations from the authors in question are taken from these texts, with page numbers given for prose passages. Occasionally, short titles are used.

The Complete Poetry and Prose of William Blake, newly rev. edn., ed. David V. Erdman, commentary by Harold Bloom (New York: Anchor–Doubleday, 1988).

William Wordsworth, ed. Stephen Gill, Oxford Authors (1984; Oxford: Oxford University Press, 1990 (with corr.)).

Coleridge: Poetical Works, ed. Ernest Hartley Coleridge (1912; London: Oxford University Press, 1967).

Byron, ed. Jerome J. McGann, The Oxford Authors (Oxford: Oxford University Press, 1986).

Percy Bysshe Shelley: The Major Works, ed. Zachary Leader and Michael O'Neill (Oxford: Oxford University Press, 2003).

John Keats, ed. Elizabeth Cook, The Oxford Authors (Oxford: Oxford University Press, 1990).

References to Shakespeare are to *The Norton Shakespeare*, gen. ed. Stephen Greenblatt (New York: Norton, 1997). The Bible is cited from the King James (Authorized) Version. Dante is quoted from the Temple Classics edition.

Introduction: 'Original Response'

I

Many of the finest poets writing after 1900 engage in strenuous tussle as they respond to Romantic poetry. The wish to be absolutely modern coexists with an intricate view of the meaning and value of tradition. The desire to escape mere self-expression cannot stifle the sense of the poem as a place where modes of self-revelation occur. If a poem serves only the autotelic circle of itself, it is also a way of happening. The political aspirations—and doubts—of the Romantics can seem inseparable from 'battles long ago' (Wordsworth, 'The Solitary Reaper', 20), yet they shape and bear on the understanding of many subsequent historical events. Stephen Spender, introducing his co-edited collection *Poems for Spain*, was able to cite as relevant Keats's words about the state of the nation in the aftermath of Peterloo as 'No contest between Whig and Tory—but between Right and Wrong'.[1] The blissful dawn of revolutionary Romantic optimism has proved hard to sustain, though Allen Ginsberg was happy to enlist Blake in his prophetic denunciations and celebrations of contemporary America. But Romanticism's accompanying apocalyptic intimations have proved highly influential. Wilfred Owen, reaching towards a visionary overcoming of militaristic enmity, turns back to Shelley's *Laon and Cythna* for the title of his 'Strange Meeting'.[2] His 'Exposure' opens with the assonantally nerve-twisting 'Our brains ache, in the merciless iced east wind that knives us', deploying what Owen's editor Jon Stallworthy calls an 'ironic echo' of the start of Keats's 'Ode to a Nightingale': 'My heart aches, and a drowsy numbness pains | My sense' (1–2). Whether the echo is, in fact, simply 'ironic' is arguable.[3] It is more the case that a Keatsian intensity unravels itself and turns out to have terrifying applicability to life in the trenches. Again, as has frequently been noted, Yeats's 'The Second Coming' derives its diagnostic

---

[1] Keats is quoted from Stephen Spender and John Lehmann (eds.), *Poems for Spain* (London: Hogarth Press, 1939), p. 9.
[2] Compare *Laon and Cythna* [*The Revolt of Islam*], 5, st. 14, in *Shelley: Poetical Works*, ed. Thomas Hutchinson, rev. G. M. Matthews (London: Oxford University Press, 1970).
[3] Owen is quoted from Wilfred Owen, *The Poems*, ed. and intro. by Jon Stallworthy (London: Hogarth Press, 1985). Editor's comment is on p. 163.

language, 'The best lack all conviction, while the worst | Are full of passionate intensity' (7–8), from the Fury's temptation in Shelley's *Prometheus Unbound*, Act I: 'The good want power, but to weep barren tears. | The powerful goodness want: worse need for them' (625–6). But he also draws his nightmarish sense of the shape of things to come, 'a vast image' (12) that 'Troubles my sight' (13), from Wordsworth's experience of 'huge and mighty Forms' as 'the trouble of my dreams' (*The Prelude*, 1805, I. 425, 427).[4]

The result of these reactive and responsive interplays is often what might be termed a post-Romantic doubleness of vision, one marked by a generous scepticism, by an inclusive irony that shares with its Schlegelian forerunner the view that 'The romantic kind of poetry . . . recognizes as its first commandment that the will of the poet can tolerate no law above itself'.[5] There are complications. T. S. Eliot, for example, wrestles with the desire that poetry should be itself and not another thing, and the belief that there is a Logos beyond human language. Yet it is only through poetry that poetry is conquered in his work. Moreover, no poet is more aware than Eliot is that 'the communication | Of the dead is tongued with fire beyond the language of the living' ('Little Gidding', I).[6] The lines cheat the ear into hearing a 'communication' between 'the dead' and 'the living'. But for Eliot, the dialogue is not straightforward; any poetic Pentecostal visitation will be accessed only with great difficulty. Yet those who, 'tongued with fire', ride above and alongside the chariot of his own work include, despite his ostensible and ostentatious hostility, the Romantic poets.

An aspect of Romanticism's legacy is the way in which its major poets compose a ghosting presence in subsequent writing. In 'Skylarks' Ted Hughes confronts and exorcizes a Shelleyan wraith. But he also invites us to reconsider 'To a Skylark', a poem which, set against Hughes's 'Skylarks', emerges as Neoplatonist in its pursuit of disembodied essence and surprisingly deft in its realism. 'Bird thou never wert' (2), the Romantic poet exclaims in his 'To a Skylark'; yet his stanza form moulds itself effortlessly to the bird's soaring flight and its sustained song. In the following chiastic alexandrine, Shelley captures the bird's dual achievement: 'And singing still dost soar, and soaring ever singest' (10). His skylark is at once natural object and adequate, even reproving symbol; it exists in relation to the poet's alienated subjectivity as an unreachable spur, prompting questions and envious assertions.

[4] Yeats is quoted from W. B. Yeats, *The Poems*, ed. Daniel Albright (London: Dent, 1990) from which all Yeats's poems are quoted.
[5] Friedrich Schlegel, 'Athenaum Fragments', 116, in *The Origins of Modern Critical Thought: German Aesthetic and Literary Criticism from Lessing to Hegel*, ed. David Simpson (Cambridge: Cambridge University Press, 1988), p. 193.
[6] T. S. Eliot, *The Complete Poems and Plays* (London: Faber, 1969). Unless indicated otherwise, this edition is used for all quotations from Eliot's poetry and drama.

Although Hughes, writing one and a half centuries after Shelley, abandons regularity of metre, he rehearses in a revitalizing, original way many of the impulses and dilemmas at work in the Romantic poem. He appears to deliver a devastating retort to Shelley's symbol-mongering when, in his poem's first section, he speaks of the skylark as

> A whippet head, barbed like a hunting arrow
> But leaden
> With muscle
> For the struggle
> Against
> Earth's centre.⁷

Yet the twin processes of legacy and renewal, highlighted throughout the present study, kindle this passage into poetic life. Hughes writes to his present and in an idiom satisfyingly true to the speech of his present, as that eye-on-the-object image of the 'whippet head' bears witness. At the same time, this present is aware of the past as anything but another country. Deep in the poem's bones is a conviction that we perceive the natural world in the light of our concern with origins, with the struggle to survive which led primitive human beings to invent 'a hunting arrow'. To the degree that Romanticism participates in Enlightenment dreams of progress, Hughes's poem acts as a salutary check. His bird is part of a natural cycle that is far removed from the benignly unbetraying Nature of Wordsworth's 'Tintern Abbey'. In section II, as 'A towered bird, shot through the crested head | With the command, Not die', it is said to be 'Obedient as to death a dead thing'. And yet Hughes serendipitously shows his alliance with Romantic practice when, in the lines just quoted from section I, he produces a homespun reworking and mirror-image of Shelley's stanza. Instead of four short lines in trochaic metre followed by an alexandrine, Hughes supplies a long line followed by five short ones, describing the 'struggle | Against | Earth's centre'. There, the preposition 'Against' takes a good deal of emphasis. Fighters against 'Earth's centre', the skylarks have much in common with one kind of Romantic poetry, a poetry nerved with and by would-be transcendental aspiration, a kind often associated with Shelley. Arguably, this kind is figured in section VI's account of the birds as 'The mad earth's missionaries', a phrase that attributes madness both to the earth and the birds that seek escape from it, and plays its own variation on Shelley's attribution to the bird of 'harmonious madness' (103).

The poem's form opens itself to the dynamic provisionality and fascination with process central to the Romantic project. Hughes recognizes that his own

---

⁷ Quoted from Ted Hughes, *Collected Poems*, ed. Paul Keegan (London: Faber, 2003). The text includes two sections (IV and VIII) 'not present in the *Wodwo* [1967] text, but . . . added to the poem as reprinted in [*Selected Poems, 1957–1967* (1972)]', p. 1252.

hunger for verbal apprehension of reality generates a sprawl of conflicting meanings. Use of different sections suggests that there are, if not thirteen, then more than one way of looking at a skylark. In one section the 'sun will not take notice' (IV), indifferent to the lark's frantic efforts; in the next it is the aspiring bird's only ally as the section alights on the unexpected grace of a long, flowing, 'endless' line: 'Only the sun goes silently and endlessly on with the lark's song' (V). As in 'The Ancient Mariner', cosmic imagery shifts in accordance with states of feeling.[8] Moreover, similes and metaphors announce the work done by a poet searching for ways of grasping his subject. The skylark in both Hughes and Shelley embodies a spontaneity of song that contrasts with the human poet, who, Hamlet-like, looks 'before and after' ('To a Skylark', 86). 'I suppose you just gape and let your gaspings | Rip in and out through your voicebox', Hughes asserts, sardonically yet admiringly in section III, his own voice mimicking the bird's vocalizing energy as it relishes the enjambed 'Rip'. In the same section, his comment on the song turns it into a fascinating emblem of lyric poetry: 'O song, incomprehensibly both ways— | Joy! Help! Joy! Help!'. '[I]ncomprehensibly both ways' describes how many poems in the post-Romantic tradition engage with Romantic poetry. They have it 'both ways', honouring the past even when tenaciously at odds with it, enacting a response of nuanced flexibility that rationalist paraphrase finds 'incomprehensible'.

John Beer sees Romanticism as dealing with and bequeathing the 'question of being', a question 'raised by a disparity between a world created by conscious rational organization and one which might be less amenable to mental analysis'.[9] Hughes's vision is viscerally alert to this 'disparity', and it chimes with Shelley's sense that the bird's knowledge is of a different, higher order than that of humans: 'Thou of death must deem | Things more true and deep | Than we mortals dream, | Or how could thy notes flow in such a crystal stream?' (82–5). But Hughes affectingly hears in the song a simultaneous doubleness, an exclamation that communicates 'Joy' and a cry for 'Help'. Shelley's doubleness, as affecting, centres on the gap between the bird's 'clear keen joyance' (76) and the human condition, one in which even art depends on 'pain' (89), so that 'Our sweetest songs are those that tell of saddest thought' (90). Hughes's skylark embodies a force that demands sympathy, ignites empathy, and yet establishes the natural as obeying its own laws. In the second of two added sections, VIII, the last in the poem, the lark appears as a rebuke and comforter to fallen heroism, and Hughes's poem performs a not dissimilar

---

[8] Hughes has written with idiosyncratic power and insight on Coleridge in his introduction to his selection *A Choice of Coleridge's Verse* (London: Faber, 1996), in which he asks whether Coleridge thinks 'something wonderful has happened to the Mariner, or something terrible—unspeakable' (p. 62).

[9] John Beer, *Post-Romantic Consciousness: Dickens to Plath* (Basingstoke: Palgrave, 2003), p. 3.

role in relation to Romantic poetry. At the close, the poem itself sheds any burden of influence; like the descending birds, it, too, is 'Weightless, | Paid-up, | Alert, | | Conscience perfect'. It has entered its own poetic territory; there is no servile imitation of the Romantic; yet this book's case is that, without the Romantic inheritance, it would not have taken its particular shape.

Robert Frost's enigmatic 'The Most of It' remodels Wordsworth's account (which ended up in *The Prelude*, 1805, v. 389–422) of the Boy of Winander who 'Blew mimic hootings to the silent owls | That they might answer him' (398–9). Frost unearths, in his search for 'counter-love, original response', an 'embodiment' that is experienced as other, even threatening: an unexpectedly disturbed and disturbing presence.[10] In the dialogue that takes place between Romantic and post-Romantic poems, each can find in the other both 'counter-love, original response' and an 'embodiment' that challenges preconceptions. 'Scatter . . . my words among mankind' (66–7) is Shelley's plea at the close of 'Ode to the West Wind', a scattering that concedes his relinquishing of authorial control over words which will be 'modified', as Auden has it, 'In the guts of the living' ('In Memory of W. B. Yeats'). 'Romanticism', notoriously a protean term and post-facto construction, reshapes itself in the light of later ghostlier demarcations, finding itself more truly and more strange when viewed from the perspective of poetry written in its wake. Above all, its affirmations, about the self and its innate and potential grandeur, about the mind's capacity to enter into relationship with and to transform understanding of reality, and about the significance of poetry and the imagination, can be seen to involve themselves in a poetically productive drama. Jerome McGann asserts that 'in romantic poems . . . tensions and contradictions appear as experiences to be undergone, as a drama of suffering', and one need not endorse the conception of a Romantic ideology in which Romantic poets were supposedly complicit to see the value of his description; it is later rewritings of Romantic poetry—by Bishop of Wordsworth, or Muldoon of Byron—that allow us to see how 'deeply self-critical' the Romantic were all along.[11]

'It seems', writes Lisa M. Steinman, 'that both Romantic practice and the caricatured ghosts of Romanticism continue to haunt contemporary poetry.'[12] As Steinman half implies, the vagaries of reception make such distinctions perilous. Even apparent simplifications and misreadings yield new possibilities.

---

[10] Quoted from Robert Frost, *Collected Poems* (London: Cape, 1943).

[11] Jerome J. McGann, 'Romanticism and its Ideologies', *Studies in Romanticism*, 21 (1982); repr. in *Romanticism: Critical Concepts in Literary and Cultural Studies*, ed. Michael O'Neill and Mark Sandy, 4 vols. (London: Routledge, 2006), ii. 127.

[12] Lisa M. Steinman, Introduction to *Romanticism and Contemporary Poetry and Poetics*, ed. Lisa M. Steinman for the Romantic Circles Praxis Series, series ed. Orrin Wang, July 2003, online, para. 5.

Partial understandings of the Romantic open up unforeseen vistas of interpretation. Parody wittily makes the case. In 'Upon Finding *Dying: An Introduction*, by L. E. Sissman, Remaindered at Is', the poet takes as his point of departure Wordsworth's 'I wandered lonely as a cloud': 'I wandered lonely as a cloud in Foyles | Of incandescent, tight-knit air' (1–2), the poem begins, mocking the poem's persona and transferring that mockery, in turn, to the Wordsworthian original. The lyrical tetrameter used by Wordsworth gains a deliberately near-bathetic final foot in Sissman's rewording. And the syntax, comically stumbling where Wordsworth soared, means that it might be the poet himself who is 'a cloud ... | Of incandescent, tight-knit air', a knot of authorial hopes and anxieties amusingly and cruelly cut when he comes across his own book in a remainder pile, 'a snip under a blackleg sign' (11).[13] No host of golden daffodils meets his gaze, only a sign of his own literary mortality. The sonnet signs off with the couplet, 'Well, if you | Preach about dying, you must practice, too' (13–14). Dying here is an art of self-deprecating wit, yet the poem's humour exposes to our inward eye questions of literary legacy. Its own accomplishment is to concede the author's perishability, even as it reminds us of the quotable riches bequeathed by a major Romantic poet. Sissman's piece glimpses and drolly avoids the solipsistic cul-de-sac of self-preoccupation, and it enhances awareness that in the Wordsworthian original the self is a means of relationship with a world elsewhere.

The legacy of the Romantic poets lures and liberates writers in the decades after 1900. Returned to after Victorian moderations and swoon-laden acquiescence, after the arcane torchlight playing on the faces of French and English Symbolist poems, after and amidst Modernist repudiation, canonical Romantic poems often play a duplicitous game with some brilliantly double-minded readers. Romantic poetry emerges as a place of primary inspiration from which later poetry is necessarily at a remove. However, illuminated by such poets as W. H. Auden or Geoffrey Hill, it turns out to be shot through with contradictions, at times distant from the inspiration it avows, and yet inspired by that distance. In this context, Coleridge's 'Dejection: An Ode' is a quintessentially tangled Romantic poem. The lamented suspension of the poet's 'shaping spirit of Imagination' (86) gives fresh impetus to that spirit. As Frank Kermode noted in one of the major studies of Romantic legacies, 'But of course there is always a last victory; and that is the Romantic poet's Dejection Ode, which exhausts him.'[14] While 'exhausts' is a Yeatsian verb, at the heart of 'Two Songs from a Play' ('The herald's cry, the soldier's tread | Exhaust his glory and his might', 13–14), the final Yeatsian riposte to exhaustion is creative

---

[13] Quoted from *The Norton Anthology of Poetry*, 4th edn., ed. Margaret Ferguson, Mary Jo Salter, and Jon Stallworthy (New York and London: Norton, 1996).

[14] Frank Kermode, *Romantic Image* (London: Routledge, 1957), p. 11.

renewal. Reconfiguring Shelley's image of Intellectual Beauty as paradoxically supplying 'human thought' with 'nourishment, | Like darkness to a dying flame' (version A, 44–5), 'Two Songs from a Play' concludes thus: 'Whatever flames upon the night | Man's own resinous heart has fed' (13–14). The flame consumes the 'resinous heart', yet it challenges 'the night'. Shelley's hovering between humanism and spiritual intimation has become a quasi-Nietzschean assertion of imaginative force. In 'The Circus Animals' Desertion', Yeats completes his enumeration of imaginative depletion with a counterbalancing momentum of rhythm and image that culminates in a couplet that daringly rhymes 'start' and 'heart' (III. 7, 8). If the poem has come to the end of the symbolist-mythic road, it also looks ahead to the point where the consciously remade self meets the confessional psyche.

'Dejection: An Ode' shows Romantic poetry thriving on its disengagement with any unifying poetics or ethics. Coleridge's imagination asserts itself in the act of denying its efficacy, but it is chastened by 'each visitation' (84) of anxiety and self-doubt. In 'Rejoinder to a Critic', Donald Davie, writing in the shadow of Hiroshima, borrows the Romantic poet's self-administered and knowingly inadequate nostrum. Davie incorporates into his poem the Coleridgean lines supposedly quoted at him by a critic reproaching his work for absence of feeling, ' "And haply by abstruse research to steal | From my own nature all the natural man" ' (3–4).[15] In fact, Davie concedes that the lines may, as the critic alleges, be '*My* sole resource' (5), also quoted (though this time without quotation marks) from 'Dejection: An Ode' (91). Allowing, albeit disbelievingly, that others may 'have a better plan' (6) Davie commits himself, at this stage of the poem, to what the Romantic poet calls his 'only plan' ('Dejection: An Ode', 91). In his witty, savage final stanza, Davie returns to rhymes on the word 'plan', pointing that 'Half Japan' (14) has been 'injured' (13) by '"feeling"' (16), and concluding that we must 'Appear concerned only to make it scan' (17). Yet the poem's very vehemence consciously complicates its adherence to emotional numbness: 'Appear' is a loaded word; no more than Coleridge can Davie remain wholly content with a self-crippling rejection of 'the natural man'. But his poem shows how Romantic poetry cannot be simply identified with uninhibited expression of feeling. It brings out, as many poems studied in this book do, that the complexities of response to, or of stances made possible by, Romantic poetry correspond to complexities central to Romantic poetry.

A. O. Lovejoy made the point some time ago that 'we should learn to use the word "Romanticism" in the plural'.[16] There is common sense in the view, yet

---

[15] Quoted from Donald Davie, *Collected Poems* (Manchester: Carcanet, 1990).
[16] Arthur O. Lovejoy, 'On the Discrimination of Romanticisms', *PLMA* 39 (1924); repr. in *Romanticism: Critical Concepts in Literary and Cultural Studies,* ed. O'Neill and Sandy, i. 40.

the plurality of meanings packed into the words 'Romanticism' and 'Romantic' serve to explain their resilience and persistence. Gene Ruoff says of 'romanticism' that 'words which do not name still may have a remarkable power to provoke and evoke'.[17] His edited collection of essays sought to address that provocative and evocative 'power'; so, too, does the present book, which seeks throughout to preserve a sense of the 'Romantic' as that which valorizes process, the new, and the ever-changing, and retains, throughout its displacements and transvaluations, a commitment to imaginative vitality.

None of Romanticism's great poets or poems exists as one thing only for later writers. So, Wordsworth is a figure composed of multiple poetic elements. 'He'll never fail nor die', says Sidney Keyes in his 'William Wordsworth',

> And if they laid his bones
> In the wet vaults or iron sarcophagi
> Of fame, he'd rise at the first summer rain
> And stride across the hills to seek
> His rest among the broken lands and clouds.[18]

Keyes allows the verse movement to shepherd the abstraction, 'Of fame', to the touchline of the passage; the real life of the poetry lies in his depiction of an imagined resurrection that has its own 'striding' energy. '[T]he broken lands and clouds' are both descriptive of nature and speak of the stormy historical weather endured by both poets. The Romantic poet may 'seek | His rest', but the enjambment implies that seeking rest may be as close as the great Wordsworth (for Keyes, 'a stormy day, a granite peak | Spearing the sky') would ever come to the 'repose' (40) for which he longs in his 'Ode to Duty'. At once an ethical exemplar and an aesthetic model, Wordsworth speaks with two voices for Keyes: one issues in 'Words' that 'flower like crocuses in the hanging woods'; one confronts us as enduringly as a 'bony face', an underpresence discernible in the poetry.

Nor does Wordsworth require endorsement to be influential. His quarrel with 'The world' in 'The world is too much with us' is itself contested by Denise Levertov in 'O Taste and See'. 'The world is | not with us enough', replies Levertov: her short lines hurry towards advocacy of immersion in 'being | hungry', where the ontological enjoys a momentary sovereign space before the line-ending.[19] Yet what is striking is how frequently Wordsworth's visionary explorations give licence to later imaginings. Anthony Hecht's menacing transition from straggling ordinariness to sensory black-out in

---

[17] Gene W. Ruoff (ed.), *The Romantics and Us: Essays on Literature and Culture* (New Brunswick, NJ: Rutgers University Press, 1990), p. 1.

[18] Quoted from Sidney Keyes, *The Collected Poems*, ed. with a memoir and notes by Michael Meyer (London: Routledge, 1988).

[19] Quoted from *Norton Anthology of Poetry*.

'A Hill' is unthinkable without Wordsworth's experience of 'blankness' and invasion by 'huge and mighty Forms that do not live | Like living men' (*The Prelude*, 1805, I. 425–6). Hecht relies on a sublime dissolve much as Wordsworth does:

> And then, when it happened, the noises suddenly stopped,
> And it got darker; pushcarts and people dissolved
> And even the great Farnese Palace itself
> Was gone, for all its marble; in its place
> Was a hill, mole-colored and bare. (15–19)[20]

Hecht's diction—words such as 'Was' and 'bare' throwing into relief the arresting 'mole-colored'—pays tribute to Wordsworth's practice. He stops short, however, of the earlier poet's celebration of memory, writing, instead, 'at last, today, | I remembered that hill; it lies just to the left | Of the road north of Poughkeepsie; and as a boy | I stood before it for hours in wintertime' (37–40). The specificity of place means that something is pinned down, but the poet refuses to analyse explicitly why 'as a boy | I stood before it for hours in wintertime'. He leaves himself and the reader with the bare fact, an economical, stoic restatement for a post-Freudian era of De Quincey's belief in the 'brain' as a 'natural and mighty palimpsest'.[21] For Hecht, it is less the mind's 'might' that is illustrated than its inexplicability, and yet the two mental attributes are near neighbours.

II

My purpose in *The All-Sustaining Air* is to explore ways in which Romantic poetry both renews itself and is creatively used, contested, and reworked in a range of twentieth-century, and some twenty-first-century, poetry. It studies poets from Yeats to the present, looking at the Romantic bequest as a dominant influence in American, British, and Irish poetry. Romantic poetry celebrates the particular and reaches into the 'world which is the world | Of all of us' (*The Prelude*, 1805, X. 725–6); it has sown seeds in different national soils, contributing in localized and individual ways to processes of poetic and cultural self-definition. Part of my purpose is to allow that wider sense of its influence, as demonstrated in the workings of particular poems, to emerge. In considerations of Romanticism's creative displacements, W. B. Yeats demands

---

[20] Ibid.
[21] *Suspiria de Profundis: The Palimpsest* (extract), in Duncan Wu (ed.), *Romanticism: An Anthology*, 3rd edn. (Oxford: Blackwell, 2006), p. 830.

pride of place, his self-making and capacity for poetic renewal dependent on his creative appropriations of Romanticism as he fashions his identity as the poet who would 'write for my own race' ('The Fisherman', 11). In Hart Crane, 'the Shelley of our age', in Robert Lowell's phrase,[22] and Wallace Stevens, twentieth-century American poetry boasts determinedly ambitious post-Romantic poets. In Lowell, there is admiration for Crane, whose passionate American Romanticism demands an answerable response, requiring the reader to 'lay his heart out for my bed and board' ('Words for Hart Crane').[23] Elizabeth Bishop works at a lower pitch; the irony that hums round her inflections can sound anti- rather than post-Romantic. Yet, as Chapter 1 suggests, her irony is more than reductive wariness; it involves sustaining a double responsiveness, offering not just a belated knowingness, but also an authentic knowing of the Romantics themselves. Post-Romanticism sees its own face in the mirror held up by Romanticism; but it persuades us, too, that Romanticism's features were always ready to grow into the expressions worn by the post-Romantic. Comparable double-takes are at work in Northern Irish poets such as Seamus Heaney and Derek Mahon, while Patrick Kavanagh and Paul Muldoon are quick to sense the usefulness of Byronic comedy, influenced here by Auden's practice in his *Letter to Lord Byron*. Mainland British poetry often takes its cue from the emigré American T. S. Eliot's blend of consciously wary antagonism towards and covertly powerful interest in the Romantic, as is studied in different ways in the accounts of Auden, Spender, Hill, and Fisher.

The book affirms the capacity of poems to attain highly individualized artistic identities, examining Romantic legacies from the perspective of a delight in aesthetic achievement that attributes to such achievement, especially when it displays an intricate self-awareness, something close to an ethically alert engagement with experience. 'Post-Romantic' is, in its way, as uncertain and fluid a term as 'Romantic'; it is a necessary term, however, since, even as poets such as Stevens seek to renew the Romantic for a later age, they are conscious of differences from Romanticism. 'Post-Romantic', too, allows one to see Modernism as existing in a relationship to the Romantic that is subtler and more varied than some of the more trenchant pronouncements of its leading figures would seem to permit. Albert Gelpi is persuasive when he argues that 'the epistemological, and so the aesthetic, divisions within Romanticism itself

---

[22] Robert Lowell, 'Words for Hart Crane', in *Collected Poems*, ed. Frank Bidart and David Gewanter, with the editorial assistance of DeSales Harrison (London: Faber, 2003).

[23] For a recent discussion of twentieth-century American Romanticism (with stimulating analysis of William Carlos Williams), see David Herd, 'Pleasure at Home: How Twentieth-Century American Poets Read the British', in *A Concise Companion to Twentieth-Century American Poetry*, ed. Stephen Fredman (Oxford: Blackwell, 2005), pp. 33–54, esp. 43–6.

anticipate and lead to the divisions within Modernism', and even more so when he suggests that the 'slipperiness' of the terms 'Romanticism' and 'Modernism' 'manifests itself in their ability to mask and unmask one another, to slide into one another only to polarize again': phrasing which captures the relationships more broadly sustained between the poets studied in this book and Romantic poetry.[24]

A key emphasis in the book is the attempt to re-conceive the idea of influence, to stress that it involves individuality within relationship and a model of creative reading. A theme running through the book is that of 'poetry as literary criticism', of the poem as a place where the finest and most nuanced reading of a previous poem or poetry occurs.[25] Throughout, the book views authorship as the product and embodiment of legacy. The critical method that flows from this view is a mode of close reading that allows attention to both individuality and relationship. My approach inevitably incurs debts to Harold Bloom's body of work on influence. Bloom has defended poetry at a time when criticism has been in thrall to modes of hermeneutical suspicion; his books and essays show superb, if intermittently eccentric, resourcefulness as they demonstrate that 'The meaning of a poem can only be another poem', and that 'Criticism is the art of knowing the hidden roads that go from poem to poem'.[26] Yet my position in the book is post-Bloomian, in that I conceive of influence, not as a quasi-Freudian struggle between male egos, but as involving an interplay between indebtedness and individuation. In my readings, the desire to establish difference and originality is productive not only of anxiety but also of acknowledgement and admiration. Moreover, even if a poem is a house whose doors are always open, its architecture is unique, a hard-won prize, individualized, with its own inscape: features celebrated in my accounts.

My analyses are often in dialogue with the insights and methods of other critics of the Romantic period; but they seek to make a distinctive contribution to the understanding of Romantic and post-Romantic literature by virtue of their engagements with the texts themselves. Their aim, when bringing texts together, is not to imply some intertextual solution in which the individual nature of particular authors and works dissolves, but to remain alert to what in *The Prelude* Wordsworth calls 'the shades of difference | As they lie hid in all exterior forms' (1805, III. 158–9). Similarly, dialogue with other critics is

---

[24] Albert Gelpi, *A Coherent Splendor: The American Poetic Renaissance, 1910–1950* (1987; Cambridge: Cambridge University Press, 1990), p. 2.
[25] See my 'Poetry as Literary Criticism', in *The Arts and Sciences of Criticism*, ed. David Fuller and Patricia Waugh (Oxford: Oxford University Press, 1999), pp. 117–36.
[26] Harold Bloom, *The Anxiety of Influence: A Theory of Poetry* (1973; London: Oxford University Press, 1975), pp. 94, 96.

designed to clarify the precise nature of my own critical response. Drawn from Shelley's *Prometheus Unbound,* the book's title suggests the cultural and literary persistence of the Romantic, even as it allows for and celebrates the multiple, even fractured nature of that notion. Above all, it is meant to intimate the possibility of an autonomy of voice drawn from a sustaining air. The title also alludes to, without acquiescing in, a once dominant critical tradition of reading Romanticism, notably that embodied in works such as M. H. Abrams's *The Correspondent Breeze,*[27] and throughout, as I explore the creative legacy bequeathed by Romantic writing, I reflect on the implications of different attempts to respond critically to that legacy.[28]

Northrop Frye expresses the view that 'Poetry can only be made out of other poems'.[29] Yet just as to think about genre is necessarily to think about genius, so to reflect on intertextuality is to meditate on the intra-textual. 'A poet', writes Shelley in his Preface to *Prometheus Unbound,* 'is the combined product of such internal powers as modify the nature of others, and of such external influences as excite and sustain these powers; he is not one, but both' (p. 231). It is no accident that Shelley emerges as the Romantic figure central to the book's thinking about influence, since he is the most self-conscious theorist of

---

[27] M. H. Abrams, *The Correspondent Breeze: Essays on English Romanticism* (New York: Norton, 1984).

[28] Critical literature on the Romantic legacy composes a genre of its own. Along with other works touched on in this Introduction, particular mention must be made of the work of Harold Bloom (also discussed in the Introduction), who, in studies such as *Poetry and Repression: Revisionism from Blake to Stevens* (New Haven: Yale University Press, 1975), applies his theory of 'revisionary ratios' to readings of the major Romantic poets and their heirs. As suggested already, my book differs from Bloom's work, in that it does not sustain a largely pessimistic thesis about influence. Other significant recent works include Edward Larrissy (ed.), *Romanticism and Post-Modernism* (Cambridge: Cambridge University Press, 1999), a collection that considers Romanticism's endurance from a different perspective from the present book's and in relation to different texts, and the same author's *Blake and Modern Literature* (Basingstoke: Palgrave, 2006). Christopher Ricks, *Allusion to the Poets* (Oxford: Clarendon Press, 2002), is also relevant to my project. Ricks offers characteristically alert and nuanced readings concerned with the ways in which allusiveness often functions in contexts that have connections with the process of allusion—poems concerned, for example, with succession or inheritance. The essays on Burns, Wordsworth, and Byron are of particular interest, as is his book's emphasis on 'the similarity within difference' apparent in 'the art of allusion' (p. 12) and illustrated by Dryden's line 'How like the former, and almost the same' (*Aeneid* VI. 1195). Two central, and seminal, studies are Carlos Baker, *The Echoing Green: Romanticism, Modernism, and the Phenomena of Transference in Poetry* (Princeton: Princeton University Press, 1984), and George Bornstein, *Transformations of Romanticism in Yeats, Eliot, and Stevens* (Chicago: University of Chicago Press, 1976). See also three stimulating studies to appear in recent years: Fiona Stafford, *Starting Lines in Scottish, Irish, and English Poetry: From Burns to Heaney* (Oxford: Oxford University Press, 2000); Deborah Forbes, *Self-Consciousness in Mid-Twentieth-Century American Poetry* (Cambridge, Mass.: Harvard University Press, 2004); and Damian Walford Davies and Richard Marggraf Turley (eds.), *The Monstrous Debt: Modalities of Romantic Influence in Twentieth-Century Literature* (Detroit: Wayne State University Press, 2006).

[29] Northrop Frye, *Anatomy of Criticism: Four Essays* (Princeton: Princeton University Press, 1957), p. 97.

influence among the canonical Romantics and since his work, as has been shown by critics from Earl R. Wasserman to Stuart Peterfreund, owes its power and subtlety to its ceaseless interplay with other texts and cultural productions.[30] In *Adonais* he writes an elegy that is remarkably allusive, but also communicates a sense of the poetic career as vitally dependent on individual aspiration, offering a model of solitariness amid company which later writers will find fruitful.

The book's intention is not the forlorn hope of completeness, but the wish to open up possibilities and intersections. Chapter 1 offers a reading of the efforts of a number of twentieth-century poets, including Yeats, Eliot, Crane, Stevens, Bishop, and Rich, to 'sustain' Romanticism, or forms of it, in a post-Romantic age. It touches, too, on Sylvia Plath's darkly entrammelled response to Romantic poetry in a piece such as 'Lady Lazarus'. It seeks to value continuities while attending to transformations and variations. Chapters 2 and 3 begin the process of more detailed exploration of the responses of individual poets to Romantic poetry. They focus on Yeats and Eliot, respectively, the latter apparently shunning the Romantic, the former seeming to embrace it, but both responding with acute subtlety and individuality to the Romantic bequest. Chapter 2, on Yeats, explores the work of his mid-to-late career; it begins by examining 'Ego Dominus Tuus', a pivotal poem written in a crucial period for Yeats, and one in which he sharpens his response to Romantic culture by setting that response in dialogue with his evaluation of Dante. The chapter's second half explores in detail the nature of his self-declared status as a 'last Romantic' in relation to a number of later poems. Chapter 3 argues that Eliot's poetry is illuminated by studying him in terms of a 'counter-Romanticism' which he discerns in Baudelaire and enacts in a variety of ways in his poems; it also attends to the Romantic ground of his beginnings as a poet. As with all the chapters, the intention is not neatly to re-package the poet, but to find appropriate ways of describing, evoking, and valuing the poetry. It helps, for example, in thinking about the achievement of 'What the Thunder said' to set it in relation to the apocalyptic ambitions of major Romantic poems. Chapter 4 discusses the poetry of W. H. Auden and Stephen Spender, exploring the complex response of both to the Romantic, focusing on a variety of texts by Auden, including his *Letter to Lord Byron,* in order to bring out his complicatedly post-Romantic poetic voice in his Thirties poetry. It looks, too, at Spender's attempts to preserve a Romantic lyric voice in the modern age.

Chapter 5 sustains this attention to particular poems and poets; it argues that Wallace Stevens's 'Esthétique du Mal' should be read as a work that illuminates

---

[30] See Earl R. Wasserman, *Shelley: A Critical Reading* (Baltimore: Johns Hopkins University Press, 1971), and Stuart Peterfreund, *Shelley among Others: The Play of the Intertext and the Idea of Language* (Baltimore: Johns Hopkins University Press, 2002).

the writings of the major Romantics, especially about evil and suffering. Chapter 6 returns to a broader sweep as it investigates the response of a range of contemporary poets from or associated with Northern Ireland to Romantic poetry (poets discussed include Kavanagh, Heaney, Mahon, and Carson). Chapter 7 discusses Paul Muldoon's dealings with Byron and other Romantics in 'Madoc: A Mystery', and looks at the degree to which Muldoon interweaves a post-modern absorption in textuality with a post-colonial critique and emerges with a post-Romantic re-commitment to imaginative power, here re-conceived as fictive linguistic play. Chapter 8 focuses on two British poets, Geoffrey Hill and Roy Fisher, to suggest their fascinating relationships with Romantic poetry, tense and tensed in Hill's case, troubled and energized by the ongoing question of subjectivity in Fisher's. Fisher seems at two removes from Romanticism, in that his practice takes its theoretical cue from a poet such as William Carlos Williams who shed his early Keatsian allegiance, forswearing metaphorical projection in favour of an Objectivist poetics. Yet Fisher, like Williams, strays into the force-field of Romantic poetry. In 'Spring and All' Williams's delicate use of metonymy represents a Modernist updating of Wordsworth's fidelity to the local that reminds one of Keats's cunningly inverted 'The poetry of earth is ceasing never' ('On the Grasshopper and Cricket', 9). Indeed, it does not cease; neither does the urge to invest particulars with larger metaphorical suggestions, such as inhere in lines describing 'entrance' in Williams's poem: 'They enter the new world naked', 'But now the stark dignity of | entrance'.[31] If a new poetry for a 'new world' covertly announces itself here, so too does an entrance made possible by the practice of British Romantics for whom 'Spring' is potently symbolic. Fisher, too, slips the leash of anti-Romantic strictures, and explores self and reality with a boldness that belies the deceptive modesty and quietness of his poetry's surface tone.

The idioms of the poets studied in the book differ strikingly; their concerns vary. All bear witness to the Romantic as a necessary angel; all suggest, through their very achievements, that there is an array of as yet unrealized possibilities awaiting later poets as they breathe the sustaining air of Romantic poetry. In words that fuse elegiac admiration with mockery as they allude to 'Ode to the West Wind' and the last stanza of *Adonais,* Robert Lowell says in 'Second Shelley': 'dying, he left the wind behind him.' It is as good an epigraph as any for the pages that follow.

---

[31] Quoted from William Carlos Williams, *Selected Poems,* ed. with intro. by Charles Tomlinson (Harmondsworth: Penguin, 1976).

1

'The All-Sustaining Air': Variations on a Romantic Metaphor

I

'Shakespearean fish swam the sea, far away from land; | Romantic fish swam in nets coming to the hand; | What are all those fish that lie gasping on the strand?'[1] The effect of Yeats's countdown triplet is not merely one of diminishment. The image of modern poems as fish out of water, gasping on the strand, evokes, too, a bracing austerity, the need to adapt to a new, harsh element, to vaporize past oceans into a breathable air. Certainly, though, Yeats's lines indicate the difficulty of being 'reborn as an idea, something intended, complete'.[2] Few poems convey this difficulty as affectingly as Hart Crane's 'The Broken Tower' does. The poem is interpretable as an elegiac celebration of Crane's poetic career, in particular his entrance as a latter-day American Romantic into 'the broken world | To trace the visionary company of love, its voice | An instant in the wind'.[3] 'To trace the visionary company of love' means, as the verb and wistfully elongated rhythm intimate, a brave attempt to track, copy, or emulate a 'company' of beckoning and dissolving shadows. In 'the broken world' Crane is outside any Romantic 'world to which the familiar world is as a chaos', in Shelley's phrase from *A Defence of Poetry* (p. 698), and in search of a lost wholeness, a search made possible by the experience of fragmentation.

Crane's poem openly proclaims its anxiety of influence, thus severing any supposedly necessary link between poetry and repression: 'My word I poured. But was it cognate, scored | Of that tribunal monarch of the air | . . . ?' Here the 'tribunal monarch of the air', if allegorized as the Romantic tradition, suggests

---

[1] W. B. Yeats, 'The Nineteenth Century and After'. The poem is cited by W. Jackson Bate in *The Burden of the Past and the English Poet* (Cambridge, Mass.: Harvard University Press, 1970) as one of four examples of authorial fear that 'poetry has been cultivating progressively smaller plots or concentrating on less general interests' (p. 60).

[2] 'A General Introduction for My Work', in W. B. Yeats, *Selected Criticism and Prose*, ed. A. Norman Jeffares (London: Pan in association with Macmillan, 1980), p. 255.

[3] Quoted from Hart Crane, *The Complete Poems and Selected Letters and Prose of Hart Crane*, ed. Brom Weber (New York: Liveright, 1966).

a Jupiter-like superego. But Crane's 'poured' word hangs for more than 'An instant in the wind' of inspiration by virtue of his exalted, punishing sense of poetic vocation. Reliant on a 'dynamics of inferential mention', his poem 'score[s]' a new music that is in complex harmony with, say, Shelleyan figurative orchestrations (as in the earlier image of stars 'caught and hived in the sun's ray').[4] More poignantly, it is 'scored' (in the sense of marked or slashed) by its very ambition. At the same time, the capacity to be wounded has humanized the poet's soul and underpins the poem's trust in the 'latent power' stirred by 'sweet mortality'.

Healed by the poet's capacity to be wounded, Crane's work exemplifies the intricacy of relations between Romantic and post-Romantic poetry, relationships which occur within an 'all-sustaining air'. A pervasive and polysemous metaphor in this chapter, the phrase occurs twice in Shelley's *Prometheus Unbound*: once when Ione beholds the final two Spirits of the Human Mind in Act 1, and again when Asia says of 'love' that 'Like the wide heaven, the all-sustaining air, | It makes the reptile equal to the God' (2. 5. 40, 42–3). The air we breathe is a hackneyed phrase, revivified by Shelley, for whom the 'world-surrounding ether' (1. 661) serves as an image of the way in which human beings are affected by, and affect, prevailing climates of thought and belief. Asia's words catalyse the near-identification of 'air' and 'love' that her simile describes; a '*Voice (in the air, singing)*' (stage direction before 2. 5. 48) celebrates the way Asia is different and inextricable from the 'atmosphere divinest' (2. 5. 58) that surrounds her. In the lyric exchange between the Voice and Asia, Shelley affirms what in *A Defence of Poetry* he calls the capacity of poetry to 'transmute' its materials, so that 'every form moving within the radiance of its presence is changed by wondrous sympathy to an incarnation of the spirit which it breathes' (p. 698). So, Asia imagines 'Realms where the air we breathe is love' (2. 5. 95), near-identification now becoming complete.

Prometheus Unbound is an exercise in deep breathing, an eco-utopian search for and journey into a transformed, no longer polluted ideological atmosphere. Inhalings and exhalings of 'oracular vapour' (2. 3. 4), at once inspiringly and ambivalently Dionysian, gust through the awakening world of the second act.[5] Pollution vanishes in the Utopian conditions of the last two acts, but the subliminal fear that 'vapour' has turned, and therefore can turn, pestilential is evident throughout the work. Shelleyan 'air' is always ready to rhyme with 'despair' as in Ione's lines, even if it is 'despair | Mingled

---

[4] Quoted from Hart Crane's 'General Aims and Theories', in *Complete Poems*, p. 222; the image of starlight fading into sunlight is a favourite of Shelley's: see *Prometheus Unbound*, 2. 1. (17–25); 'To a Skylark', 18–20; and *The Triumph of Life*, 77–9.

[5] See Kelvin Everest's notes in Percy Bysshe Shelley, *The Poems of Shelley*, ii: *1817–1819*, ed. Kelvin Everest and Geoffrey Matthews (Harlow: Longman, 2000), esp. to 2. 3.

with love and then dissolved in sound' (1. 756–7). Shelley's lyrical airs alert us to the desirability of keeping a check on the air we metaphorically breathe. Indeed, his use of the word 'air' is alert to the spectrum of quasi-symbolic suggestions that the word can imply. When in the fourth act of *Prometheus Unbound* Panthea hears 'The music of the living grass and air' (4. 257), she verges on the pantheism of Wordsworth's 'living air' (99) in 'Tintern Abbey' or 'Lines Written in Early Spring' ('And 'tis my faith that every flower | Enjoys the air it breathes', 11–12). But when the Poet in *Alastor*, contemplating the swan, laments that he is condemned to waste 'these surpassing powers | In the deaf air' (288–9), the word anticipates the bleak reality that for Stevens challenges and provokes what his Ozymandias in *Notes toward a Supreme Fiction* ('It Must Change', VIII) calls 'A fictive covering'.[6] 'How cold the vacancy', Stevens writes in 'Esthétique du Mal' (section VIII), echoing the Poet's plight in *Alastor*, 'When the phantoms are gone and the shaken realist | First sees reality'. Arguably, Shelley's Poet in *Alastor* elicits a mixture of blame and praise because of his refusal to accept that 'vacancy' is 'reality'. For Stevens, 'air' bodies forth the real, yet it is a reality that must be imagined for it to exist, as well as being an atmosphere that sustains the mind's fictions and a figure for the breath of inspiration. 'Esthétique du Mal', a major post-Romantic text to grapple with the problem of evil (and the subject in this context of Chapter 5), concludes with a question that gathers momentum and dispenses with a mark of interrogation:

> And out of what one sees and hears and out
> Of what one feels, who could have thought to make
> So many selves, so many sensuous worlds,
> As if the air, the mid-day air, was swarming
> With the metaphysical changes that occur,
> Merely in living as and where we live.

That meaning is invested in an endless reshaping ('So many selves, so many sensuous worlds') of the ordinary involves a radiant if hard-won and conditional post-Romantic illumination. The 'mid-day air' swarms with revelations that suggest Stevens's intricate engagement with the project of Romanticism.

Locating value in 'the weather, the mere weather, the mere air', as *Notes toward a Supreme Fiction* ('It Must Be Abstract', VI) has it, is a major task for Stevens, whose very repetition of 'mere' paradoxically invests the 'weather' with significance. Stevens seems convinced of the need to leave behind the old mythologies, especially the myth of religious belief: 'To see the gods dispelled in mid-air and dissolve like clouds is one of the great human experiences,' he

---

[6] Quoted from Wallace Stevens, *Collected Poems* (London: Faber, 1955); unless indicated otherwise, this edition is used for all quotations from Stevens's poetry.

writes with sardonic tranquillity in 'Two or Three Ideas'.⁷ Yet the phrasing endows the dispelled gods with a presence even as it repudiates the idea of such presence. 'The god approached dissolves into the air' is William Empson's equivalent in 'Doctrinal Point', where 'dissolves' works to establish air as the illusory token as well as destroyer of deity in a piece that finishes with a dark, ebullient flurry of rhymes on 'air', the poem's last word, and comprises a sardonic reworking of Shelley's dome image in *Adonais*:

> That over-all that Solomon should wear
> Gives these no cope who cannot know of care.
> They have no gap to spare that they should share
> The rare calyx we stare at in despair.
> They have no other that they should compare.
> Their arch of promise the wide Heaviside layer
> They rise above a vault into the air.⁸

Empson's note to the poem suggests that it is a tissue of analogies for coverings and layerings.⁹ The passage teases jokily, yet builds powerfully, the 'They' growing less specific as the rhymes mount, until the line 'They have no other that they should compare' describes the predicament of a post-Romantic culture that has grown entirely sceptical of any transcendent 'radiance of Eternity' (*Adonais*, 463). At their most imaginatively daring and heterodox, the Romantics at once see 'the gods dispelled in mid-air' and that 'The god approached dissolves into the air'. The shared experience of a dispossession that empowers a sense of possible sublimity links Romantic poems with many poems of a later climate. There is a side of Stevens that thrives on the attempt to assert, as he does in the elegant metaphysical spring-cleaning performed by 'A Clear Day and No Memories', that 'Today the air is clear of everything. | . . . | it flows over us without meanings':¹⁰ here 'air' is the Romantic tradition and that which supplants such a tradition, as Stevens adopts the tone of the letter-writer who says, a shade misleadingly, 'while [. . .] I come down from the past, the past is my own and not something marked Coleridge, Wordsworth, etc.',¹¹ or who would contend with Emerson that 'there remains the indefeasible persistency of the individual to be himself'.¹²

---

⁷ Wallace Stevens, *Opus Posthumous by Wallace Stevens*, ed. Samuel French Morse (New York: Vintage, 1982), p. 206; hereafter cited in the text as *OP*.
⁸ Quoted from William Empson, *Collected Poems* (London: Hogarth Press, 1984).
⁹ Ibid. 103–4.
¹⁰ Quoted from Wallace Stevens, *The Palm at the End of the Mind: Selected Poems and a Play by Wallace Stevens*, ed. Holly Stevens (New York: Vintage, 1990); hereafter *Palm*.
¹¹ Wallace Stevens, *Letters of Wallace Stevens*, ed. Holly Stevens (New York: Knopf, 1966), p. 292.
¹² Ralph Waldo Emerson, 'Quotation and Originality', in *Emerson's Prose and Poetry: Authoritative Texts, Contexts, Criticism*, ed. Joel Porte and Saundra Morris (New York: Norton, 2001), p. 329.

Stevens, an inveterate 'scholar', to use his word, of Romanticism, asserts in 'Evening without Angels' that

> Air is air,
> Its vacancy glitters round us everywhere.
> Its sounds are not angelic syllables
> But our unfashioned spirits realized
> More sharply in more furious selves.

Manifesto here turns epiphanic, as 'glitters' and the chiming 'everywhere' suggest. Stevens's serio-comic lecture goes on to remind us that we 'repeat antiquest sounds of air | In an accord of repetitions'. For all the anti-transcendental drift of the writing (it is 'light | That fosters seraphim'), the phrasing mimics 'The gaiety of language' ('Esthétique du Mal', XI) that Stevens uses to concede, and yet free himself from, allegiance to 'antiquest sounds of air'. Should 'we' repeat what the Romantics were saying (for example), it is because we are always making it new. This is one implication of Stevens's use of the very Romantic trope of the 'wind | Encircling us' that 'speaks always with our speech'. Stevens contrives to make the word 'air' serve a double purpose: to sustain our link with the past and to shore up our trust in our ability to find fresh significances. In 'Evening without Angels' the very sound of the word sponsors the trust that 'Bare night is best. Bare earth is best. Bare, bare'; the poem's air resonates with the 'voice that is great within us'. As so often in Stevens, the anti-transcendent ('Air is air') coexists with a recognition of possibilities that it seems right to call sublime. 'Air', here, is 'An abstraction blooded, as a man by thought', as Stevens will say in *Notes toward a Supreme Fiction* ('It Must Be Abstract', VI): the imaginative 'abstraction' is 'blooded' by re-entering the world that engages the mind and senses, until an abstraction (such as the Supreme Fiction) and the 'mere weather' blend, 'making visible | The motions of the mind' ('Evening without Angels').

'I slowly start again in the open air,' writes Philippe Jaccottet (in Derek Mahon's translation) at the close of an untitled poem about poetry. Mahon sees Jaccottet's 'Airs' (the punning title of one of his collections) as dealing with an idea 'familiar to us since the Romantics', and quotes Jaccottet's 'The limitless is the breath which gives us life [. . .] Poetry is the word which this breath sustains and carries, whence its power over us'.[13] The 'mere air' gives promise of origins, yet it does so by retaining a capacity to house the sublime, the limitless, to hint, even in Stevens, at traces of dispelled presence, as it does in Keats, elegist of an 'air' that was once 'haunted' (*Lamia*, II. 236) or 'Holy' ('Ode to Psyche', 39) and is now in danger of being 'emptied' by 'Philosophy' (*Lamia*, II. 236, 234). Mallarmé's 'Azure' with its 'serene irony', canopies the earth of much modernist and modern poetry: that 'irony' takes the form of

---

[13] Derek Mahon, Introduction, in *Selected Poems: Philippe Jaccottet* (Harmondsworth: Penguin, 1988), p. 10. This edition is the source of the quotation from Jaccottet's poem, p. 95.

mocking the poet with an 'absolute that is simultaneously perfection and nothingness', in Henry Weinfeld's words.[14] Even an apparently anti-Romantic poet such as Larkin is haunted in 'High Windows' by the thought of 'deep blue air, that shows | Nothing, and is nowhere, and is endless', much as Mallarmé asserts at the end of 'L'Azur': '*Je suis hanté. L'Azur! L'Azur! L'Azur! L'Azur!*'[15]

II

'I made it out of a mouthful of air,' Yeats asserts in an alliterative compacting of poetry's newness and capacity to last. 'He Thinks of Those Who Have Spoken Evil of His Beloved', the poem from which the line comes, finds that a song made of air will 'weigh' more than 'the great and their pride' (4), a phrase that loses air like a deflated balloon when repeated. For the youthful Yeats, *Prometheus Unbound* was 'among the sacred books of the world', and his poetic breathings are sustained by his lifelong engagement with Shelley's poetry and Romantic poetry more generally.[16] In later work he relishes pungent variations on Shelleyan themes. The swan of *Alastor* and Asia's lyric in *Prometheus Unbound* where the soul is 'like a sleeping swan' (2. 5. 73) transmogrifies into the terrifying swan who assaults Leda in a poem that is concerned, like *Prometheus Unbound*, with the inauguration of a fresh cycle. Unlike *Prometheus Unbound*, however, 'Leda and the Swan' tramples Utopian dreams into the dust. 'The brute blood of the air' (12) is Jupiter returned to take revenge on the Shelleyan creed of redemption through love and forgiveness. Against, and yet in subtle accord with, the 'dragon-ridden' destruction of civil war, Yeats sets the Romantic Image of Loie Fuller's Chinese dancers unwinding their 'shining web' until it seemed 'a dragon of air | Had fallen among dancers' ('Nineteen Hundred and Nineteen', II. 2–4): art has the power to find an image for turbulent chaos. But 'Nineteen Hundred and Nineteen' opens itself to such chaos at its close, when what emerges from the air, from 'the labyrinth of the wind' (VI. 9), is the lurching image of 'That insolent fiend Robert Artisson' (VI. 16). 'The disentangled Doom', in Shelley's phrase, is well and truly out of the 'pit' (*Prometheus Unbound*, 4. 569, 564).

Yeats, the self-styled last romantic (in 'Coole and Ballylee, 1931'), is led to exalt art, yet, as in the Keatsian odes which lie behind his Byzantium poems, he

---

[14] Stephane Mallarmé, *Collected* Poems, trans. Henry Weinfeld (Berkeley: University of California Press, 1994), p. 163. I have substituted 'Azure' for Weinfeld's 'Sky'.

[15] Philip Larkin, *Collected Poems*, ed. with intro. by Anthony Thwaite (London: The Marvell Press and Faber, 1988).

[16] Yeats, 'The Philosophy of Shelley's Poetry', in Yeats, *Selected Criticism*, p. 53.

discovers the limits of seeking to exist in a world 'All breathing human passion far above' (Keats, 'Ode on a Grecian Urn', 28). His Byzantium, a place that disdains 'All that man is' ('Byzantium', 6), in a terse, contempt-filled line, turns out to be a place too ghostly, too virtual, a place where 'Breathless mouths' (14) are too at home, and a series of trance-wrecking images leaps to the defence of the 'unpurged' (1) in the final stanza, in which 'bitter furies of complexity' (37) flood back into the poem with a vengeance. Indeed, Yeats is sensitized by Romantic poetry to an inescapable war of contraries, as will be explored further in Chapter 2.

For the moment, two Yeatsian quotations will help to develop this point. The first is from 'Blood and the Moon': 'And Shelley had his towers, thought's crowned powers he called them once' (II. 3); the second comes from the end of the final poem in 'Meditations in Time of Civil War': 'The abstract joy, | The half-read wisdom of daemonic images, | Suffice the ageing man as once the growing boy' (VII. 38–40). The allusion to Shelley in the first quotation is to *Prometheus Unbound*, Act 4, where the Chorus of Spirits sing of how they have come 'From those skiey towers | Where Thought's crowned powers | Sit watching your dance, ye happy Hours' (4. 102–4). The second passage echoes Wordsworth's 'Ode: Intimations of Immortality', in which the poet laments that 'Shades of the prison-house begin to close | Upon the growing Boy' (67–8). Yeats quotes Shelley in support of a defiantly idealist and Anglo-Irish perspective and a consciously arrogant 'mockery of a time | Half dead at the top' ('Blood and the Moon', I. 11–12); Wordsworth's phrase serves a deeply plangent dying fall. In both cases, Yeats uses the Romantic poem for his own ends. Shelley's phrase, snatched from its Promethean context, is made to serve a vision that is powerfully if dangerously contemptuous of the present. 'Meditations' finishes with Wordsworth's phrase, as though Yeats were denying the Romantic poet's narrative of growth through loss. Yet it is the bitterness of Yeats's self-characterization that keeps his poetry alive: 'A poet, when he is growing old', Yeats writes in 'Anima Hominis', 'will ask himself if he cannot keep his mask and his vision without new bitterness, new disappointment.'[17] But 'new bitterness, new disappointment' is what, for Yeats, creates, in Stevens's words from one of his *Adagia*, 'a romantic that is potent' (*OP*, p. 180), and in the prose passage, as in the poem, he turns on his dreams of escaping bitterness: 'Then he will remember Wordsworth withering into eighty years, honoured and empty-witted, and climb to some waste room and find, forgotten there by youth, some bitter crust.'[18] Wordsworth's supposed failure sustains Yeats's new lease of imaginative life.

In both Yeatsian poems a Romantic poem serves as a point of light, however ironized, that enables the later poet's imagination to assert its presence. Harold

---

[17] Yeats, *Selected Criticism*, p. 179.   [18] Ibid. 180.

Bloom, the hierophant of such assertions and the tortuous misprisions they may involve, has made us familiar with the notion that post-Enlightenment poetry traces a curve of quasi-inevitable decline: 'it seems just to assume', he writes, 'that poetry in our tradition, when it dies, will be self-slain, murdered by its own past strength'.[19] As its title suggests, the present chapter swerves from Bloom's work in seeing Romantic poetry as often 'sustaining' a supply of imaginative oxygen to later poems. To put the point differently, Bloom's generous shrewdness emerges most persuasively when he contends that the imagination is always making a final reckoning, that every new poem battles to bring something original into being, and that possibilities other than the ironic or the diminished are forever luring poets. Hence he ends *Poetry and Repression* with the fascinating claim that Wallace Stevens, for all his limitations, is 'the authentic twentieth-century poet of the Sublime' and rejects the view of Stevens as 'an ironist, as a wry celebrant of a diminished version of Romantic or Transcendental selfhood'.[20] This is well said, and suggests why George Bornstein's unmelodramatic term—'transformations'—is as helpful as any in describing uses made of the Romantic legacy by twentieth-century poets.[21] That those transformations can tap into and be shaped by Romanticism's 'poetics of disappointment' has been explored by Laura Quinney, and yet, when in 'Long and Sluggish Lines', Stevens writes, 'Wood-smoke rises through trees, is caught in an upper flow | Of air and whirled away. But it has been often so', assonance serves as a minimal guarantee that repetition is not merely diminishment; 'the upper flow | Of air' is an emblem of inspiration's availability, the imagination's capacity for fresh conceptions. 'A comic infanta among the tragic drapings' is a felicitous description of the poem that emerges from the 'tragic drapings' of post-Romantic dejection; like many of Stevens's poems, its verbal gaudiness invites us to value the possibility of poetic re-creation. For Quinney, the poem's moral is more depressing, since, for her, the poem's upshot is that Stevens 'finds that thought is incorrigibly self-confident; it is perpetually emerging from its haze and thinking to start again', and is thus a 'species of delusion'.[22] Yet Stevens does not find merely that 'thought' is 'thinking to start again'; he discovers that language itself, poetry, in all the estranging richness of its vocables, is able to stage recurrent enactments of newness, even if, in an image which recalls Keats and Shelley, the poet sees himself or his poem as not 'born' 'now, in this wakefulness inside a sleep'. That 'now' allows us to enter a paradoxical no-place, the virtual reality of a poem whose theme is that it is yet to come into existence: 'The life of the poem in the mind has not yet begun.'

---

[19] Bloom, *Anxiety of Influence*, p. 10.   [20] Bloom, *Poetry and Repression*, p. 282.
[21] Alluding to the title of George Bornstein's *Transformations of Romanticism in Yeats, Eliot, and Stevens* (Chicago: University of Chicago Press, 1976).
[22] Laura Quinney, *The Poetics of Disappointment: Wordsworth to Ashbery* (Charlottesville: University Press of Virginia, 1999), p. 103.

The effort to bring about transformations is Wallace Stevens's concern. His great gift is not only to talk about the need for poetry to 'be living, to learn the speech of the place', but, as he does here in 'Of Modern Poetry' to create a poetry that persuades us that 'the act of finding | What will suffice' is at work. In the poem's words, the poet or poem 'has | To construct a new stage' and 'be on that stage'. The poem enacts its theme, especially through the workings of a quirkily, even comically inventive diction and a highly complex syntax that gives the air of inspecting its unfurlings. As the poem takes possession of 'the delicatest ear of the mind', the reader grows conscious of 'Sounds passing through sudden rightnesses': sounds that have at and as their centre the word 'mind'. Near the end Stevens modulates from the vehement 'It must | Be the finding of a satisfaction' to the relatively playful 'and may | Be of a man skating, a woman dancing, a woman | Combing'. As at the close of 'Among School Children', these images seek to express the 'satisfaction' that occurs when analysis is defeated and we cannot distinguish between 'dancer' and 'dance' (Yeats, 'Among School Children', VIII. 8) or agent and act, or poem and the mind. Yet the poem's satisfactions are not complacent or repeatable, and are distinctly provisional: a hallmark of Stevens's 'new romanticism'.[23]

Stevens says that '[f]or the sensitive poet, conscious of negations, nothing is more difficult than the affirmations of nobility, and yet there is nothing that he requires of himself more persistently'. 'Nobility', apparently 'false and dead and ugly', is, in fact, 'a force and not the manifestations of which it is composed'. It shows itself wherever we are conscious of 'a violence from within that protects us from a violence without'.[24] This fraught defence of 'nobility' comes close to explaining the continual hold of Romantic poetry over twentieth-century poets, however strong the urge to jettison the past. Recapturing the 'almost disbelieving wonder' she felt at encountering the poetry of Adrienne Rich, Helen Vendler echoes Stevens's plea for poetry to be 'living' when she writes: 'I had not known till then how much I had wanted a contemporary and a woman as a speaking voice of life.' She goes on to quote Wordsworth's *Prelude*, 1805, IV. 145–6: 'Strength came where weakness was not known to be, | At least not felt.'[25] The tribute expresses the continuity between Romantic poet, twentieth-century poet, and twentieth-century critic. In her *Midnight Salvage: Poems 1995–1998* (1999), Rich has a poem made up of flayed units of prose and poetry called 'A Long Conversation', and the title points up the

---

[23] For Stevens's use of the phrase 'new romantic', see *Letters*, p. 277.
[24] Wallace Stevens, 'The Noble Rider and the Sound of Words', in *The Necessary Angel: Essays on Reality and the Imagination* (London: Faber, 1960), pp. 35–6.
[25] Helen Vendler, 'Ghostlier Demarcations, Keener Sounds', in *Adrienne Rich: Poetry and Prose: Poems, Prose, Reviews and Criticism*, ed. Barbara Charlesworth Gelpi and Albert Gelpi (New York: Norton, 1993), p. 300.

protracted dialogue between Romantic and twentieth-century poets. More immediately, Rich's conversation is between poetry and politics, poet and reader, and moves towards a troubled defence of poetry. At the core of this defence is the belief that 'All kinds of language fly into poetry', a belief in direct if distant descent from the Preface to *Lyrical Ballads*, and a conviction—enabling for Rich as for Shelley—that 'the words have barely begun to match the desire'. Rich's stance in this poem is that of a tough-minded, modern-day Romantic, her economical, intense style catching the force of 'desire' and her eloquent, principled refusal to settle for an illusion of aesthetic mastery. She organizes her poem through allusions: to Marx, Nixon, and Mandelstam, and, vitally, to Blake and Coleridge. The first poem in the unnumbered and unsectioned sequence sets the 'warm bloom of blood in the child's arterial tree' against the parental warning against catching '*your death of cold*'. She finishes this first section of the poem with the parenthetical phrase '(energy: Eternal Delight)', referring to Blake's *Marriage of Heaven and Hell*. Amidst the war of feeling in the poem, the phrase serves as a beacon of revolutionary purpose. Later, she quote a famous letter from Coleridge to Wordsworth, in which Coleridge anticipates the very terms used about him by hostile critics in his day and ours: '*I wish*', he says to Wordsworth, as lineated by Rich, '*you would write a poem | addressed to those who, in consequence | of the complete failure of the French Revolution | have thrown up all hopes | of the amelioration of mankind | and are sinking into an almost epicurean | selfishness, disguising the same | under the soft titles of domestic attachment | and contempt for visionary philosophes.*' In subsequent lines, failure, rebuff, and repetition are Rich's emphases, yet it is when 'the cold fog blows back in' that the chances of a new imaginative breathing present themselves in the dense, suggestive, and generously mocking lines that follow: 'Your lashes, visionary! screening | in sudden rushes this | shocked, abraded crystal.' The visionary 'screens' a reality tinged with possibilities, 'this | shocked, abraded crystal', and in the double meaning of 'screens' (covering and showing) Rich suggests obliquely a double response to Romanticism's visionary quest.

Many twentieth-century writers wear bifocal lenses as they contemplate the legacy of Romanticism. In Elizabeth Bishop's 'Sandpiper', the poet chooses as her hapless, obsessive surrogate a bird who 'runs to the south, finical, awkward, | in a state of controlled panic, a student of Blake'.[26] Here, a Blakean distillation gives way to a 'finical' condition. The opening lines of the Romantic poet's 'Auguries of Innocence'—'To see a World in a Grain of Sand | And a Heaven in a Wild Flower | Hold Infinity in the palm of your hand | And Eternity in an hour'

---

[26] Quoted from Elizabeth Bishop, *The Complete Poems, 1927–1979* (London: Hogarth Press, 1984).

(1–4)—ironically ghost Bishop's poem, a poem much concerned with whether it is possible 'To see a World' at all, let alone 'in a Grain of Sand'.²⁷ The sandpiper is 'a student of Blake', knows about the possible significance of 'minute particulars', but it is in a panicky state, however controlled the panic, because the particulars seem to open into nothing more than themselves. In places, mirroring this inability to make or find coherence, the diction offers a Modernist updating of Coleridge's notion of Fancy as having 'no counters to play with, but fixities and definites'.²⁸ Thus, the second stanza opens, 'The beach hisses like fat': the hissing fat and the roaring beach are neatly connected, but the writing calculatedly does not move, here, beyond 'fixities and definites'. As 'he stares at the dragging grains', meaning seems to be chance-ridden and fortuitous: 'The world is a mist. And then the world is | minute and vast and clear.' There, the clarification, across the line-ending, promises the double vision ('minute and vast') previously eluding the bird; but the subsequent, 'he couldn't tell you which', suggests a collapsing back into uncertainty. The bird's problem is that of the poet for whom particulars are all that can be trusted, yet merely add up to a heap of disconnected objects. He is less oblivious to history, if one so allegorizes the Atlantic beside which he runs, than uncurious about it: 'the roaring alongside he takes for granted'. But while Bishop may stand at a laconic, severely charitable arm's length from her surrogate ('Poor bird'), she won't deny the residual post-Romantic ardour of his search: 'he is preoccupied, | | looking for something, something, something'. Romantic 'somethings'—one thinks of Wordsworth's 'something far more deeply interfused' ('Tintern Abbey', 99) or 'something evermore about to be' (*The Prelude*, 1805, VI. 542)—cloak themselves in an aura of sublime indeterminacy. Bishop's triple repetition suggests more the twitchy routine of a neurotic. Yet, as though she had taken to heart a later Blakean maxim from 'Auguries of Innocence'—'If the Sun & Moon should Doubt | Theyd immediately Go out' (109–10)—Bishop concludes with a forceful and transformative vision that half-justifies the bird's obsession: 'The millions of grains are black, white, tan, and gray, | mixed with quartz grains, rose and amethyst.' Half-justifies: the bird may be missing what is under his eyes, and that final off-rhyme ('obsessed' and 'amethyst') may be saying as much. Or the 'rose and amethyst' vision may sanction the obsession: for Seamus Heaney, it is though the quartz, rose, and amethyst 'had escaped

---

²⁷ For searching commentary on this poem and Bishop's work more generally, see Jamie McKendrick, 'Bishop's Birds', in *Elizabeth Bishop: Poet of the Periphery*, ed. Linda Anderson and Jo Shapcott (Newcastle upon Tyne: Bloodaxe, 2002), pp. 123–42.

²⁸ Samuel Taylor Coleridge, *Biographia Literaria, or, Biographical Sketches of my Literary Life and Opinions*, ed. James Engell and W. Jackson Bate, 2 vols. (London: Routledge, 1983), vols. 7.1 and 7.2 of *The Collected Works of Samuel Taylor Coleridge*, gen. ed. Kathleen Coburn, 16 vols. (Princeton: Princeton University Press, 1969–2002), i. 305. This edition is used for all quotations from *Biographia Literaria*; references to volume and page numbers are given in the text.

from the light-drenched empyrean of Dante's *Paradiso*.[29] But a steady poise is kept: any Dantescan or transformative vision is tempered by a sense of the 'millions of grains' as implying a potentially nightmarish infinity of particulars, the opposite of that 'effect of reducing multitude to unity' (*Biographia Literaria*, ii. 23) which Coleridge saw as a proof of original genius in the use of images.

In her insightful study of Bishop's perceptions, Bonnie Costello claims that the poet 'dismantles the transcendent gaze of Romanticism'.[30] But Costello also quotes the poet's letter to Robert Lowell in which she says wryly, 'I find I'm really a minor female Wordsworth'.[31] Her subtle, agnostic poetry refuses to be neatly corralled, and is finely attuned to the way in which Romantic poetry itself resists easy categorizing. Wordsworth, read through lenses supplied by Bishop, seems as much a poet of disconcerting juxtaposition as of visionary climax.[32] 'Crusoe in England', Bishop's version of the Robinson Crusoe story, depicts Crusoe recollecting emotion once taken off the island, but tranquillity eludes him. Bishop has her character say:

> I tried
> reciting to my iris-beds,
> 'They flash upon that inward eye,
> which is the bliss . . .' The bliss of what?
> One of the first things that I did
> when I got back was look it up.

The bliss of solitude eludes Crusoe trapped in a post-Darwinian nature that has no particular care for him; he suffers nightmares of 'infinities of islands, islands spawning islands'.[33] Still, the recollecting, isolated self of the poem, as he recalls, say, looking at the waterspouts and remarks wryly, 'Beautiful, yes, but not much company', has something in common with the

---

[29] Seamus Heaney, '*from* Counting to a Hundred: Elizabeth Bishop', in *Finders Keepers: Selected Prose, 1971–2001* (London: Faber, 2002), p. 340.

[30] Bonnie Costello, *Elizabeth Bishop: Questions of Mastery* (Cambridge, Mass.: Harvard University Press, 1991), p. 6.

[31] Ibid. 8.

[32] See Charles Rzepka, 'Elizabeth Bishop and the Wordsworth of *Lyrical Ballads*: Sentimentalism, Straw Men, and Misprision', in 'The "Honourable Characteristic of Poetry": Two Hundred Years of *Lyrical Ballads*', ed. Marcy L. Tanter, an online volume in the Romantic Circles Praxis Series, series ed. Orrin Wang, Nov. 1999, for helpful commmentary on Bishop's relationship with Wordsworth, a relationship explored as well, as Rzepka notes, by critics such as Robert Pinsky, 'The Idiom of a Self: Elizabeth Bishop and Wordsworth', *American Poetry Review*, Jan.–Feb. 1980, pp. 6–8; Willard Spiegelman, 'Landscape and Knowledge: The Poetry of Elizabeth Bishop', *Modern Poetry Studies*, 6 (1975), pp. 203–24; Helen Vendler, *Part of Nature, Part of Us* (Cambridge, Mass.: Harvard University Press, 1980); and David Bromwich, 'Elizabeth Bishop's Dream Houses', *Raritan* 4/1(1984), pp. 77–94.

[33] The allusion does not merely bring the word 'solitude' to mind. Christopher Ricks notes that Bishop's iris makes 'a strange oeillade at Wordsworth's "inward eye" ' (*Allusion to the Poets*, p. 272).

Coleridge of 'Dejection: An Ode', who saw, not felt, how beautiful the natural scene was.

In 'The Unbeliever', Bishop produces a parable of types of poet: the unbeliever, who 'sleeps on the top of a mast | with his eyes fast closed'; the cloud, 'Secure in introspection'; and the gull, who 'remarked that the air | was "like marble" '. A discernible but sympathetic irony governs the poem. Bishop is concerned with stances and strategies associated with Romantic poetry, and implicitly mocks the buoyancy of Shelley's speaker in 'The Cloud'. At the same time, the fear experienced by the unbeliever is as subjective as the confidence of cloud and gull, and when the gull decodes the unbeliever's 'dream', what opens up is a post-Romantic abyss in which the solitary 'I' battles with a malevolent other: ' "I must not fall. | The spangled sea below wants me to fall. | It is as hard as diamonds; it wants to destroy us all"'. Metaphoric projection has turned paranoid; Urizen's 'unseen conflictions with shapes | Bred from his forsaken wilderness' (*The [First] Book of Urizen*, 3. 14–15) may come to mind, but his desire—'a solid without fluctuation' (4. 11)—is the unbeliever's terror.

Bishop's poem, like Blake's, empathizes even as it critiques. It is one thing to satirize the gull's figurative impulse to see 'the air' as ' "like marble" ', another to forsake the poem as a space where 'before unapprehended relations of things' (Shelley, *A Defence of Poetry*, p. 676) can come into being. Bishop's self-reflexive poetry composes an observer's sceptical *ars poetica*. For a Romantic belief in the one life, she substitutes her own 'one art' in a villanelle of that title. In this poem 'the art of losing' is available both to author and to things. Dualism gives way, not to some Heideggerean condition of dwelling, but to a unifying capacity for loss. For such loss, there is always the recompense that Bishop finds in her imperative at the close: 'It's evident | the art of losing's not too hard to master | though it may look like (*Write* it!) like disaster.' 'In the Waiting Room' also ironically invokes oneness: 'What similarities', the young girl thinks, sickeningly fascinated by photos in a *National Geographic* magazine, 'held us all together | or made us all just one.' Costello asserts that in the poem 'Bishop clearly separates herself from Wordsworth, whose "Ode: Intimations of Immortality" decries the fall into difference and social definition and takes comfort in the promise of spiritual oneness derived from recollections of childhood'.[34] Still, if Wordsworthian intimations dissolve into a sense of identity as appallingly inexplicable ('Why should I be my aunt, | or me, or anyone?'), the Romantic poet's 'obstinate questionings | Of sense and outward things' (144–5) help to shape Bishop's poem. Her search for a language adequate to negative wonder ('How—I didn't know any | word for it—') results in the self-consciously inadequate 'how "unlikely" ';

---

[34] Costello, *Elizabeth Bishop*, pp. 123–4. Costello argues, too, for a close fit between Bishop and Coleridge: 'Bishop's gothic and grotesque qualities, her moods of anxiety and dejection, her sense of otherness, all identify her as a modern Coleridge' (p. 124).

a low-key replay of Wordsworth's 'Fallings from us, vanishings' (146). Bishop's lines pass into another 'how', this time an obstinate questioning: 'How had I come to be here, | like them, and overhear | a cry of pain that could have | got loud and worse but hadn't?' The half-echo (involving repetition of the same sound) of Keats's inhabiting of a 'Here, where men sit and hear each other groan' ('Ode to a Nightingale,' 24) reminds us again that the Romantics cannot be turned into poets of transcendent flight. Theirs is also a poetry of 'The weariness, the fever, and the fret' (23), as Keats's Ode has it.

It is, too, a poetry of passion. In an example of a twentieth-century poet responding to work by female Romantic poets, Bishop's 'Casabianca' returns to Felicia Hemans's poem of the same title, one of the few poems by one of the most popular poets of her day to survive in the culture's memory before the salvaging work of recent critics and editors. Hemans extols the boy's self-sacrificing commitment to duty, 'The boy stood on the burning deck | Whence all but he had fled' (1–2), awaiting a command, that never comes, from his father who has died.[35] Quietly the sacrifice exacted by a system founded on obedience to the Father (capitalized in Hemans's text) is also communicated. Like many poems by Hemans, 'Casabianca' balances on a knife-edge between celebration and the faintest stirrings of critique, critique founded on the perception that the very system which exalts domestic affections is capable, when war so demands, of destroying them. Here the air is full of a pyrotechnical display at the centre of which is the fragmented body of the son: 'The boy—oh! where was he? | Ask of the winds that far around | With fragments strewed the sea!—'(34–6). Bishop's 'Casabianca' is responsive to the duality of feeling in Hemans's poem. There is an element of parody as Hemans's heroics appear to be reduced to an elocution lesson: there may even be in the opening the suggestion that 'Love' is inevitably part of a linguistic system, as it haplessly attempts to recite words mimetic of its condition. But the conclusion, associating all those involved in the scenario of the original, suggests love's width of significance, while the conclusion, 'And love's the burning boy', rewrites Hemans's lines to create a sense that love exists in the midst of passion's flames. The coolness and control of tone are excitingly at odds with Bishop's reassertion of a Romantic commitment to passion. The poet needs air to breathe her 'stammering elocution' in the midst of existential disaster (figured in the line 'while the poor ship in flames went down').

Here Bishop anticipates the darker post-Romanticism of Sylvia Plath's poetry. 'Lady Lazarus' concludes with a seemingly triumphant flourish, a rising from the

---

[35] Felicia Hemans, *Selected Poems, Letters, Reception Materials*, ed. Susan J. Wolfson (Princeton: Princeton University Press, 2000). See Emma Mason, ' "Love's the burning boy": Hemans's Critical Legacy' in *The Monstrous Debt*, ed. Davies and Turley, for a discussion of the way in which 'Bishop seems to be deliberately draining Hemans's poem of its emotion in order to lay bare the loss such an action effects' (p. 219).

dead that 'echoes Coleridge's description of the possessed poet in "Kubla Khan" ':[36] 'Out of the ash | I rise with my red hair | And I eat men like air.'[37] Christina Britzolakis argues that the poem exposes, in fact, the way that 'Lyric inwardness is "prostituted" to the sensationalism of "true confession" '.[38] This judgement is alert to Plath's mimicry of self-unwrapping, the poem's textualized 'big striptease', in which the 'artiste' plays her role 'exceptionally well'; the poem, its eye firmly on its beholder, deftly interweaves a show of 'lyric inwardness' with a mocking imitation of ' "true confession" '. All is gesture, sound, and fury, signifying and sardonically playing up the alienated status of the poet and of 'art'. Yet the performance does not merely deconstruct a Romantic commitment to what Keats in a letter of 21 September 1819 calls 'the true voice of feeling' (p. 493), since Romanticism itself is often alert to the difficulty of claiming and enacting such a voice, one yearned for, rather than confidently possessed, by Keats himself. Even the close of 'Kubla Khan' is itself fraught and riven; it is, for one thing, a conditional imagining; for another, it shows the poet as estranged from and feared by his audience. Plath offers a post-Romantic poetry of retaliatory vengeance, in which the speaker eats 'men like air', feasting on figures such as 'Herr Doktor' and 'Herr Enemy', or 'Herr God, Herr Lucifer', all of whom represent a patriarchal rule or a hostile male poetic canon. Eating men 'like air' recalls the desire to 'build that dome in air' in 'Kubla Khan'; it also reworks an earlier image in 'Lady Lazarus', one drawn, not from the air, but from the earth: 'Soon, soon the flesh | The grave cave ate will be | At home on me.' Flesh being devoured after death represents one extreme of human impotence; converting flesh to air has the ring of an Ariel-like or a Shelleyan transformation. And yet any final affirmation deliberately tastes of and like the 'ash' that the poem's imagery has—again in a deliberate way—tastelessly associated with the Holocaust. A Romantic extremism performs and passes judgement on itself in this as in many late Plath poems.

III

In 'The Monument' Bishop also rewrites for a later age the drama of artistic creation enacted in Coleridge's 'Kubla Khan'. At one stage in Bishop's poem, an imagined sceptical voice asks, commenting on the ramshackle monument:

> 'Why did you bring me here to see it?
> A temple of crates in cramped and crated scenery,

---

[36] Christina Britzolakis, *Syvia Plath and the Theatre of Mourning* (Oxford: Clarendon Press, 1999), p. 155.
[37] Sylvia Plath, *Ariel* (1965; London: Faber, 1968).
[38] Britzolakis, *Sylvia Plath and the Theatre of Mourning*, p. 156.

>   what can it prove?
>   I am tired of breathing this eroded air,
>   this dryness in which the monument is cracking.'

'[T]ired of breathing this eroded air' might suggest one response to the sense of belatedness, of coming after the Romantics. But Bishop finds a way out of anxiety and exhaustion. Coleridge's poem is brought in when Bishop speaks of an 'artist-prince', who might have wanted, looking at the seascape running behind the monument, to 'make | a melancholy or romantic scene of it'. Yet her monument resists the decree of any such artist-prince; no stately pleasure-dome, it is more a matter of 'piled-up boxes', a wooden, box-like structure with warped poles at the top, a makeshift installation that emphasizes its materiality. It is a shape, though, and here Bishop begins her surreptitious rediscovery of purpose, that teases the viewer in and out of thought. Art has ceased to be iconic or symbolic of unageing intellect. The monument, rather, is 'the beginning of a painting, | a piece of sculpture, or poem, or monument, | and all of wood'. It is subject to, and made out of, the contingent, and requires the observer's sceptical involvement: 'Watch it closely' is how the poem ends. Yet for all its deflation of 'Kubla Khan', the poem's cunning insertion of the phrase 'or poem' reminds us that Bishop has written a monument and has, in her own unshowy way, fulfilled Coleridge's just-quoted desire to 'build that dome in air' ('Kubla Khan', 46).[39]

Poems about art bring sharply into focus poetic responses to the Romantic legacy. Stevens's 'Anecdote of the Jar' works its ambiguous way to what he himself calls 'The American Sublime' by replacing Keats's Grecian Urn with a 'jar' that is not only comically 'round upon the ground', but is also unignorably if awkwardly present, 'tall and of a port in air'. Its uncomfortable dominion is marked by the precipitation of rhymes on 'air': 'It took dominion everywhere. | The jar was gray and bare.' Here, art's nonsense pierces us with strange relation. Of all post-Romantic poets Stevens is the most concerned, in his oblique relations with the Romantic, to make the air breathed by his poems uneroded, unstale, not filled with spent images. The weather, and especially air, however much they may stand for 'reality', that troublesome term in Stevens, imply the workings of that equally troublesome term, 'imagination'. When in an intricate passage in *Notes toward a Supreme Fiction* Stevens asserts: 'The air is not a mirror but bare board' ('It Must Be Abstract', IV), he is building on his existential conviction that 'we live in a place | That is not our own and, much more, not ourselves'. The distinction between 'mirror' and 'bare board' both holds and collapses: if the air were a mirror, it would merely give us back our reflections; as a bare board or stage, it serves as a place where

---

[39] See Costello, *Elizabeth Bishop*, p. 218, for a comparison between 'The Monument' and 'Kubla Khan'.

plots not of our devising can unfold. Yet the fact that Stevens uses one metaphor to discredit another may suggest that the strongest impression conveyed by the line and the passage is of support for one of the *Adagia*: 'Reality is a cliché from which we escape by metaphor' (*OP*, p. 171). When Stevens rejects the air, as in 'Poem with Rhythms', he sculpts a post-Romantic rhetoric of the sublime that verges on solipsism; here the mind's figurations emerge as clothing the mind '*in the powerful mirror of my wish and will*', '*Not as in air, bright-blue-resembling air*'. The italicized assertion sways between the grand and the grandiloquent, and seems vulnerable to scepticism about the final power of the doubled '*wish and will*'.

As James Longenbach has shown,[40] Stevens articulates the friction between the claims of politics and those of poetry. It is at once a Romantic and a post-Romantic dilemma, but one which, treated by Stevens, turns quickly into metapoetic commentary. In 'Mozart 1935' Stevens feels the lure of 'That lucid souvenir of the past, | The divertimento; | That airy dream of the future, | The unclouded concerto'. The word 'airy' works to suggest a lack of reality, and Stevens instructs his poet, by way of Shelley's 'Ode to the West Wind', 'be thou, be thou | The voice of angry fear, | The voice of this besieging pain'. In the 'Bethou' section of *Notes toward a Supreme Fiction* ('It Must Change', VI), however, Stevens ironizes Shelley's urgent prayer to the wind: 'Be thou, Spirit fierce, | My spirit! Be thou me, impetuous one!' (61–2). The prayer's failure is tacitly conceded by the very form of the plea. Stevens's canto concludes: 'Bethou him, you | And you, bethou him and bethou. It is | A sound like any other. It will end.' The sparrow's 'Bethou' is spoken against the 'ké-ké' of the other birds, but the attempt to assert an original sound and the significance of the self fades as all voices turn into 'A single text, granite monotony'. It is a typical and sardonic Stevensian parable about poetry, about its continual capacity for entropy. Yet, as with Coleridge's 'Dejection: An Ode' or Shelley's *The Triumph of Life*, the theme of poetic entropy sparks a creative resurgence.

Stevens's imagining of a supreme fiction, 'the fiction of an absolute' as he calls it in *Notes toward a Supreme Fiction* ('It Must Give Pleasure', VII), shows the mind in the act of finding what will suffice. In this section of the poem Stevens takes to an elaborated extreme a fictive impulse in Shelley. True, he does not say, as Shelley does in the Conclusion to 'The Sensitive-Plant', 'It is a modest creed, and yet | Pleasant if one considers it' (13–14). But as he works his way in section VIII of 'It Must Give Pleasure' through conditional clauses towards central questions and the eruption of the subjective 'I'—'Am I that imagine this angel less satisfied? | Are the wings his, the lapis-haunted air?'— he tentatively asserts his creation of the 'air' his poem breathes: 'I have not but

---

[40] James Longenbach, *Wallace Stevens: The Plain Sense of Things* (New York: Oxford University Press, 1991).

I am and as I am, I am'. Coleridge's Primary Imagination is not far in the background, and yet Stevens's echo of Jehovah's self-titling looks dispossession squarely in the eye: 'I have not' lets go of ownership (of the angel, the lapis-haunted air, and so forth) in order to assert identity, 'I am'. That identity is the basis for the 'reflections' and 'escapades of death' with which the section wryly yet not wholly reductively concludes. 'Cinderella fulfilling herself beneath the roof' may seem auto-erotic to a damaging degree, yet 'external regions', the poem makes us aware, are sustained by poetic 'reflections'.

Fortuitously, the end of Stevens's late poem 'The Course of a Particular' read, in its original printing in *Opus Posthumous:*

> It is the cry of leaves that do not transcend themselves,
> ...
> In the absence of fantasia, without meaning more
> Than they are in the final finding of the air, in the thing
> Itself, until, at last the cry concerns no one at all.
> (*Palm*, p. 367 n. 9).

Subsequent printings have 'the final finding of the ear', but the misprint is peculiarly suggestive. The poem dramatizes in miniature Stevens's response to his own 'fantasia' and to that of Romanticism; in this response, 'There is a conflict, there is a resistance involved.' Stevens appears to want to capture a step-by-step withdrawal from imaginative projection, to reach a state in which the cry of the leaves 'concerns no one at all'. 'Final finding of the ear', in a sense, wants to be 'final finding of the air': 'air' would imply that the mind has been subsumed by 'the | Thing itself' (quoted from *Palm*). As it is, we are left with that mind as it rehearses a major theme in Stevens since 'The Snow Man', the wish to behold 'Nothing is not there and the nothing that is.' But this wish is never quite realized. Stevens's leaves may refuse the metaphoric transformations undergone by Shelley's leaves in 'Ode to the West Wind', and yet there is a conflict, a resistance involved in the American poet's project. For one thing, his negations show him involved in a mode of thinking officially outlawed by the poem: 'It is not a cry of divine attention, | Nor the smoke-drift of puffed-out heroes, no human cry.' For another, the sentence 'The leaves cry' will not divest itself, despite the poem's best efforts, of associations—desire, torment, and longing—produced by the verb.

In 'The Noble Rider and the Sound of Words' Stevens distinguishes between a pejorative sense of the word 'escapism' ('where the imagination does not adhere to reality') and a nobler sense of the word wherein poetry is a way of 'resisting or evading the pressure of reality'.[41] The intricate evasions of *as*, embodied in Stevens's 'syntactic provisionality'[42] and supplying an endless motive for metaphor, are forms of such resistance and evasion. Instead of accepting 'blank space', a Lockean void, poetry can reshape reality, as in Wordsworth's

---

[41] Stevens, *Necessary Angel*, pp. 31, 30. [42] Bornstein, *Transformations*, p. 205.

sonnet on Westminster Bridge, quoted by Stevens to show how the poet 'creates the world to which we turn incessantly and without knowing it'. And it is intriguing that the Wordsworthian lines, as quoted by Stevens, conclude with a vision of London 'All bright and glittering in the smokeless air'.[43] That 'smokeless air' is object and medium of Wordsworth's vision of what is 'bright and glittering', and it is such an expansion into supra-sensuous transparency that is often signalled by Stevens's images of air. Wordsworth's lines are freshly romantic, as Stevens wants his lines to be, and as he claims Marianne Moore's are in 'A Poet That Matters'. Moore's ways of making it new are the reverse of 'the sense in which the romantic is a relic of the imagination'. By contrast, she 'hybridizes by association', disconcerts expectation and is 'romantic' in the positive sense, 'meaning always the living and at the same time the imaginative'. The romantic in this sense 'is a process of cross-fertilisation, an immense process [. . .] of hybridization' (*OP*, pp. 248, 249).

Hybridization, in Stevens's sense, is a fitting image for the way in which twentieth-century poets enter into sustaining dialogue with the great Romantic poets. Mrs Alfred Uruguay may wipe away the romantic moonlight like mud, but Stevens's sympathies are always with the figure of capable imagination who passes her. In his 'Final Soliloquy of the Interior Paramour' Stevens offers a conversation as well as a monologue. So, Coleridge's 'The Eolian Harp' and his near-pantheist affirmation in chapter 13 of *Biographia Literaria* appear to be alluded to, in lines that compare poetry's warmth to 'A light, a power, the miraculous influence' and assert, albeit tentatively, 'We say God and the imagination are one . . .'.[44] Blake, too, suggests himself as a probable forebear. At the same time, Stevens concedes how his own reassertion of Romantic hope coexists with awareness that hope is creating from its own very possible wreckage: it is 'for small reason' that we think 'The world imagined is the ultimate good'; it is on account of our poverty that we wrap ourselves in 'the miraculous influence'; 'We say' is a phrase which reminds us that our words are sounds that will end like any other; our candles light up an immense darkness. Yet, at the last, 'We make a dwelling in the evening air.' Here Stevens makes poetry 'the song that names the earth', in Jonathan Bate's words;[45] but it is such a song, the poetry suggests, because post-Romantic poetry is often, and at its greatest, concerned, as Ezra Pound has it, 'To have gathered from the air a live tradition' (canto LXXXI).[46]

---

[43] Stevens, *Necessary Angel*, p. 31.
[44] Compare 'The Eolian Harp': 'A light in sound, a sound-like power in light' (28); and *Biographia Literaria*, where the 'primary IMAGINATION' is said to be 'a repetition in the finite mind of the eternal act of creation in the infinite I AM' (i., 304).
[45] Jonathan Bate, *The Song of the Earth* (London: Picador, 2000), p. 282.
[46] Ezra Pound, *The Cantos* (London: Faber, 1968).

2

'A Vision of Reality': Mid-to-Late Yeats

I

The young Yeats, 'a romantic in all', began his career as an enthusiastic admirer of Blake and Shelley.[1] As George Bornstein points out, however, for Yeats, 'not only Romanticism but even one's own Romanticism would change over time', and it is the later poet, the poet whose remarkable post-Romantic work is ushered in with the refrain 'Romantic Ireland's dead and gone' ('September 1913'), on whom this chapter will mainly concentrate.[2] 'September 1913' enacts an allegiance in the process of lamenting a loss. 'Romantic Ireland' is an idea out of Shelley and John O'Leary, known mainly as it has seemingly vanished, composed of a celebration of the nation in the light of ideals drawn from Romanticism. At the same time as affirming a seemingly now-lost idea, the poem involves Yeats in writing about all that affronts the imagination. This strategy brings Yeats close to the 'cadences of literary Modernism', as Bornstein argues, but it is recognizable in Wordsworth's encounters with the poor, in Blake's visions of contemporary London as a loathsome sewer, and in Shelley's confrontation with grimmer aspects of post-Waterloo European history in *The Triumph of Life*.[3] My purpose is not to deny Yeats's complicated affinities with Modernism, but to argue that his form of belated Romanticism is close kin to that impulse in English Romantic poetry to see poetry as an arena of struggle between poetic desire and recalcitrant reality. Like the Romantic poets, Yeats in 'September 1913' does not yield the victory to such reality, staging a last-minute fight-back that sounds elegiac but also reasserts the values of 'Romantic Ireland':

> They weighed so lightly what they gave.
> But let them be, they're dead and gone,
> They're with O'Leary in the grave. (30–2)

---

[1] W. B. Yeats, *Memoirs*, transcribed and ed. Denis Donoghue (New York: Macmillan, 1972), p. 19.
[2] George Bornstein, 'Yeats and Romanticism', in *The Cambridge Companion to W. B. Yeats*, ed. Marjorie Howes and John Kelly (Cambridge: Cambridge University Press, 2006), p. 21.
[3] Ibid. 28.

The heroes may be 'with O'Leary in the grave', but this reworking of the poem's refrain is silent about the fate of 'Romantic Ireland', an abstraction whose possible resurrection is embodied in the very carriage of the poem.

Yeats's development, as critics such as Harold Bloom and George Bornstein have demonstrated, relates closely to his readings and misreadings of Shelley, a poet whom he links and contrasts with Dante, and in this section I offer a rereading of Yeats as a reader and misreader of Shelley, in order to demonstrate Yeats's fierce wish to grapple with a major predecessor. I then provide in the chapter's second section more detailed accounts of a small number of his later poems.[4] Yeats's mid-career and later poems vex intriguingly his own exaltedly transhistorical account of the romantic as 'freedom of the spirit and imagination of man in literature'.[5] In 'Ego Dominus Tuus' Yeats distinguishes between, yet links, Dante and English Romantic poetry as he articulates the notion that 'art | Is but a vision of reality'; 'vision' bespeaks the student of Shelley and Blake, even as 'reality' swithers between a quasi-occultist sense of the real and a glance at a would-be unillusioned Modernism. The wisdom imagined in 'Ego Dominus Tuus' is hugged to itself by the poem's close, where Ille fears the hostile response of 'blasphemous men', and this secretive ending recalls the conclusion of another dialogue poem, Shelley's 'Julian and Maddalo', possibly the most striking pre-Yeatsian poem of self and anti-self: 'I urged and questioned still, she told me how | All happened—but the cold world shall not know' (616–17).

In 'Ego Dominus Tuus' the second speaker, Ille, offers this view of Dante:

> I think he fashioned from his opposite
> An image that might have been a stony face
> Staring upon a Bedouin's horse-hair roof
> From doored and windowed cliff, or half upturned
> Among the coarse grass and the camel-dung.
> He set his chisel to the hardest stone.
> Being mocked by Guido for his lecherous life,
> Deriding and derided, driven out
> To climb that stair and eat that bitter bread,
> He found the unpersuadable justice, he found
> The most exalted lady loved by a man. (27–37)

Eric Griffiths chides Yeats for believing that 'he would have recognised Dante anywhere, however infernal the press or celestial the throng', adding that the Florentine master 'looks quite like a well-fed hamster in many of the early illuminated

---

[4] Harold Bloom, *Yeats* (New York: Oxford University Press, 1970); George Bornstein, *Yeats and Shelley* (Ithaca: Cornell University Press, 1970); *idem*, *Transformations*.

[5] Yeats, *Unpublished Prose*, ed. J. P. Frayne (New York: Macmillan, 1970), i. 183.

manuscripts'.⁶ This is an entertaining put-down of a kind that Yeats seems often to invite. But it misses wholly one of the points of Yeats's lines, that the 'spectral image' by which Dante is best known may well not have resembled 'The man that Lapo and that Guido knew' (phrase and line also from 'Ego Dominus Tuus', 25, 26). The relationship between that 'stony face' and Dante the man, 'the bundle of accident and incoherence', to borrow the famous formulation from 'A General Introduction for My Work', who sat down 'to breakfast', is, says Ille, one of opposition.⁷ The lines offer an understanding of self-creation or self-fashioning central to Yeats and his relations with Romantic poetry as well as Dante: the notion that anything shaped, a self, a poem, a culture, is made from a conscious effort to 'imagine ourselves as different from what we are', to move against the grain of what is natural, easy, straightforward, 'the passive acceptance of a code'. This idea appeals to Yeats as the source of modern heroism, of what in the same section of *Per Amica Silentia Lunae* he calls 'Active virtue'.⁸ Such 'virtue' is heroic because it involves wrestling continually with 'new bitterness, new disappointment' (*Per Amica*, p. 15); it entails a fight for imaginative life with the 'Daimon' (Yeats's term for the anti-self at its most imperious and occult), who 'delivers and deceives us' (*Per Amica*, p. 11).

Yet what alliteration ('delivers and deceives') joins together, Yeats's keen self-awareness has already put asunder. Arguably, it is the defeats that lie in store for his treasured, desperate notion of the anti-self, after the breakthrough of 'Ego Dominus Tuus', which make him a poet of power and great pathos. Yeats argues, through his conception of the anti-self, that the poet does not find himself so much as discover an image that embodies the capacity to imagine the self as different from what it is, thus escaping the restrictions of viewpoints, personalities, cultural horizons. That, at any rate, is the idea; but in Yeats's finest poems it is rarely unimperilled by contrary impulses. All that is opposed by the anti-self fights back in, say, 'A Dialogue of Self and Soul'. Ille and Hic reappear, in somewhat altered guises, as the poet's Soul and Self in the poem. The Soul, a good student of *A Vision*, urges the poet to 'Fix every wandering thought upon | That quarter where all thought is done' (6–7); the Self chooses 'emblems of the day' (29) and, in response to the Soul's contempt for 'the

---

⁶ Eric Griffiths, 'The Divine Comedy Collides with the Modern "Vision Thing"', *The Guardian Review*, 8 Jan. 1998. *Guardian Unlimited*. Online.

⁷ Quoted from W. B. Yeats, *Later Essays*, ed. W. H. O'Donnell, with assistance from E. Bergmann Loizeaux (New York: Charles Scribner's Sons, 1994), p. 204. In *Later Essays*, the essay is entitled 'Introduction', with the following subtitle, '(w. 1937) For the never-published Charles Scribner's Sons "Dublin Edition" of W. B. Yeats; published in *Essays and Introductions* (1961) as "A General Introduction for My Work"'.

⁸ *Per Amica Silentia Lunae*, quoted from W. B. Yeats, *Later Essays*, p. 10; subsequent references to *Per Amica* are drawn from this edition; page numbers are given parenthetically in the main body of the text.

crime of death and birth' (24), claims 'A charter to commit the crime once more' (32). Yeats uses his roomy, eight-line stanza, with its quickening shorter lines towards the close, to accommodate both positions. But in the poem's second half, Soul drops away, and Self comes to the fore, uttering a tormented yet pugnacious defence of life, and concluding with a vision of unesoteric blessedness that emerges from the previous acceptance of the 'blind man's ditch' (II. 19), Yeats's image for life at its most 'unpurged' ('Byzantium', 1). True, the final blessedness in 'A Dialogue of Self and Soul' requires a casting out of 'remorse' (II. 28), but this casting out feels less like a return to the Soul's wisdom than a rejection of its disdain for quotidian experience. With more disenchanted knowingness, 'The Circus Animals' Desertion' records a comparable process, though not without backsliding in favour of the dream of art. When Yeats asserts, 'It was the dream itself enchanted me' (II. 20), the line does many things at once in a way that is characteristic: to employ the two nouns which give Conor Cruise O'Brien's well-known essay on Yeats its title, but to unite them in a more positive manner than O'Brien does, 'passion' weds itself to 'cunning'.[9] Yeats writes lines that are deliberate, even majestic, and yet shot through with a mercurial elusiveness. In this case, the 'dream itself' takes on a value of its own, facing down the poet's own post-Freudian awareness; at the same time, 'enchanted' speaks not only of legitimate imaginative mastery, but also of possible deception.

For all its moments of declarative force, 'Ego Dominus Tuus' bears out Yeats's assertion in *Per Amica Silentia Lunae* that 'we sing amid our uncertainty' (p. 8).[10] It is clear from other associated prose writings that the side of Yeats which was critical of his belief in occult wisdom was never silenced during the years during which he wrote 'Ego Dominus Tuus' and was effectively engaged in a remaking of the self. In 'The Poet and the Actress' (unpublished until 1991), the Poet prevails with his belief in the need for 'a violent antithesis' in 'our natures, and the circumstances that surround us', but the Actress is for most of the dialogue unpersuaded of the need to wear a mask.[11] A few months later, in December 1916, Yeats wrote a letter to 'Leo Africanus', his supposed occult alter ego. As R. F. Foster points out, 'It is a strangely irresolute text.'[12] If

---

[9] Conor Cruise O'Brien, 'Passion and Cunning: An Essay on the Politics of W. B. Yeats', in *In Excited Reverie: A Centenary Tribute to William Butler Yeats, 1865–1939*, ed A. N. Jeffares and K. G. W. Cross, (London: Macmillan, 1965), pp. 256–63.

[10] See A. Norman Jeffares on the way in which in *Per Amica* Yeats 'undercuts . . . affirmations with questions, so that he often leaves his options open' (*W. B. Yeats: A New Biography* (London: Continuum, 2001), p. 169).

[11] Yeats ' "The Poet and the Actress": An Unpublished Dialogue by W. B. Yeats', ed. David R. Clark, in *Yeats Annual No. 8,* ed. Warmick Gould (Basingstoke: Macmillan, 1991), p. 136.

[12] Roy Foster, *W. B. Yeats,* ii: *The Arch-Poet, 1915–1939* (Oxford: Oxford University Press, 2003), p. 72; hereafter Foster.

it contains Leo's vehement assertion that he really exists—'it is only because I am your opposite,' he says in Ille-like tones (as Foster points out), 'your antithesis because I am in all things furthest from your intellect & your will, that I alone am your Interlocutor'—it closes with this characteristic stricken qualm on Yeats's part: 'I am not convinced that in this letter there is one sentence that has come from beyond my imagination.'[13]

In the poem itself, Ille brushes aside Hic's scorn. Picking up, instead, on Hic's final phrase, 'Magical shapes' (7), set apart as if to foil its speaker's conscious intentions, and making a highly rhetorical poetry out of the quarrel with the self, Ille develops the idea of the anti-self, reached through 'the help of an image' (7). Ille does not quite 'call up'. Less peremptorily, he 'call[s] to my own opposite' (8), and there is pleading—and stasis—in the summons. When at the end Ille 'call[s] to the mysterious one who yet | Shall walk the wet sands by the edge of the stream' (70–1), there is progression; the abstract 'opposite' has become a being of spectral flesh and blood, but there is a sense, too, of progression as punishingly incremental, 'yet' drawing to itself a charge of still unfulfilled hope. The poem is a prelude to vision.

Yeats's 'Magical shapes', as Bloom and Bornstein have noted, are Shelleyan in origin, deriving from Cythna's account in *Laon and Cythna,* canto 7, of her recovery from madness, which involved her drawing on the sand 'Clear, elemental shapes, whose smallest change | A subtler language within language wrought: | The key of truths which once were dimly taught | In old Crotona' (3111–14).[14] Yeats, too, searches for a 'subtler language within language', dimly taught by many predecessors, at the head of whom one might place Shelley. Indeed, it is arguable that Shelley, rather than Leo Africanus, shadows that 'mysterious one' who is both double and anti-self at the poem's close. Yeats's 'subtler language' emerges from the pressure brought to bear on plain but active verbs, words such as 'call' and, crucially, 'find' and its cognates. Wishing to 'find myself and not an image' (10), Hic provokes an attack by Ille on 'the gentle, sensitive mind' (12) that has cost us 'the old nonchalance of the hand' (13). Ille is at once among those afflicted by the modern condition ('We are but critics' (15), he laments, and the pronoun is telling), and a seeker after that 'old nonchalance', gestured towards in the fine carelessness with which 'old nonchalance of the *hand*' fails to avoid an obtrusive repetition soon after Ille's wish to 'summon all | That I have *handled* least' (8–9; emphases added).

The quest to 'find' is central to the poem. Yeats does not lazily assume knowledge of a body of ideas outside his poetry; he works towards them through the words he uses, and the insistence with which 'find' (or cognate forms of the

---

[13] S. L. Adams and G. Mills Harper (eds.), 'The Manuscript of Leo Africanus', in *Yeats Annual No. 1* (1982); quoted in Foster, p. 74.

[14] See Bloom, *Yeats,* pp. 200–2, and Bornstein, *Yeats and Shelley,* p. 91.

verb) is used tells us that this is an inward, post-Romantic poem, concerned with imaginative exploration. At the same time, the fascination with doubleness and division has a muted but inescapable political relevance. In a lecture given a decade earlier, Yeats suggests the connections between his fascination with inner conflict and Ireland's troubled political landscape: 'England sometimes taunts us with our divisions,' he told his American audience, 'divisions that she has done her best to foment; as if she herself was ever united, as if it was natural for any country to be united. No land lives out a wholesome life, full of ideas and vitality, that is not fighting out great issues within its own borders.' Yeats in this lecture expresses reservations about 'an unnatural unity' achieved at great cost under a leader such as Parnell; such a 'unity' 'broke up explosively', since 'underneath were emotions, forces, seeking to express themselves'.[15] One way of looking at the idea of self and anti-self in Yeats is to regard it as a means of channelling and regulating contrary 'emotions, forces, seeking to express themselves'. Throughout 'Ego Dominus Tuus' Yeats transforms Freudian thought and sub-textual political strife into a drama consonant with the drives that underpin imaginative discovery. Whereas Freud sees the sovereign ego as failing to exercise mastery in its own household, Yeats views the self as capable of 'a vision of reality' through summoning its 'opposite'.

So, Ille imagines how Dante 'fashioned from his opposite | An image'. The verb, picked out by the iambic emphasis, implies that Dante both 'moulded' and 'gave shape to' (to give the relevant *OED* meanings); it intimates that Dante brought something (or someone) new into existence, and that this something (or someone) new was already there, *in potentia*. That the 'fashioning' involves imaging and imagination is brought out by the twofold process of the making: first, the meeting with, that involves a summoning up of, the poet's 'opposite'; then the finding for that 'opposite' of 'An image'. Bloom is right to say that the poem's 'strength . . . is that Yeats evades the constriction of his still rudimentary doctrine'.[16] Moreover, as already indicated, Hic has his moments, and surely the poem's choice of exempla, Dante and Keats (whatever one makes of Ille's views about them), confirms a strong element of truth in Hic's assertion that 'A style is found by sedentary toil, | And by the imitation of great masters' (65–6). At any rate, 'sedentary toil' was necessary for Ille's understanding of the two poets' careers, even if the passive voice ('is found') counters Ille's trust in subjective quest. Hic's 'found' is in touch with the need for foundations; Ille's kiss is given to the void.

A Dantescan clarity finds expression in Ille's 'He set his chisel to the hardest stone'. The line, end-stopped even as it implies endless labour, acts as a 'stone'

---

[15] Yeats, 'Four Lectures by W. B. Yeats, 1902–4', ed. Richard Londraville, in *Yeats Annual No. 8*, pp. 105, 106.
[16] Bloom, *Yeats*, p. 198.

in the midst of the stream of two swirling long sentences; it brings out the work involved in imagining an image of one's opposite: Yeats avoids saying that Dante successfully carved or sculptured or wrought or even chiselled an image. Rather, he takes us back to the process of work, the act of chiselling. If the poem's thinking about Dante mingles supposed biography with the idea of art as 'a hollow image of fulfilled desire' (*Per Amica*, p. 7), Ille's lines carry conviction because their rhythms and allusions participate in the fictional construction that is their subject. Didactic exposition turns into imaginative drama. So, the alliteration of 'Deriding and derided, driven out | To climb that stair and eat that bitter bread' helps to underscore the to-and-fro sways that beset a man compelled to live out his destiny. 'Deriding and derided, driven out', he may be, but he is also the agent of two infinitives. The last two lines are all active, and the use of 'found' pulls away from the idea of wish-fulfilment: 'He found . . ., he found.' In a draft, Yeats wrote, 'He saw the unpersuadable justice in a vision.'[17] But, wanting to hold back the word 'vision' for Ille's next speech (see 48), he elected to cut the echo of 'Kubla Khan' ('A damsel with a dulcimer | In a vision once I saw', 37–8), with its suggestion of unrecoverable inspiration and domes in air. His Dante not only 'saw', he 'found'. At the same time, ambiguity of a kind familiar in Romantic poetry surrounds the would-be unambiguous emphasis on finding. Did Dante find what was there? Or did he find, as we say, what he was looking for? The repetition of 'found' betrays the 'driven' nature of Dante's quest.

Yeats places Dante and Shelley (and himself) in phase 17 of his system in *A Vision*, differentiating between his two predecessors in ways that favour Dante over Shelley. As Bornstein points out, Yeats's 'interpretation of Dante's personality . . . assumes particular importance for understanding both Yeats's own ambitions and his view of Shelley'.[18] But the exaltation of Dante for being able to attain 'Unity of Being' cannot disguise Yeats's recognition of affinity with and indebtedness to Shelley.[19] Shelley, too, develops as a poet through the assimilation of a range of influences, central among which is the poetry of Dante. Dante's work sponsors a series of daringly metaphorical imaginings in the Romantic writer's later works, especially *Adonais* and *The Triumph of Life*. At the end of *Adonais* the atheistic Shelley plunders the Catholic medieval

---

[17] Yeats, '*The Wild Swans at Coole*': *Manuscript Materials*, ed. Stephen Parrish (Ithaca: Cornell University Press, 1994), p. 277.

[18] Bornstein, *Yeats and Shelley*, p. 220. See n. 53 on the same page for the comment that 'Richard Ellmann told me in conversation that Mrs. Yeats said her husband regarded himself as a man of phase seventeen.'

[19] Yeats, *A Vision* (London: Macmillan, 1962), p. 144, where Dante is said to have 'attained, as poet, to Unity of Being', while, on Yeats's reading, Shelley is a poet 'in whom . . . as poet unity was but in part attained'.

poet for images that suggest a secularized heaven.[20] In turn, Yeats, heavily indebted to Shelley, turns away, as already suggested in Chapter 1, from Shelley's political optimism in poems such as 'Leda and the Swan' and 'Nineteen Hundred and Nineteen'. Yeats criticizes Shelley through an understanding of Dante as a poet who was, as he puts it in *A Vision*, 'content to see both good and evil'. By contrast, Shelley, drawn like Dante, to '"simplification through intensity"' (hence his Mask is a figure like Ahasuerus or Athanase or Dante's 'gaunt' self-representation), is said, as will be noted and discussed in Chapter 5, to have 'lacked the Vision of Evil', and not to 'conceive of the world as a continual conflict, so, though great poet he certainly was, he was not of the greatest kind'.[21] Admittedly, all poets compared with Dante seem like sunspots compared with the sun, but Yeats ignores that sceptical restlessness in Shelley which makes him refuse to come to ultimate judgements about the origin of evil, a restlessness at work in the Romantic poet's most Dantescan poem, *The Triumph of Life*, and analysed in Chapter 5's discussion of Stevens's 'Esthétique du Mal'.

The longer one stays with 'Ego Dominus Tuus', the more Shelley's features obtrude. The Romantic poet cited by Hic as proving the capacity of artists simply to express inner happiness and by Ille to show that all happy art is compensation for experiential unhappiness is Keats. But Keats makes an easier target for Yeats than Shelley does. Ille caricatures Keats 'as a schoolboy . . . | With face and nose pressed to a sweet-shop window' (55–6), though, as often in Yeats, the tone of brutal, overriding assertion concedes that assertion is grounded in subjective impressive ('I see a schoolboy when I think of him', 55). Ille starts with the question—surely a perceptive question so far as Keats is concerned—'His art is happy, but who knows his mind?' (54). Then, deploying that *'affirmative capability'* which Ellmann discovers in Yeats, Ille tells us what he 'sees' when he thinks of Keats.[22] 'Certainly' comes later in the speech (57). So, if the lines seem reductive about Keats—he made 'Luxuriant song' (62) because he was 'Shut out from all the luxury of the world' (60)—they offer themselves as little more than trenchant opinion.[23]

If in the poem Yeats seems to take issue with a debased 'romantic' notion of art as self-expression, he exempts the practice of the Romantics from this debased romantic notion. Greatness is conceded to Keats, if not greatness of the

---

[20] Among many other relevant works, see Peter Vassallo, 'From Petrarch to Dante: The Discourse of Disenchantment in Shelley's *The Triumph of Life*', *Journal of Anglo-Italian Studies*, 1 (1991), pp. 102–10, and Michael O'Neill, 'Cathestant or Protholic? Shelley's Italian Imaginings', *Journal of Anglo-Italian Studies*, 6 (2001), pp. 153–68.

[21] Yeats, *A Vision*, pp. 142, 141, 144.

[22] Richard Ellmann, *The Identity of Yeats* (London: Macmillan, 1954), p. 238.

[23] For a similar view of Keats as 'like a a boy with his face glued to the glass window of a sweet shop', and as someone who has altered 'the history [and] the direction of our poetry', see ' "The Poet and the Actress"', p. 134.

highest kind: Dante is a tragic hero of the antithetical creative life; Keats is that life's inspired fool, tricked by needing to sublimate interiorized feelings of social rejection into a 'happy art', to use Yeats's phrase from *Per Amica*, 'Anima Hominis', section 4, that cannot include within itself recognition of its origins in misery. Or, as Yeats says in the same section of *Per Amica*, the 'lineaments' of Dante's art 'express also the poverty or the exasperation that set its maker to the work' (p. 7), where 'set' chimes with the poem's use of the same verb in 'He set his chisel to the hardest stone'.[24] And yet, though in March 1916 Yeats wrote to his father, 'I think Keats perhaps greater than Shelley and beyond words greater than Swinburne because he makes pictures one cannot forget & sees them as full of rhythm as a Chinease [*sic*] painting', Shelley is Yeats's true Romantic 'opposite'.[25] Yeats was fascinated by Shelley as a poet of doubles. It is intriguing that 'The Poet and the Actress' alludes to a story about Shelley that one can sense ghosting the final lines of 'Ego Dominus Tuus'. Yeats speaks of Synge as keeping before him in his final months 'death . . . , and the answer Shelley gave, when the spirit came to him in a dream before his drowning and said are you satisfied. Both [Shelley and Synge or his tragic heroine, Deirdre] answered "I am satisfied".'[26] That final touch is an addition to the story, since, as David R. Clark points out, there is no mention in the original account of Shelley making any such answer.[27] The addition shows Yeats's unappeasable demand that Shelley should share his quest for a 'group of images, which obeys us, which leaves us free, and which satisfies the need of our soul'.[28] Yet, as Yeats himself says in *Per Amica Silentia Lunae* in a meditation on how the heart of a poet cannot be satisfied: 'The poet finds and makes his mask in disappointment, the hero in defeat. The desire that is satisfied is not a great desire, nor has the shoulder used all its might that an unbreakable gate has never strained' (p. 12). 'Finds and makes' is a phrase that rehearses the twinning of discovery and invention which supplies 'Ego Dominus Tuus' and *Per Amica* with their enabling inner quarrel. Yeats, who reruns the same Shelleyan story in 'Are You Content?', a poem which concludes, 'But I am not content' (24), and who in 'The Circus Animals' Desertion', entertains with an audible snarl the notion that 'I must be satisfied with my heart' (4), subtly condescends to Shelley in having him reply to the double who portends death, 'I am satisfied', because, as he taught many others to see, Shelley is a poet of 'infinite desire' who sought 'more in life than any understood'.[29]

---

[24] See Albright in his note on l. 25 of the poem for a comparison with Yeats's 'The Phases of the Moon', l. 40: 'He follows whatever whim's most difficult' (p. 587).
[25] Quoted from Foster, p. 36.   [26] Yeats, ' "The Poet and the Actress" ', p. 136.
[27] Ibid. 143.   [28] Ibid. 136.
[29] Yeats's phrase and his quotation from Shelley's unfinished late lyric 'The Zucca' occur in 'The Philosophy of Shelley's Poetry', p. 78.

'Ego Dominus Tuus' knows better than the anecdote in 'The Poet and the Actress'; it knows that the 'mysterious one', both double and anti-self, is longed for rather than attained, that the poem's drama has emerged out of Yeats's bitter soul. In 'Anima Mundi', the second half of *Per Amica*, Yeats writes as if in possession of a comparable knowledge: 'When I remember that Shelley calls our minds "mirrors of the fire for which all thirst", I cannot but ask the question all have asked, "What or who has cracked the mirror?" I begin to study the only self that I can know, myself, and to wind the thread upon the perne again' (p. 31). Shelley, too, in *Adonais*, from which Yeats quotes (484–5), moves between the burden of selfhood and the longing for transcendence. In the final stanza, he is still 'the only self that [he] can know', a self 'borne' perilously towards the 'soul of Adonais', with the anxiety-ridden question, 'What Adonais is, why fear we to become?' (492, 494, 459), still ringing in the reader's ear.

Yeats says of Shelley that 'he can never see anything that opposes him as it really is'.[30] But then Yeats had problems seeing for what they really are those aspects of Shelley's poetry which opposed the younger man's mystical desires. Bloom makes a related point about Yeats's account in 'The Philosophy of Shelley's Poetry' of the conclusion of 'The Sensitive Plant' as constituting 'a reference to a palpable spirit-world, a universe of squeaking phantasms that can be invoked by a Soho medium or a self-induced trance'.[31] One notes in this essay that for Yeats a symbol is a means of accessing a 'mystical state of the soul', whereas one might feel that for Shelley an image or symbol is often fretting away at, rather than confirming, ancient associations. Yeats himself comments that he does not know whether Shelley 'understood that the great Memory is ... a dwelling-house of symbols, of images that are living souls', and he revealingly, if beautifully, misreads 'Mont Blanc' when he describes it as 'an intricate analogy to affirm that the soul has its sources in the "secret strength of things which governs thought, and to the infinite dome of heaven is as a law"'.[32] It is revealing that he stops short of considering the poem's final twist, its recognition that all depends on the 'human mind's imaginings' (143). But, at his acutest, Yeats is alert to a strain of quest in Shelley that makes him an apt illustration of the admission in *Per Amica* that the poet 'may not stand within the sacred house but lives amid the whirlwinds that beset its threshold' (p. 9).

In *Adonais* Shelley writes of the 'one Spirit's plastic stress' (381), 'compelling there | All new successions to the forms they wear' (382–3). Shelley's trance of waking thought in *The Triumph of Life*, where all is time-bound and no 'One' beckons, allows little escape from 'successions', experiences endlessly crying out for and refusing to be accorded causal explanations. Figuration in the

---

[30] Yeats, *A Vision*, p. 143. [31] Bloom, *Yeats*, p. 61.
[32] Yeats, 'Philosophy of Shelley's Poetry', pp. 65, 57–8.

Commedia brings into play associations and makes demands on the reader's intellectual and emotional resources. But it does not involve the reader in tracking the process of mental unravelling and ultimate bewilderment that occurs in *The Triumph*'s use of images. In Dante, the starlings borne along and the cranes chanting their songs to whom the 'ombre' (shades) are compared at the outset of the Paulo and Francesca episode; the suggestive comparison between Dante and Virgil and people 'who ponder o'er their road, who in heart do go, and in body stay' (*Purg.* 2. 11–12), full of the deferred longing typical of *Purgatorio*; the climactic account of 'the scattered leaves of all the universe— again something the pilgrim says he 'saw'—'bound by love in one volume' (*Par.* 33. 85–7): all these moments crystallize and bind together feeling and thought.[33] What Shelley gives in *The Triumph* are similes that trace the curve of shifting consciousness. When Yeats says of phase 17 that in it, by contrast with phases 13 and 14, 'where mental images were separated from one another that they might be subject to knowledge, all now flow, change, flutter, cry out, or mix into something else', he might be describing the way in which in *The Triumph* the narrator experiences the dawning sun as both radiant and dispiriting, or the chariot of life as at once majestic or menacing—or, indeed, Rousseau's experience of the 'shape all light' (352) as now entrancing, now devastating, now deeply desired.[34] In the Preface to *Prometheus Unbound*, Shelley asserts that 'The imagery which I have employed will be found, in many instances, to have been drawn from the operations of the human mind, or from those external actions by which they are expressed', and he singles out Dante's writing as particularly full of such images (p. 230). In *The Triumph* those mental 'operations' are enigmatic; so, in Rousseau's encounter with the 'shape all light', simile leads from one emotion to another, changes possibly explained by Rousseau's own shifting states of mind, possibly due to the shifting nature of the shape, possibly the product of his own projections—but all true to the difficulty of final judgement, final explanation.[35]

In a late essay, 'Prometheus Unbound', Yeats comes close, albeit inadvertently, since his overt intention seems hostile, to doing justice to the side of Shelley that is never 'satisfied' when he comments: 'Shelley was not a mystic, his system of thought was constructed by his logical faculty to satisfy desire,

---

[33] Dante is quoted from the translations in the Temple Classics edition (see Note on Texts).
[34] Yeats, *A Vision*, p. 141.
[35] Stuart Curran's fine 'Figuration in Shelley and Dante', in *Dante's Modern Afterlife: Reception and Response from Blake to Heaney*, ed. Nick Havely (Basingstoke: Macmillan, 1998), stresses the affinity between the two poets' use of 'figuration', both seen as using it to 'disconcert' and enforce 'an act of questioning as prior to any agreement that may be struck between signifier and signified' (p. 55). My emphasis is on the way in which 'figuration' in Shelley's *The Triumph of Life* demands that we relate it back to the workings of a consciousness that may be divided against or even, at moments, incomprehensible to itself.

not a symbolical revelation received after the suspension of all desire. He could neither say with Dante "Thy will is my peace", nor with Finn in the Irish story "the best music is what happens".'[36] Shelley may wish to 'satisfy desire', but Yeats suspends him between the Dante capable of intuiting and acquiescing in divine purpose and the Finn who accepts 'what happens'. Yeats may deny 'symbolical revelation' to Shelley, but he gives us a Shelley who lives through incompleteness. Indeed, Yeats makes his peace with Shelley both at the end of this essay, where he says that 'When in middle life I looked back I found that he and not Blake, whom I had studied more and with more approval, had shaped my life',[37] and in one of his last poems, 'Cuchulain Comforted', which shapes a direct line between Dante, whose *terza rima* is used for the only time by Yeats, Shelley whose resistance to closure is also honoured by the poem, and Yeats. As Peter Vassallo and others have pointed out, the cowards sewing in the afterlife, Cuchulain's antithetical anti-selves, recall Dante's image of an old tailor peering at his needle which precedes his recognition of Brunetto Latini in the *Inferno* (15. 20–1).[38] Yeats subjects his heroic ideal to majestic diminishment in this poem, as he anticipates an afterlife in which Cuchulain must submit to the rule of the Shrouds. The opening sets up a contrast that is also an unlikely correspondence between the hero and the Shrouds, an asymmetrical relationship to which Yeats's *terza rima* attunes itself. The hero seems first to hold centre-stage, 'Violent and famous' (2), leaning 'upon a tree' (5), but the Shrouds, introduced as 'the dead' in the unrhymed second line of the first tercet, begin eerily to steal the show.

Post-mortal encounter is the theme of this *terza rima* poem, as in Dante's *Commedia* and Shelley's *The Triumph of Life*. But Yeats reacts against Dante and Shelley by stripping the dead of their individuality. Shifting patterns of sound subtly mimic the neutralization of heroic energy: the active virtue of 'strode' (2) must cope with the passivity of 'dead' (2) and the fearful spectatorship of 'stared' (3), before the word 'Shrouds' (4) casts its shapeless folds over the scene, a scene dominated by the fact that their being 'afraid' (15) gives them power over the person who induces fear. This sound-cluster transforms itself towards the close, when out of its ashes emerges, phoenix-like, the true rhyme of 'words' (23) and 'birds' (25). The Shrouds themselves undergo a further transformation in the metamorphic last line, 'They had changed their throats and had the throats of birds' (25), as though they (and Cuchulain with them) were able to take on the power of poets. Fragile and spectral as the

---

[36] Yeats, *Later Essays*, p. 120.

[37] Ibid. 121–2; see Bloom, *Yeats*, for the view that the moving turn-around at the essay's end shows that 'Yeats's subject ... tended to be his relation as poet to his own vision, in Shelley's mode rather than Blake's, for Blake largely centered on the content of the poetic vision itself' (p. 63).

[38] See Peter Vassallo, 'T. S. Eliot, W. B. Yeats and the Dantean "Familiar Compound Ghost" in Little Gidding', *Journal of Anglo-Italian Studies*, 6 (2001), pp. 243–4.

poem's vision of companionship is, it issues a rebuke to the image of heroic isolation which has sustained Yeats and which, in different ways, he projected on to Dante and Shelley. This vision finds a focus in the use of 'Came': at first the staring eyes 'were gone' (3); then 'certain Shrouds' (4), where 'certain' makes use of the double meaning that Yeats gives the same word in 'Man and the Echo' (12), 'Came and were gone' (5); finally, and no less authoritatively for their 'creeping' (10) motion, other 'Shrouds' (9) 'Came creeping up because the man was still' (10). Almost as though recalling the Wordsworth for whom vision was often a gift offered the soul when 'still', the 'still' hero sees the gathered 'Shrouds', an unintended but significant by-product of his apparent attempt to 'meditate on wounds and blood' (6).

'All we do | All must together do' (16–17): acting in 'common' (24), the Shrouds represent the antithesis of Yeatsian heroism, as the creepingly incremental phrasing shows. The pressure to conform in 'must together' is strong; read metapoetically, the lines slap down any post-Romantic notion of poetic individuality. Yet, a further turn of the wheel, a further progress along the labyrinth of 'the *Shiftings*' (described in *A Vision* as a state 'where the *Spirit* is purified of good and evil'), and Yeats will be on his own again.[39] So, ultimately, the poet figures his union with previous poets and asserts his own 'final isolation', in Bloom's phrase, much as in *Adonais* Keats is absorbed into 'The splendours of the firmament of time' (388), but Shelley is left voyaging 'darkly, fearfully, afar' (492) on his own quasi-Dantescan, solitary quest.[40] Yeats speaks affectingly about such isolation amid company at the end of the first paragraph of *Per Amica*, 'Anima Hominis', section 5, where the 'We' that has governed most of the paragraph drops away and the first-person singular takes centre-stage: 'I shall find the dark grow luminous, the void fruitful when I understand that I have nothing, that the ringers in the tower have appointed for the hymen of the soul a passing bell' (p. 9). The editors of *Later Essays* direct us to Shelley's 'Julian and Maddalo' for those 'ringers in the tower', and one might wish to assert, too, that for the Yeats of *Per Amica* no poet speaks so eloquently of 'the hymen of the soul', the soul's marriage with 'reality', as the Dante of the *Vita Nuova* and the *Commedia*.[41]

II

If Yeats seeks a 'marriage with "reality"', he thrives on conflict and dispute, on the possibility of divorce between mind and externality, as, for him, did at

---

[39] Yeats, *A Vision*, p. 231. See Bloom, *Yeats*, pp. 463–4.   [40] Ibid., p. 465.
[41] Yeats, *Later Essays*, p. 296.

least one of his Romantic avatars: William Blake. Canny as ever, Yeats seeks to guide us to the heart of the matter when in *A Vision* he writes in a passage broken in upon by a diagram illustrating the 'Primary' and 'Antithetical' movements of the gyres:

I had never read Hegel, but my mind had been full of Blake from boyhood up and I saw the world as a conflict—Spectre and Emanation—and could distinguish between a contrary and a negation. 'Contraries are positive', wrote Blake, 'a negation is not a contrary', 'How great the gulph between simplicity and insipidity', and again, 'There is a place at the bottom of the graves where contraries are equally true.' (*A Vision*, p. 72)

Yeats quotes and slightly misquotes the reversed writing in Plate 30 of Blake's *Milton*, which opens, 'How wide the Gulf & Unpassable! between Simplicity and Insipidity', before the mirror-written assertions, 'Contraries are Positives' and 'A Negation is not a Contrary'; he also alludes to *Jerusalem*, chapter 2, Plate 48: 13–14: 'Beneath the bottoms of the Graves, which is Earths central joint, | There is a place where Contrarieties are equally true'. Yeats's misquotations, one might argue, allow him to build a theory of creative 'conflict' out of Blake's pronouncements, yet to avoid too slavish an adherence to a Blakean system. The rewriting, 'Contraries are positive', is especially marked. Blake's plural noun, 'Positives', yields to a Yeatsian adjective; Blake is made strange by being made 'conventional'. A similar process is at work in the rewriting of *Jerusalem*, where Blakean plurality—'the bottoms of the graves'—again passes into Yeatsian fixity: 'a place at the bottom of the graves'. Important as 'contraries' are to Yeats, he intuits the fact that a theory of creative conflict can grow complacent. As Essick and Viscomi remark in relation to the first lines of *Milton*, Plate 30, 'There is a place where Contrarieties are equally True | This place is called Beulah': 'If "Contrarieties" are equally true, then there is peace but perhaps no "progression"' (the allusion is to Blake's comment in Plate 3 of *The Marriage of Heaven and Hell*, 'Without Contraries is no progression').[42]

The later Yeats sculpts poems out of 'contraries', but he does not impose any Blakean theory on his poetic creations. 'Contraries' flourish in the roomy spaces of the *ottava rima* stanzas preferred by Yeats in many of his later meditative poems, poems such as 'Coole and Ballylee, 1931'. For the middle-aged Yeats, looking back in elegiac mode, it seemed like a form of spiritual nobility to claim to be a Romantic. Defiant, almost defeated by the 'darkening flood' of modernity, he concludes 'Coole and Ballylee, 1931' with this stanza:

> We were the last romantics—chose for theme
> Traditional sanctity and loveliness;
> Whatever's written in what poets name

---

[42] William Blake, *Milton: A Poem*, ed. with intro. and notes by Robert N. Essick and Joseph Viscomi (London: William Blake Trust/Tate Gallery, 1993), p. 182.

> The book of the people; whatever most can bless
> The mind of man or elevate a rhyme;
> But all is changed, that high horse riderless,
> Though mounted in that saddle Homer rode
> Where the swan drifts upon a darkening flood. (41–8)

To be, or, more precisely, to know that you were a 'last romantic' is to elegize, rather than to reassert faith in, the 'theme' of 'Traditional sanctity and loveliness'. It is, above all, to place the poet's lonely, disenchanted consciousness to the poem's fore. The past tense of 'chose for theme' speaks of Yeats's inability simply to choose that theme again in any unselfconscious way. Again, to appeal to 'what poets name | The book of the people' is to concede the fancifulness as well as the nobility of the poets' naming, while the final term of the romantic triad—'whatever most can bless | The mind of man or elevate a rhyme'—calculatedly recalls a Shelleyan rhetoric of generalized aspiration, as when the Romantic poet invokes 'aught that for its grace may be | Dear, and yet dearer for its mystery' ('Hymn to Intellectual Beauty', version A, 11–12). That the word 'rhyme' off-rhymes with a once-chosen 'theme' and a tradition in which 'what poets name' has authority reveals that Yeats now feels a gap opening up between himself and his past self, even as that past self is only fully defined in the poem's present. Writing in *ottava rima* stanzas like Byron in his satires, composing without Byron's satirical edge, but with his ability to run together conversational momentum and syntax (Byron had, said Yeats in 1924, sought to attain the 'syntax and vocabulary of common personal speech'[43]), Yeats makes us aware of a major legacy of Romanticism: poetic self-consciousness and awareness of the mind's imaginings in the discovery or projection of significance. That awareness and self-consciousness come to the fore in the last three lines, where 'all is changed' applies Yeats's complex refrain in 'Easter, 1916', 'All changed, changed utterly' (15), to a further 'change' in his own perspective, and recalls the reworking of the very word 'changed' in Wordsworth's 'The Ruined Cottage'.[44] The use of self-quotation is a practice common among the Romantics (as when Shelley alludes to the 'Ode to the West Wind' at the start of the last stanza of *Adonais*), and if Pegasus is to be ridden, the lines intimate, it is by someone with the Romantic tradition in his bones. The echo of his own work and the glance towards Romantic practice confirm Yeats's quasi-Byronic sense that the poetic career involves fate and freedom, that freedom to 'create' derives from reaction against the antagonism of 'fate'. Pegasus ('that high horse') may be 'riderless',

---

[43] Yeats, *The Letters of W. B. Yeats*, ed. Allan Wade (London: Rupert Hart-Davis, 1954), p. 710.
[44] For commentary, see Jonathan Wordsworth, *The Music of Humanity* (London: Nelson, 1969). Wordsworth would have known 'The Ruined Cottage' as the first book of *The Excursion*, presumably among the 'nearly all Wordsworth' which Pound tells us in canto LXXXIX that Yeats heard during their stay at Stone Cottage 'for the sake of his conscience'.

but one poetic equestrian at least recognizes his existence (*'that* high horse'); indeed, the very syntactical awkwardness which makes one want to supply a subject for 'mounted' implies that Yeats's hands are on the bridle, as does the magnificence of the final line. There, Yeats finds an image for a personal and a cultural predicament; if the 'swan drifts' and the 'flood' is perceptibly 'darkening', the poem remains in control. It reveals this control by its reworking of the premonitory close of Blake's 'The Ecchoing Green', a reworking achieved by detonating the implications coiled within the poem's fourth line, which describes a double darkness—one bespeaking underground forces and hinting at Homeric-like creativity—as the waters run 'darkening through "dark" Raftery's "cellar" drop'.

Yeats may have been unemulous of Byron's satiric edge, but there is sardonic comedy of a kind in the way he parades his symbolizing bias at the end of the poem's first stanza. He describes the movement of waters that 'Spread to a lake and drop into a hole' (7), before adding, as though it were a self-evident gloss, the question, 'What's water but the generated soul?' (8). The question may evoke the world of Neoplatonic symbols discussed in 'The Philosophy of Shelley's Poetry', in which we learn that Porphyry 'contends that fountains and rivers symbolise generation'.[45] But the alliterative 'What's water' inflects a query that mocks both the uninitated and the symbol-mongerer in Yeats himself. Yet it prepares us, too, for the final 'darkening flood', itself 'water' that bears witness to the 'generated soul' of the poem. Again, the second stanza might be sponsored by Coleridge's 'Dejection: An Ode' in its awareness of the external as a mirror of the internal: 'And all the rant's a mirror of my mood' (13), writes Yeats, a fraction less explicit about the mind's responsibility for meaning than the Coleridge who asserts, 'O Lady! we receive but what we give, | And in our life alone does Nature live' (47–8), but equally aware of a poem as a drama in which the principal actor is the poetic self. The drama, for Yeats as for Coleridge, tempts towards melodrama. Coleridge apostrophizes the wind in 'Dejection' as 'Thou Actor, perfect in all tragic sounds' and as a 'mighty Poet, e'en to frenzy bold' (108, 109). In so doing, he concedes his own rhetorical manipulations; psychological troubles motivate tropes. Yeats, too, suggests Nature's willingness to play its allotted part in 'For Nature's pulled her tragic buskin on' (12). The 'tragic buskin' is a phrase that hams things up; it assumes an exaggeratedly thespian air. Yet Yeats rises to the challenge he has set himself, and draws on his memories of Shelley's swans to suggest his own 'mounting', self-aware intensity of feeling:

> At sudden thunder of the mounting swan
> I turned about and looked where branches break
> The glittering reaches of the flooded lake. (14–16)

[45] Yeats, 'Philosophy of Shelley's Poetry', p. 68.

'A symbol of inspiration I think': Yeats's account of the 'mounting swan' has an attractive unsureness.[46] The swan pulls the poem beyond and out of the theatrical narcissism threatened by previous lines. Yet the switching between tenses suggests that the default position to which the poet's consciousness returns is one in which awareness of symbol-making dominates. In the recent past the poet has 'turned about and looked', shaken out of self-concern, as in so many Romantic lyrics, by the presence of a world beyond the mind. But at this pivotal point in 'Coole and Ballylee, 1931' the poet discovers and enacts the inevitable, even ruthless law of his imaginative creations: that the external must always obey the whim of the internal, that 'all the rant's a mirror of my mood'. The poem moves beyond narcissism by virtue of its encounter with its threat, however, so that when in the next stanza the poet concedes his emblem-hunting, he does so with perceptible self-mockery:

> Another emblem there! That stormy white
> But seems a concentration of the sky;
> And, like the soul, it sails into the sight
> And in the morning's gone, no man knows why ... (17–20)

The opening exclamation serves as one epigraph for post-Romantic poetry. Symbols have turned into emblems, Coleridgean organicism into De Manian disillusion.[47] Emblems bear witness to the mind's longing for meanings and hint at that longing's frustration. Further meditation, though, outspeeds self-mockery as 'emblem' passes into something closer to 'excited reverie', the word 'seems', catalyst of many Romantic epiphanies, allowing for the swan's merging with the larger dimension of 'the sky'. The stanza's third line brings the 'soul' before us; 'sight', where one might, subconsciously, expect 'night', holds the soul-like swan in front of the poem's eyes. Remarkably, the writing twists out of a self-referential labyrinth, making of the swan, belatedly but triumphantly, an image 'So arrogantly pure' (23) that it serves to clarify or 'concentrate' our understanding of what is at stake. If the swan has a whiteness that 'can be murdered with a spot of ink' (24), two stanzas later the murdering 'spot' turns, through a wry process of verbal play, into an imperilled 'spot whereon the founders lived and died'. Lady Macbeth's 'Out, damned spot!' (v. i. 30) ghosts the text, both in its recall of her earlier fantasy of control and in her benightmared longing for eradication of the signs of guilt. Not that Yeats wishes that Coole Park should be destroyed; more that the Shakespearean allusion links complexly with the poem's investigation of legacies, how pride in past glories is linked with and, indeed, triggers awareness of their imminent fall in the present.

---

[46] Quoted in Yeats, *The Poems*, ed. Albright, p. 712.
[47] See Paul De Man, 'Image and Emblem in Yeats', in *The Rhetoric of Romanticism* (New York: Columbia University Press, 1984), pp. 145–238.

The swan of the second and third stanzas has flown straight from the pages of Shelley's *Alastor*, where the Poet asserts, in relation to the 'beautiful bird': 'And what am I that I should linger here, | With voice far sweeter than thy dying notes' (285–6).[48] Yeats's 'swan', unlike Shelley's, is as homeless as the Poet: 'like the soul, it sails into the sight | And in the morning's gone, no man knows why'. Yet, as in Shelley, there is the same note of ultimate ignorance, here about the soul-like swan's fate, 'gone, no man knows why'. Yeats has turned Shelley's Romantic lament into his own post-Romantic performance. If he is histrionic, he is affecting, too, since the poem openly declares its need for a rhetoric to convey the poet's sense of tumultuous loss. Indeed, the final stanza's invocation of later 'loveliness' is the more powerful because earlier (here in stanza 3) the swan is 'so lovely that it sets to right | What knowledge or its lack had set awry' (21–2). There, Yeats plays 'sets to right' against 'set awry' with a conscious sense that the Romantic Image can undo what is 'awry'.

Like many of Yeats's poems, 'Coole and Ballylee, 1931' engages in continual intertextual dialogue with Romantic poetry, even as its images are fresh and new. The swan is 'So arrogantly pure', for example, 'a child might think | It can be murdered with a spot of ink' (23–4). The appeal to the child's perspective is Romantic; yet, if the child is father to the man, it is because the child anticipates the adult's capacity for violence. That final image is Romantic just as Wallace Stevens thought the romantic should be—that is, unstale and unspent, excitingly drawn from the present yet impossible to grasp without a sense of a child as not trailing Wordsworthian or Rousseauist clouds of glory.

Alastor, once touched on, may persist as a haunting presence in Yeats's poem. The elegiac end of Shelley's poem involves an eloquent turning against eloquence : 'Art and eloquence | And all the shows o' the world are frail and vain | To weep a loss that turns their lights to shade,' asserts the Narrator. 'It is a woe too "deep for tears"' (710–13), he continues, echoing the close of Wordsworth's 'Ode: Intimations of Immortality'. Yeats moves into elegiac mode in the fourth stanza, but with a sense that 'Art and eloquence' are 'frail and vain'. Instead, dispensing with a main verb, he offers an inventory that is at once tight-lipped and admiring, conscious throughout of legacy, pastness, and age:

> Sound of a stick upon the floor, a sound
> From somebody that toils from chair to chair;
> Beloved books that famous hands have bound.
> Old marble heads, old pictures everywhere;
> Great rooms where travelled men and children found
> Content or joy; a last inheritor

---

[48] Harold Bloom reads the poem as 'one of Yeats's series of revisionary swerves away from *Alastor*' (*Yeats*, p. 381).

> Where none has reigned that lacked a name and fame
> Or out of folly into folly came. (25–32)

The stanza manages affectingly to convey both the painful movement of 'somebody that toils from chair to chair' and the toil-won bequest of value from generation to generation. What matter, in the end, are not individual names, but a culture. If 'somebody' at first seems to relegate Lady Gregory to unaccommodated anonymity, it also suggests that she is 'somebody' by belonging to the house that she is continuing to sustain. This is a late Romanticism in which the light of meaning and value flashes out from a world in the process of disintegration. Whatever the reader makes outside the poem of the aristocratic Protestant ascendancy, the world that is celebrated and mourned by the poet compels the imagination as the details accumulate: the 'Beloved books', where 'Beloved' has a Wordsworthian plangency (compare 'Beloved Friend', *The Prelude*, 1805, VII. 13); the 'famous hands'; the room, the men and children; and, finally, and serving as a surrogate for the poet himself, 'a last inheritor'.

The Romantic-period writer whom Yeats recalls most vividly here is his Anglo-Irish forebear Edmund Burke and his counter-revolutionary lament for 'the princes of the blood, who, . . . held large landed estates', now 'in lieu of their stable independent property, reduced to the hope of some precarious, charitable pension'.[49] Burke sponsors the later poet's exaltation of the Coole Park milieu, and, as Bloom points out, for all the poem's Shelleyan motifs, the poem swerves from Shelley in blaming the poet's 'alienation from nature and society' on 'a historical process of decline'.[50] Shelley, one feels, would have resigned himself to the sweeping away of 'A spot whereon the founders lived and died' (33).

Yeats, then, as a self-described 'last Romantic', lamenting the loss of 'great glory spent' (39), uses his self-created Romantic identity to protest against change and to concede its 'darkening' inevitability. In 'Easter, 1916', as Elizabeth Cullingford has shown, a flurry of Shelleyan echoes aids Yeats in his attempt to articulate the oxymoronic nature of the rebels' achievement: the 'terrible beauty' (16, 40, 80) may derive from 'the tempestuous loveliness of terror' which makes the air 'a mirror | Of all the beauty and the terror there' (33, 37–8) in Shelley's 'On the Medusa of Leonardo da Vinci'. Moreover, the 'excess of love' (72), which may have half-exoneratingly 'Bewildered them till they died' (73), recalls the Poet whose strong limbs in *Alastor* 'sickened' across a line ending with 'excess | Of love' (181–2).[51] The near-solipsistic quester of *Alastor* turns out to be

---

[49] Edmund Burke, *Reflections on the Revolution in France*, ed. with intro. by Conor Cruise O'Brien (Harmondsworth: Penguin, 1968), p. 260.

[50] Bloom, *Yeats*, p. 382.

[51] Elizabeth Cullingford, *Yeats Annual No. 4* (1986); cited in Yeats, *The Poems*, ed. Albright, pp. 610, 611. Shelley's poem is quoted from *Shelley: Poetical Works*, ed. Thomas Hutchinson, rev. edn. G. M. Matthews (London: Oxford University Press, 1970).

twinned, in Yeats's imagination, with those revolutionary freedom fighters who fought the British state, their sacrificed hearts possibly turning to stone in the process. But in the earlier poem Yeats is master of his poetic domain, for all his openness to ambivalence. A few lines from the poem's close, the poet declares, 'I write it out in a verse' (74), making something happen, whatever Auden in his elegy for Yeats says to the contrary about poetry. The close of 'Easter, 1916' certainly mimes, in Auden's words, 'A way of happening'. In its assertion of the poet as memorializer and giver of meaning, it looks back to that decisive moment in the struggle between poet and inspiring wind when Shelley harnesses his self-created deity's power to his own purposes, saying to the wind: 'And, by the incantation of this verse, | Scatter, as from an unextinguished hearth | Ashes and sparks, my words among mankind' (65–7). Indeed, Yeats inherits from Shelley and the Romantics more generally a sense of the poem as 'A way of happening'. Poems are events of a kind, artistic creations that are also processes of consciousness: the poet is both controller of and participant in his own poems, and at moments of climactic self-awareness, as in the lines just quoted, Yeats's sense of poetry's difficult value as a declarative act makes clear what is at stake for him in writing poetry.

This is the Yeats for whom in 'A General Introduction for My Work' the poet 'is never the bundle of accident and incoherence that sits down to breakfast; he has been reborn as an idea, something intended, complete', a credo with its roots in the Romantic tradition.[52] Through poetry the accidental grows coherent, just as the secondary imagination, for Coleridge, 'struggles to idealize and to unify' (*Biographia Literaria*, i. 304). Yet Yeats's 'coherence' strives to acknowledge the claims of the 'accidental', rather as it is the Coleridgean 'struggle' to idealize and unify which often holds our attention.[53] Indeed, in Yeats's case, it may be that it is the struggle towards being 'something intended, complete' that affects the reader. Pose or masking will seem at odds with Romantic self-expression only if we pay insufficient attention to the Romantics' sense of the quicksilver alliance and difference between the man who suffers and the poet who creates, as when Byron asserts in *Childe Harold's Pilgrimage* III. 6: 'What am I? Nothing; but not so art thou, | Soul of my thought! with whom I traverse earth' (50–1).

Yeats went to the Romantics, in part, because he sensed that, in them, 'self-expression' involved what he would think of as antithetical discipline. So, in his initial phase, recorded in 'The Philosophy of Shelley's Poetry', he saw Shelley as a poet who understood the importance of symbols, saying, in his characteristically dialectical way: 'It is only by ancient symbols, by symbols that have numberless meanings besides the one or two the writer lays an emphasis

---

[52] Yeats, *Later Essays*, p. 204.
[53] See Seamus Perry, *Coleridge and the Uses of Division* (Oxford: Clarendon Press, 1999), p. 152.

upon, or the half-score he knows of, that any highly subjective art can escape from the barrenness and shallowness of a too conscious arrangment, into the abundance and depth of Nature.'[54] Yeats tempers subjectivity with symbolism in poems such as 'The Secret Rose', which ends with an image deeply suffused with Shelleyan inflections:

> I, too, await
> The hour of thy great wind of love and hate.
> When shall the stars be blown about the sky,
> Like the sparks blown out of a smithy, and die?
> Surely thine hour has come, thy great wind blows,
> Far-off, most secret, and inviolate Rose? (27–32)

This apocalyptic Yeats, afire for, yet ambivalent about, change, has, as Bloom points out, the Shelley of the 'Ode to the West Wind' in his thoughts.[55] The sparks blown out of the smithy recall the 'Ashes and sparks' (67) to which Shelley compares his words; but whereas Shelley's sparks will rekindle hope in the minds of his readers, Yeats's sparks will be extinguished (he half-hopes, half-fears) as 'thy great wind blows'. Yeats's stars no doubt belong to the 'star-world of [Blake's] Urizen', in Bloom's phrase.[56] But his questions (as so often) betoken a counter-current of feeling, a reluctance fully to unleash the forces of millennial destruction.

Even when Yeats wishes to engage in a 'movement downwards upon life' (letter of 1906), to pull off the vertigo-inducing trick of uniting 'a Shelley and a Dickens in the one body',[57] the Romantic figures as a necessary if partial presence. The consequence is a protracted, complex dialogue, as is shown by central poems in *The Tower*. Broodingly, imperiously, Yeats dwells on the role of the poet in section III of 'Nineteen Hundred and Nineteen': 'Some moralist or mythological poet', he begins the section, 'Compares the solitary soul to a swan' (1–2). The section serves to show what is at stake for the poet as he surveys a culture of ruined hopes and barbarous indifference or hostility to artistic beauty. The first section has asked with laconic magnificence, 'Man is in love and loves what vanishes, | What more is there to say?' (42–3). Now, in the third section, it emerges that there is much more to say: the poet is left alone with his literary memories, his legacies, one of which probably derives from Shelley's *Prometheus Unbound*, where Asia asserts: 'My soul is an enchanted

---

[54] Yeats, 'Philosophy of Shelley's Poetry', p. 72.

[55] Bloom argues that 'The passsage suggests both the great wind of creation and destruction in Shelley's ode, and the violent imagery of the opening of *Night the Ninth, Being the Last Judgment* of Blake's *The Four Zoas*' (*Yeats*, p. 131).

[56] Ibid. 132.

[57] Yeats, *Letters*, ed. Wade, p. 469; Yeats, *Essays and Introductions* (London: Macmillan, 1961), p. 296.

boat, |Which, like a sleeping swan, doth float | Upon the silver waves of thy sweet singing' (2. 5. 72–4). Asia's lines describe a perfect receptiveness, a listener borne along by the original. Yeats, as argued in relation to this poem in Chapter 1, engages in a more difficult tussle with a Romantic original. The balance of power is made to swing, through the bravado of the Yeatsian voice, in favour of the younger poet. The Romantic image-cum-symbol is consciously held before us as just that: a consciously shaped symbol. 'I am satisfied with that' (III. 3), Yeats says in best grumpy old man mode, before rejigging the symbol in his own way, as if to assert the force of his subjective control. Even as he surrenders power in the third stanza of this lyric, it is a surrender that is cunningly staged:

> The swan has leaped into the desolate heaven:
> That image can bring wildness, bring a rage
> To end all things, to end
> What my laborious life imagined, even
> The half-imagined, the half-written page. (III. 21–5).

Daniel Albright glosses these elusive lines thus: 'the poet is sick of his own vision—his imagination can terminate in no fixed or satisfying image. The poet seems ready to destroy the text of this very poem.'[58] Certainly this De Manian reading alerts us to the way in which Yeats deconstructs the pride in the poem heard so often in his own work and that of his Romantic predecessors. One hears such pride in the assertion of the memorializing work done by 'this hand alone' (2) in Yeats's tribute to Maud Gonne's 'Fallen Majesty', a tribute which recalls Keats's sense that the worth of *The Fall of Hyperion* will be known only 'When this warm scribe my hand is in the grave' (18). Yet, as an image that outstrips 'What my laborious life imagined', the swan serves to breathe new life into Yeats's vision. That openness—mid-composition—to the chances of rhyme and image is among his deepest debts to Romantic practitioners of reflexive poetry. Shelley's *Epipsychidion* depends vitally for its effect on the paradox that its greatest poetry mimes the inadequacy of poetic images. Comparably, the appeal in Yeats's lines about the 'swan' is to a reality beyond the word, a reality that is radiant in Shelley's case, 'desolate' in Yeats's, but in both cases mocking, yet spurring on, 'The half-imagined, half-written page'. It is worth noting that at such moments, and in the dismissive reference to 'The half-read wisdom of daemonic images' (VII. 39) at the close of 'Meditations in Time of Civil War', Yeats seems far removed from the mage-poet of Kermode's construction, warding off the false distinctions of the intellect through the Romantic Image. Indeed, one might feel that the close of 'Among

---

[58] Yeats, *The Poems*, ed. Albright, p. 654.

School Children' is rare in being a record of such a reconciling moment in Yeats. Even there, the final triumph—composed from the multiply organic tree and the dancer unentanglable from her dance—has to contend with the fear that the images may simply be further examples of what in the previous stanza Yeats calls 'self-born mockers of man's enterprise' (VII. 8).

The subject of Yeats's 'last Romanticism', in Bornstein's phrase, is never-ending.[59] Bloom makes the shrewd point that Yeats had learned from Blake 'how to make a poem mock its own dramatic speaker', [60] and this insight is invaluable for many later lyrics in the Yeatsian canon, even if Bloom feels that there is insufficient dramatic distance from the speaker who chants 'The gyres! the gyres'.[61] Yeats's poem greets with enthusiasm what Blake might have called 'the same dull round over again' ('There is No Natural Religion', p. 3). Certainly the Yeatsian interest in cycles and returns recalls Blake's, though Blake's view of such returns is frequently sardonic or tragic, as in 'The Mental Traveller', where 'all is done as I have told' (104). The driving insistence in Blake's poem, caught by the repetition at the end of a rhyme on 'old' (see also ll. 10, 12, 18, 20, 26, 28, 31, 86, 88, and 102), plots a terrifyingly inexorable process. Only at moments does escape seem possible, escape that is nullified by the terror-stricken cry 'the Babe the Babe is Born' (95), which may be echoed by Yeats in his first line. Still, as ever, 'The Gyres', despite its effort to the contrary, is not single-toned in its devotion to 'tragic joy' (8), itself a phrase that will not admit of a single interpretation. Yeats counts the cost of the 'fearful symmetry' shaping and evident in his 'unfashionable gyre' (24); a gyre, that is, that does not accord with contemporary fashions of thought, and also one that is beyond the control of human fashioning. In an exultantly anti-humanist and anti-Romantic gesture, the poem seems to hand the fate of humans to forces beyond the human, but if to do so excites Yeats, it induces terror in him, too.

Indeed, the poem represents late Yeats's version of encountering the sublime. It is an encounter in which the poet asserts the adequacy of 'tragic joy' as a stance, summoning to his aid an anti-self, 'Old Rocky Face' (1), who may be the Delphic Oracle, but also recalls Ahasuerus in Shelley's *Hellas*. 'The Gyres' alludes in its title to Yeats's favoured image of the interlocking spinning cones that govern historical change. Yet, unlike 'The Second Coming', the poem does not set present against past. Rather, its use of present-tense assertions mingles

---

[59] The phrase, alluding to 'Coole and Ballylee, 1931', is the title of Bornstein's chapter on Yeats in his *Transformations*, pp. 27–93, 235–40.

[60] Bloom, *Yeats*, p. 435.

[61] 'I think that the speaker of *The Gyres* is Yeats, ... and I find this makes me uncomfortable' (ibid. 435).

contemporary crisis with the death of Hector and the destruction of Troy. The gyres all converge on a single moment of declarative poetic utterance:

> For beauty dies of beauty, worth of worth,
> And ancient lineaments are blotted out.
> Irrational streams of blood are staining earth;
> Empedocles has thrown all things about;
> Hector is dead and there's a light in Troy;
> We that look on but laugh in tragic joy. (3–8)

The lines strive for and achieve an end-stopped dignity; yet they allow their sublimity, their superiority to aesthetics ('beauty') and to ethics ('worth'), to have commerce with a wild, even knockabout gusto. If in 'Tintern Abbey' Wordsworth hymned a 'presence' (95) that rolled through 'all things' (103), in 'The Gyres' Yeats summons as his conceptual guru Empedocles, apostle of conflict and chaos. The idea that 'beauty dies of beauty, worth of worth' suggests an iconoclastic view of poetic tradition (among other things), in which past 'beauty' will destroy the possibility of any further 'beauty', unless its own destruction is accepted. The poet's own position is that of Olympian spectator ('We that look on'), a spectator for whom a city afire can be described as 'there's a light in Troy'. He is, too, a would-be mage summoning and gathering diverse images in a blazing synthesis. He is also a creature of the very culture he is consigning to the void. Why else tell us that 'Irrational streams of blood are staining earth'? The use of 'staining' allies the moment with Shelley's quasi-suicidal stanza 52 in *Adonais,* in which he blames 'Life' (462) for the way it 'Stains the white radiance of Eternity' (463). And just as Shelley's lines cannot expel the attractiveness of life's staining, so Yeats's staining bloodstreams cannot simply be accepted.

In the second and third stanzas, the declarative tone is no less apparent, but now it must contend with questions that affect to be, but are not merely, rhetorical: 'What matter though numb nightmare ride on top | And blood and mire the sensitive body stain?' (9–10). The question seems to expect the answer 'It doesn't matter', but the writing unsettles 'tragic joy' and demands that the horror inflicted on the 'sensitive body' be granted its stance-changing due. Yeats affects to brush these tensions aside, again asking 'What matter?' (11, 15) in this stanza, and seeming to pin his faith on 'that one word "Rejoice!"' (16). But we note that the word—'all it knows' (16)—is spoken not by the poet but 'Out of Cavern' (15). Yeats offers us a deliberately comfortless solace, as his third stanza concedes: 'Conduct and work grow coarse, and coarse the soul, | What matter?' (17–18). Yet he places his trust in a resurrection of sorts, once that will restore order to 'all things' (repeated at the close, 23), a rebirth achieved by a combination of necessity and human effort:

'Those that Rocky Face holds dear', he says, 'shall | . . . disinter | The workman, noble and saint, and all things run | On that unfashionable gyre again' (18, 19–24). The formula for change is close to that dramatized in many Romantic works, especially *Prometheus Unbound*. Yeats implies the difficulty of his reactionary labour by separating 'shall' and 'disinter' by almost three lines; moreover, the final off-rhyme on 'run' and 'Again' keeps recurrence from seeming facile.

Yeats, it is important to note, does not return to the Romantics for a system of belief. But he draws on their practice for hints about how to dramatize conflict. In 'Byzantium', the paradoxes explored by Keats in his 'Ode on a Grecian Urn' are central to the poem.[62] Just as the lovers on the Urn are supposedly 'All breathing human passion far above' (28), so in the ghostly world explored by 'Byzantium', 'A mouth that has no moisture and no breath | Breathless mouths may summon' (13–14). That this summoning results in the emergence of the 'superhuman'—'I hail the superhuman' (15)—may give us pause, since this Nietzschean figure quickly arouses memories of Coleridge's most nightmarish figures, as Yeats engages in a deliberate act of naming: 'I call it death-in-life and life-in death' (16), he writes, as though wilfully seeking to arouse and possibly challenge the associations those terms bring with them from 'The Rime of the Ancient Mariner': 'The Night-mare LIFE-IN-DEATH was she, | Who thicks man's blood with cold' (193–4). Moreover, the line incorporates an earlier descendant of the Romantic movement, Tennyson, the phrase 'death-in-life' alluding to his 'Tears, Idle Tears': 'O death in life, the days that are no more'.[63] The poem's attempt to exult in a region that 'thicks man's blood with cold' sustains itself throughout the poem and into the Keatsian terrain of stanza 3, where the artefact scorns 'In glory of changeless metal | Common bird or petal' (22–3). As the shorter lines sharpen the antagonistic forces, we are taken back to the rival claims of change and changelessness debated in the lyrical dramas of Keats's odes.

As often in the Romantic tradition, Yeats finally turns from art as a product—'A starlit or a moonlit dome' (5)—to art as a process, much as Coleridge switches from affirming his 'miracle of rare device' (35) in 'Kubla Khan' to expressing the wistful belief that renewed inspiration would mean that he 'would build that dome in air' (46). So, as argued in Chapter 1, Yeats gives his

---

[62] For Bloom, the poem is 'the *Kubla Khan* or *Ode on a Grecian Urn* of Yeats's lyric accomplishment', but he builds his reading in *Yeats* on the view that it 'is one of the most Shelleyan of Yeats's poems' (p. 384). For Bornstein, the poem is 'a Yeatsian "Ode on a Grecian Urn" told from the point of view of a figure on the urn' (*Transformations*, p. 83). He notes on the same page that 'Romantic analogues pervade' 'Sailing to Byzantium' and 'Byzantium'.

[63] Bornstein notes the Coleridgean echo (*Transformations*, p. 83), while the echo of Tennyson is noted by Albright in *Yeats, The Poems*, p. 719.

latter-day post-Romantic ode over to the images that pour in from the raw, unpurged tides of reality, a world where 'Fresh images' (39) will not be tamed, insisting on their source in physical desire and spiritual longing, 'That dolphin-torn, that gong-tormented sea' (40). No more than Keats is his allegiance given to art's 'Cold Pastoral' (45), even if, as with Keats, it is in a poem that he stages his creatively renewing quarrel with poetry.

3

'Dialectic Ways': T. S. Eliot and Counter-Romanticism

I

The younger T. S. Eliot seems less questioning than assured in his dismissal of Romanticism. An amusing example occurs in a 1918 review when he writes, 'Because we have never learned to criticize Keats, Shelley, and Wordsworth (poets of assured though modest merit), Keats, Shelley and Wordsworth punish us from their graves with the annual scourge of the Georgian Anthology.'[1] Yet Eliot's anti-Romanticism masks a powerful affinity with Romantic poetry; his overt hostility to Romanticism connects with his complex feelings about self-expression in poetry. The high priest of impersonality turns out to be a poet of affecting emotional disclosure. Indeed, C. K. Stead is surely correct to say that Eliot's remarks in essays 'apparently about tradition, Jonson, and *Hamlet*' 'imply a kind of poetic composition at least as dependent on spontaneous "imagination" and "inspiration" as that which any of the romantic poets might have affirmed'.[2] And Stead's acute reading of the later 'Three Voices of Poetry' lecture shows Eliot engaged in a post-Romantic search, not for the stigmatized 'Inner Voice ... the voice of "opinion" ', but for 'the voice of the poet's "soul"—that part of his being which is unknowable, even to himself' and which 'expresses itself, not in "thought," but by a recreation of diverse experience into "feeling"—which in turn becomes ... the essential texture of the poem'.[3]

Stead's Eliot retreats from the self in order to discover a deeper self. 'Old men ought to be explorers' ('East Coker', v) places strong emphasis on 'ought', and about nothing is Eliot more exploratory than the nature of the self.[4] There is evidence from his earliest work of a disinclination fully to believe in the quotidian ego as the real self, a disbelief that takes one back to David Hume

---

[1] T. S. Eliot, 'Observations', *Egoist*, 5 (May 1918), p. 69.
[2] C. K. Stead, *The New Poetic: Yeats to Eliot* (1964; Harmondsworth: Penguin, 1967), p. 131.
[3] Ibid. 143.
[4] Unless otherwise indicated, all Eliot's poems and plays are quoted from Eliot, *Complete Poems and Plays*.

and his sceptical conviction that the self was merely a bundle of impulses. This conviction haunts Shelley and other Romantics even as they, especially Coleridge, seek to reject it. Humean scepticism calls into question, too, the reality of the physical universe. Modified by Shelley's reading of Berkeley and Sir William Drummond, such scepticism issues, for the Romantic poet, in what he calls 'the intellectual philosophy' in his essay 'On Life'. This philosophy swithers between vertigo and excitement as it demolishes differences between 'ideas' and 'external objects', and between 'distinct individual minds similiar to that which is employed in now questioning its own nature' (p. 635). Shelley gives solipsism the slip, much as early Eliot often endeavours to do ('To say that I can know only my own states ... is in no wise the foundation of solipsism'); but for both poets the relationships between self and world are perilous, giving rise in Shelley to a yearning for the 'One', in Eliot to initial flirtation with F. H. Bradley's notion of the 'Absolute', then commitment to the Christian God.[5]

Eliot's early poem 'Oh little voices of the throats of men', from *Inventions of the March Hare*, a notebook containing poems written in his twenties, finds a correlative for this perilous uncertainty in the sense that the world is merely 'Appearances appearances': a place where he always finds 'the same unvaried | Intolerable interminable maze' (19–20), and where appearances are 'unreal, and yet true; | Untrue, yet real' (26–7). These views are ascribed to a 'he' (25), but they have more than a smack of Shelley the sceptical Platonist. Lyndall Gordon hears the poem as a Prufrockian 'debate between two voices', an 'abject self' (speaker of the first two and the 'he' of the final paragraphs) and a 'philosophic self' who 'exhorts [the abject self] not to delay to take possession of some truth'.[6] But Gordon's brisk clarity underplays the extent to which the identities characteristically lose distinction, as occurs in 'Prufrock' when the 'you and I' of the first line hauntingly coalesce. In 'Oh little voices', Eliot's art lies in the way the voices blur, the second voice seeming to be a restatement from an objectivized stance of the first. The Romantic figure of the *doppelgänger* blends with the Laforgian practice of *dédoublement*, and, as Christopher Ricks points out in his extensive editorial annotation, Romantic poetry has bequeathed its share of phrases to Eliot's work. The 'Intolerable interminable maze' derives its adjectives from *The Daemon of the World*, Shelley's reworking of *Queen Mab*, adjectives which in the original occur in contexts describing the sublime unendingness of the physical universe, while the noun recalls 'Unending orbs mingled in mazy motion' (244; qtd from *Shelley: Poetical Works*) from the same poem. What for the youthful Shelley is a matter for awe and exaltation is for the youthful Eliot the language of ennui

---

[5] Quoted from T. S. Eliot, *Inventions of the March Hare: Poems, 1909–1917*, ed. Christopher Ricks (1996; San Diego: Harcourt, 1998); hereafter Ricks, p. 262.

[6] Lyndall Gordon, *Eliot's Early Years* (1977; Oxford: Oxford University Press, 1978), p. 48.

and exhaustion. In this respect, his attitude is closer to Shelley's sonnet 'Lift not the painted veil which those who live | Call Life' (1–2), a veil which has 'unreal shapes' (2) pictured on it: not least because 'Oh little voices', on closer inspection, flirts with the form and structure of the sonnet. It opens with fourteen lines, arranged as an octave followed by a sestet, with a *volta* in line 9, in which the poet mockingly applauds the 'Impatient tireless undirected feet' of those who make up what Coleridge calls 'the poor loveless ever-anxious crowd' ('Dejection: An Ode', 52). Sonnet form is departed from thereafter, in the poem's third and fourth paragraphs, but it makes recurrent if broken attempts to reappear: in the opening sestet of the third, in the approach to an octave made by the next eight lines, in the closing couplet of the third paragraph, and in a tendency to monorhyme which recalls something of the obssessive rhyming found in a Petrarchan sonnet's octave.

The form of the poem mimes in its approach to mimicked closure a sense that all is 'nowise real; unreal, and yet true; | Untrue, yet real' (26–7). The tongue-twisting wording suggests the slipperiness of what is 'real' and 'true'. Something may be 'unreal', lacking ontological identity, yet 'true', in that it is accepted as factually the case. Or it may be 'Untrue', false to ultimate ideas of 'truth', 'yet real', since, in the world of 'appearances', it is accepted as possessing substance. Much in Shelley and Keats corresponds to these hesitations and revisions: 'Real are the dreams of Gods' (I. 127), remarks the narrator of *Lamia* with some bitterness, and with the immediate corollary pressing upon him and the reader, that 'Unreal are the dreams of human beings'. Shelley, forever seeking to get beyond the 'veil and the bar | Of things which seem and are' (*Prometheus Unbound*, 2. 3. 59–60), and fascinated by the links and gaps between 'things which seem' and 'The gathered rays which are reality' (*Prometheus Unbound*, 3. 3. 53), speaks of a poet creating 'Forms more real than living man' (*Prometheus Unbound*, I. 748). Ricks cites this phrase as the echoic ancestor of Eliot's earlier line in 'Oh little voices', 'For what could be more real than sweat and dust and sun' (13), and the later poet's use seems grimly sardonic: the ultimate reality is the brute material world, not Platonic essences shiningly extracted from the phenomenal world.[7] But Shelley couples appearances and essences with enigmatic effect in his work, so that the relationship between his and Eliot's attitudes is finer than one of contrast. If 'We blow against the wind and spit against the rain' (12) sadly defines the fate of those who shun 'the wrinkled ways of wrong', they have behind them, serving not merely as an ironized origin, the anti-mocking courage of Blake's 'Mock on'. 'Mock on Mock on! tis all in vain! | You throw the sand against the wind | And the wind blows it back again' (2–4), asserts Blake. Eliot's 'We' may suffer

---

[7] Ricks, pp. 261, 258.

the indignity of ineffectual struggle against the wind, but the prevailing wind is coming from an opposite quarter to that which is blowing through the Blakean poem. Thus, to spit against it is to be something of a latter-day Romantic in a world inimical to Romanticism.

In 'Imperfect Critics', Eliot wrote that 'the only cure for Romanticism is to analyse it' and the formulation does much to explain the behaviour of poems such as 'Oh little voices' and up to *The Waste Land*.[8] In the same essay, he shapes confident antitheses of a kind both supported and questioned by his poetry. Thus, he argues that 'What is permanent and good in Romanticism is curiosity', but he then backtracks to say that 'Romanticism is a short cut to the strangeness without the reality, and leads its disciples only back upon themselves ... George Wyndham [for Eliot 'A Romantic Aristocrat'] had curiosity, but he employed it romantically, not to penetrate the real world'.[9] Eliot himself seeks always to objectify, to find a verbal equivalent for 'the real world'. To this degree, he is true to his anti-Romantic credo. At the same time, the 'real world' is so unstable a notion in his work, and his poetry so often occupies a 'strangeness' which is unsure what ' "the reality" is', that he can be seen to dramatize a latter-day Romantic struggle to connect with the 'real' while acknowledging, however covertly, the inseparability of 'the real' from consciousness.

Romantic poetry itself is often its own severest analyst, as is apparent in Shelley's *Alastor* and *Epipsychidion,* both poems of quest that question the quester. When Eliot's speaker in 'Oh little voices' records what 'he said', he hears the following:

> Appearances appearances he said,
> I have searched the world through dialectic ways;
> I have questioned restless nights and torpid days,
> And followed every by-way where it lead;
> And always find the same unvaried
> Intolerable interminable maze. (15–20)

Shelley provides the source for Eliot's interrogative idiom. His narrator in *Alastor* borrows from Wordsworth's 'Ode: Intimations of Immortality' as he hopes to 'still these obstinate questionings | Of thee and thine, by forcing some lone ghost | Thy messenger, to render up the tale | Of what we are' (26–9). Shelley's wording is alert, in its very syntax, to the elusive recessiveness of 'what we are', known only in the form of a 'tale', and one spun out of never-answered 'questionings'. In *Epipsychidion*, 234–8, the language is near neighbour to the frustrated searching reported by Eliot's speaker. Shelley, seeking an idealized 'Being' (190), asks ' "Where?"—the world's echo answered "where!" | And in that silence, and in my despair, | I questioned every tongueless wind

---

[8] Eliot, *The Sacred Wood* (London: Methuen, 1920), p. 31.   [9] Ibid. 31, 24.

that flew | Over my tower of mourning, if it knew | Whither 'twas fled, this soul out of my soul'.[10] The difference is acute: Shelley's tone is one of despairing ardour, Eliot's one of wearied enclosure within what feels like a mental prison, whose bars are constructed from 'dialectic' and which finally constitutes an inescapable 'maze'. But, as with all the poets studied in this book, Eliot shows the impact of Romantic modes and purposes in the act of struggling to articulate his individual vision.

Indeed, 'Oh little voices' partly shapes itself as a lament for a version of the Romantic: the 'little voices' addressed at the start 'come between the singer and the song' in a way that makes it impossible for Eliot to recover some perfect accord between 'singer' and 'song', an aesthetic Absolute hard wholly to dissociate from Romantic poetics. Coleridge comes close to identifying 'singer' and 'song' in the final section of 'Kubla Khan', where the revived 'song' (43) would confer on the narrating singer the sacred, if isolated, status imagined in the closing lines. In *Biographia Literaria*, he suggests a comparable identification when he asserts, 'What is poetry? is so nearly the same question with, what is a poet? that the answer to the one is involved in the solution of the other' (chapter 14, ii. 15). It is striking how often, in fact, Romantic echoes serve to suggest, in Eliot's work, a fascination with some flawless 'world far from ours' ('To Jane: "The keen stars were twinkling" ', 22), as Shelley calls it; fascinating, too, to note how the Romantics themselves, especially when searching for harmony between 'singer' and 'song', are conscious of a gap, of all that interposes itself. Shelley's confession of reaching limits at the close of *Epipsychidion* is one example. For the Romantics, as for Eliot, the pursuit of oneness often opens up 'dialectic ways', such as those explored by Blake in his *Songs*; for them, against their better hopes, as for the Eliot of 'Oh little voices', poetic quest is mired in frustration, to the aesthetic benefit of their poetry, converting what might be expository propaganda into drama. 'Contradiction is the debt you would collect' (21), says the voice recorded in 'Oh little voices', and one thinks of Blake's wry couplet, 'Do what you will this Lifes a Fiction | And is made up of Contradiction' (see Erdman, p. 880) in 'The Everlasting Gospel'.

Eliot's verbal antennae stir in response to Romantic poetry's intimacy with contradictory abysses, the shadow of their longing for some resplendent 'One'. Shelley's hope in his translation of 'To Stella (from the Greek of Plato)'—the Greek was placed at the head of *Adonais*— that the addressee (once the 'morning star among the living') will give 'New splendour to the dead' may appear to be snuffed out by its saddened reworking in 'Oh little voices': 'if you find no truth among the living | You will not find much truth among the dead' (32–3).[11] But, for all its yearning, *Adonais* exists, when all is said, in 'No other time but

---

[10] For the echo of *Epipsychidion* (ll. 234–6 only), see Ricks, p. 260.
[11] Ibid. 263. See *Shelley: The Major Works*, p. 798.

now, no other place than here' ('Oh little voices', 33), much as, for the Byron of *Childe Harold's Pilgrimage,* often evoked by *Adonais,* 'There woos no home, nor hope, nor life, save what is here' (IV. 105. 945). Shelley and Byron both embrace a fierce existentialism in the act of writing their poetry, the 'here' that emerges as the nearest thing to 'reality' for both poets. Eliot explores in 'Oh little voices' a bleakly proto-Modernist sense that it is in the 'here' of the poem's now, a now that involves awareness of language's history, that significance inheres, or fails to inhere. The poem's closing section draws, as Ricks again suggests, on a Shelleyan imagining of divisions and possible unification.[12] Eliot describes the phantasmagoric shapes that mock the dozing figure whose speech has just ended: 'Across the floor the shadows crawled and crept | And as the thin light shivered through the trees | Around the muffled form they danced and leapt' (39–41). And, as Ricks notes, 'the shadows' and 'form' invite comparison with lines in a passage from Act 1 of *Prometheus Unbound,* Earth's spellbinding evocation of an 'apparation' beheld by 'The Magus Zoroaster' (1. 194, 192): the lines, as quoted by Ricks, are, 'For know there are two worlds of life and death: | One that which thou beholdest; but the other | Is underneath the grave, where do inhabit | The shadows of all forms that think and live' (1. 195–8). The line after these is among the most crucial in the speech and for understanding of the allusion's force: 'Till death unite them and they part no more.' Shelley hauntingly divorces his two worlds, but imagines a final marriage between them in 'death': a point often gestured towards but never attained in his linguistic structures. If Shelley looks in Death for union, as in *Adonais,* where, mocking the marriage service, he writes, 'No more let Life divide what Death can join together' (477), he is 'borne darkly, fearfully' (492) towards it in the same poem, never quite reaching his complexly desired goal. Eliot leaves 'shadows' and 'form' in an unappeased dance, having already allowed the poem's 'he' to shut the gate against the hope of finding 'truth among the dead'.

II

Yet, 'Oh little voices' is ghosted by the hope that living and dying will crisscross, that dialectic ways will resolve into union, as, darkly and fearfully, they will do when Eliot returns to the same Shelleyan passage in *The Cocktail Party,* Act 3. There, the conversational idiom is interrupted by Reilly's request, in talking about Celia Coplestone's death, to 'quote poetry'; he speaks the lines from *Prometheus Unbound* to convey a 'sudden intuition', on first meeting

---

[12] Ibid. 265.

Celia, of 'the image' of her face showing 'the astonishment | Of the first five minutes after a violent death' (*Complete Poems and Plays*, pp. 436, 437). More generally, the longing for loss of self in Eliot's poetry bears witness to the hold over his imagination of Romantic modes. This hold wrestles with a detachment that can recall the dynamics of Romantic irony, but might be glossed more accurately by Eliot's own term, 'counter-romantic', used in his 1930 essay, 'Baudelaire'. Of the French poet, he says: 'Inevitably the offspring of romanticism, and by his nature the first counter-romantic in poetry, he could, like anyone else, only work with the materials which were there. It must not be forgotten that a poet in a romantic age cannot be a "classical" poet except in tendency.'[13] There would appear to be an element of tacit self-description here. Eliot as a 'counter-romantic' makes sense in a way that Eliot the classicist does not, for all his famous pronouncements to the contrary.

Eliot sees Romanticism through the tragic prism of Baudelaire's 'counter-romanticism'. The French poet's 'Le Voyage'[14] functions as a diagnosis of Romanticism's pathologies and a clear-sighted act of desperate commitment to the 'unknown'. The poem is lucid and eloquent, caustic but rapt, paradisal yet nightmarish, aloof and at the same time involved; it is a dialogic poem, involving different voices (ventriloquized by the poet), responses, and counter-responses. Its divided view of Romantic quest finds expression in sardonically apt metaphors and comparisons: 'We imitate, oh horror! tops and bowls | in their eternal waltzing marathon'; 'Our soul is a three-master seeking port' (II). For the splenetic, doom-laden eye it casts on Romanticism, one might cite lines such as 'Our hearts are always anxious with desire' (IV). In fact, 'the true voyagers', Baudelaire comments derisively, 'are those who move | simply to move—like lost balloons!' (I). This conviction suggests less quest than an inability to stay still, and, for Baudelaire, the human need to voyage and quest veers between the impressive and the contemptible, a sign of desire for freedom and confirmation that we are limited. An early warning note comes in the first section: 'we swing with the velvet swell of the wave, | our infinite is rocked by the fixed sea'. The taming of the infinite by the finite performed in that line is in part the whole endeavour of the poem; yet at least the poetic voyage brings 'an oasis of horror in sands of ennui' (VII). It is a bleak vision of what post-Romantic voyages may deliver. But in its implicit sense, however targeted by irony, of the purpose of writing—'Through the unknown, we'll find the *new*' (VIII)—the poem is, in its own deeply troubled way, caught up in Romantic pursuit.

---

[13] Eliot, 'Baudelaire', in *Selected Essays*, 3rd edn. (London: Faber, 1951), p. 424.

[14] Quoted from Robert Lowell's translation; text in George Steiner (ed.), *The Penguin Book of Modern Verse Translation* (Harmondsworth: Penguin, 1966). This paragraph draws on material from my essay, ' "Wholly Incommunicable by Words": Romantic Expressions of the Inexpressible', *The Wordsworth Circle*, 31 (2000), pp. 13–20.

A. David Moody notes the relevance of Baudelaire's poem to 'The Burial of the Dead', at the close of which Baudelaire is quoted ('hypocrite lecteur!—mon semblable,—mon frère!', 76) and to *The Waste Land* more generally: 'It is as if the poet had been striving to create, out of the consciousness of the experience in the hyacinth garden, *an oasis of horror in a desert of Ennui.*'[15] This assertion is close to saying that Eliot's vision in *The Waste Land* involves a negative Romanticism, one in which the lost, elegized experience of visionary intensity in the hyacinth garden stirs the poet and the reader out of the benumbed condition evoked so often in the poem, as when the poet describes and summons up the 'Unreal City' (60) in the first section. Certainly the moment in the hyacinth garden, sandwiched between the desolate intensities hinted at by the allusions to *Tristan und Isolde*, offers a distilled recollection of Romantic concerns with the inexpressible, the epiphanic, and the non-rational. The 'I' 'could not | Speak, and my eyes failed, I was neither | Living nor dead, and I knew nothing, | Looking into the heart of light, the silence' (38–41). Artful enjambments correspond to the passage's dual, ambivalent mood of recollected rapture and fear of nothingness. That the speaker 'knew nothing' links him with later figures who say that the wind is doing 'Nothing again nothing' (120) and who 'can connect | Nothing with nothing' (301–2). But it associates him, too, with the Romantics for whom experience, even 'An ordinary sight', sometimes called for 'Colours and forms that are unknown to man', and, like the Wordsworthian passage, it has its own 'visionary dreariness' (*The Prelude*, 1805, XI. 309, 310, 311). If the hyacinth girl passage is a spot of time, it annuls its meaning in the act of affirming it. Wordsworth's 'visionary dreariness' connects, however obliquely, with a conviction of having been 'Fostered alike by beauty and by fear' (*The Prelude*, 1805, I. 306). There is a destiny that shapes his ends. Eliot's negative Romanticism in *The Waste Land* owes its aching power to the absence of any guarantee that 'memory and desire' (3) have any grounds beyond themselves. Nature, Wordsworthian or otherwise, collapses beneath a weight of ironic textuality, evident in the poem's first line, or struggles to reassert itself amidst the city's man-made wilderness. Christ is a slain vegetation god, lost in a welter of competing syncretic myths. Religious longing is there, as in few other poems, but it is presented with oblique irony and as a matter of textual debris, as at the close of 'The Fire Sermon', where words from Augustine and the Buddha speak out of and to desperate human need, and are but truncated quotations. Or it surfaces as post-Rimbaudian hallucination, when the journey to Emmaus involves a 'white road' (361) haunted by 'another one walking beside you' (362), almost a description of the poem's dealings with

---

[15] A. David Moody, *Thomas Stearns Eliot, Poet*, 2nd edn. (Cambridge: Cambridge University Press, 1994); hereafter Moody, p. 84.

other cultures, with the past, and with, I would argue, English Romanticism, 'walking beside' the poem like its spectral other and ghostly begetter.[16] Political optimism has long since vanished, gone with the 'reverberation | Of thunder of spring over distant mountains' (326–7). If Winter comes, Spring might not be far behind. Yet even in Shelley's 'Ode to the West Wind', there is the repressed fear, communicating through the final question, that April may prove to be the cruellest month were 'Spring' to be a merely literal term, merely naming a stage in a seasonal cycle, having yielded up its metaphorical implications in despair.

The remarkable achievement of 'What the Thunder said' is to leave the poem poised in endlessly oscillating anbivalence between hope and despair, itself a characteristic Romantic stance. One might hear, in the poem's final collage, which is also a barrage, of allusions, a distant echo of the choric voices at the end of *Prometheus Unbound*, admired by Eliot as a moment when 'Shelley rises to the heights' in 'lines to the content of which belief is neither given nor denied'.[17] That final clause is relevant to the freedom which Eliot shapes from his poem's refusal wholly to endorse or reject, a refusal heard in the minutiae of its verbal behaviour. In praising the Shelleyan passage, Eliot has in mind, among other things, Demogorgon's injunction 'to hope, till Hope creates | From its own wreck the thing it contemplates' (*Prometheus Unbound*, 4. 573–4). The formulation implies, through its very wording, the 'creative' functioning of poetry in the face of the wreckage of its own best hopes. The stance is typical of Shelley, but it contributes to the air of residual, stoical hanging-on which marks the close of Eliot's poem. 'These fragments I have shored against my ruins' (430), says the speaker, having alluded to tragedy-touched nursery rhyme, Dantescan refining fire, the *Pervigilium Veneris*, and de Nerval at his '*tour abolie*' (429): all moments that compress into themselves what Moody calls

---

[16] Lawrence Rainey points out that Eliot's note directs us to Sir Ernest Shackleton's *South: The Story of Shackleton's Last Expedition, 1914–1917* (London: Heinemann, 1919), which contains the following: 'it seemed to me often that we were four, not three.... One feels the "dearth of human words, the roughness of mortal speech" in trying to describe things tangible, but a record of our journeys would be incomplete without a reference to a subject very near to our hearts'; quoted in T. S. Eliot, *The Annotated 'Waste Land' with Eliot's Contemporary Prose*, ed. Lawrence Rainey (New Haven: Yale University Press, 2005), p. 118. Rainey notes that the allusion is to Keats, *Endymion*, ii. 819–20.

[17] T. S. Eliot, *The Use of Poetry and the Use of Criticism* (London: Faber, 1933), pp. 92. Eliot does say that the lines can give only 'regretful pleasure' because embedded, for him, in a work that contains indifferent writing. Useful reflections on the relationship between Eliot and Shelley are offered by George Franklin, 'Instances of Meeting: Shelley and Eliot: A Study in Affinity', *ELH* 61 (1994), pp. 955–90, which argues that both writers believe that 'we cannot have any objective knowledge of an alternate, external reality' (p. 961), and Peter Lowe, *Christian Romanticism: T. S. Eliot's Response to Percy Shelley* (Youngstown, NY: Cambria, 2006).

'the aspiration, felt throughout *The Waste Land*, for the condition of music in which anguish is at once felt and transformed'.[18] This aspiration haunts 'What the Thunder said', yet Eliot keeps the poem objective; he does not say, as Shelley might have done, 'Our sweetest songs are those that tell of saddest thought' ('To a Skylark', 90). If 'These fragments I have shored against my ruins' is a line that comments on the poet's post-Romantic, post-Christian state of abandonment, it also wryly describes, metapoetically, the textual nature of the poem he has shaped.

The effect is to create a purity of feeling, in excess of any one situation, yet attaching itself over and over to the objective correlatives met with in the poem. So, in the case of female figures, post-Romantic objects of male desire and curiosity, one thinks of Marie in the mountains, of the hyacinth girl, of the neuraesthenic woman at her dressing-table, of the typist, and of the surreally imagined woman who 'drew her long black hair out tight | And fiddled whisper music on those strings' (377–8). In 'A Game of Chess', the second part of *The Waste Land*, drawing on different sources, notably *Antony and Cleopatra*, Eliot brings an ornately aestheticizing style to bear on the predicament of the nerve-terrorized woman at her dressing-table; the style mirrors the artificiality of her life, cocooned in 'strange synthetic perfumes' (87), and provides a stay against the too easy promptings of sympathy or disgust which a realistic presentation might induce. Those 'perfumes' take us into Romantic terrain when they are said to have 'troubled, confused | And drowned the sense in odours' (88–9). The immediate allusion is to two Shelleyan texts: *Prometheus Unbound*, Act 4, and Panthea's vision of a 'multititudinous Orb' (253) which gathers up all that surrounds it, including 'the wild odour of the forest flowers' (256) into 'one aerial mass | Which drowns the sense' (260–1), and *Epipsychidion*, in which 'a wild odour is felt, | Beyond the sense' (109–10). Eliot finds terror and confusion where Shelley seeks rapture; Eliot detects breakdown where Shelley celebrates breakthrough. Yet the poets both use words to challenge the limits of 'the sense'.

Eliot's women inhabit, and are the victims of, social worlds; Shelley's Emilia in *Epipsychidion* is both prisoner and emblem of spirit-winged hope, the 'Thou' who will give objective form to the poet's longing for transcendence of the social. But Shelley's quest consciously, deliberately, faces the possibility of failure; Eliot will not allow his female figures wholly to elude the aura of romantic desire. The constant movement towards and away from romantic situations and elevated diction suggests a more than merely ironizing impulse on the poet's part. Analogously, Byron, criticized by Eliot for his 'imperceptiveness to the English word', affects his practice as much, it may be, as Lafourge. His 'admirable antacid to the highfalutin' is present in an allusion made by

---

[18] Moody, p. 105.

'Goldfish (Essence of Summer Magazines)' to *Beppo*.[19] 'August, with all its faults!' (8), Eliot mocks, echoing Byron's play with Cowper's 'England, with all thy faults, I love thee still'.[20] The Romantic poet's flamboyant comic rhymes can be heard in 'Prufrock', licensing rhymes between 'ices' and 'crisis', as George Bornstein has argued.[21] And behind the switches of moods and modes in *The Waste Land* floats the wraith of Byronic satirical instability. The episode of the typist and young man carbuncular owes its impact to the poet's manipulation of shadows cast by past idioms. Keats's casements 'opening on the foam | Of perilous seas, in faery lands forlorn' ('Ode to a Nightingale', 69–70) swing listlessly open and shut behind the lines, 'Out of the window perilously spread | Her drying combinations touched by the sun's last rays' (224–5). Sub-Popean satire may characterize Tiresias's manner of seeing, but one finds, too, a Romantic or Byronic inclusiveness. A window opens into in-betweenness, of which Tiresias's own biological state ('old man with wrinkled dugs', 228) is the epitome. Satire modulates into elegiac yearning: if the 'human engine' (216) reduces humans to mechanical functionings, the passage's second use of 'throbbing', as Gareth Reeves has observed, 'reinvests the human engine with "throbbing" humanity'.[22] Inhabiting '*the* violet hour' (215; emphasis added), the poetry, like Tiresias, can be felt 'throbbing between two lives'.

Eliot's rhythms refuse simply to settle for the assurance of neo-Augustan satire. When such assurance asserts itself, it serves as defence against 'foresuffering' (see 243) and in response to Tiresias's deliberately foreshortening verb 'foretold' (229). Before that, the syntax 'throbs' between hovering uncertainty and attempted resolution, sustaining a sense of imminence in 'the violet hour' that focuses on how, as well as what, Tiresias 'can see'.[23] The foresuffering onlooker takes us into a world of near-voyeuristic loneliness, disgust, and desire, and opens the poem into other registers, much as Byron does with his switches of tone in *Don Juan*. So, in canto IV, we move from the affecting impact of Haidée's death to the shock of 'But let me change this theme, which grows too sad, | And lay this sheet of sorrows on the shelf' (74. 585–6), Byron consciously

---

[19] Eliot, 'Byron', in *On Poetry and Poets* (London: Faber, 1957), pp. 201, 202.
[20] Ricks, p. 149.
[21] Bornstein argues that 'Prufrock' 'reverses Eliot's earlier imitations of romanticism point for point. . . . Only Byronic rhymes like "ices" and "crisis" survive the sea change, and the context transforms even them into something rich and strange' (*Transformations*, p. 130). See also Jo Moyle, ' "A New Byronism": T. S. Eliot's "Bored But Courteous" Poetry', *Byron Journal*, 26 (1998), pp. 74–81, for a suggestive comparison that stresses the importance of 'boredom' (p. 76) for both poets.
[22] Gareth Reeves, *T. S. Eliot's 'The Waste Land'* (New York: Harvester Wheatsheaf, 1994), p. 69.
[23] For valuably detailed discussion of Eliot's 'syntactical feats' in the passage, see ibid. 69–71; Reeves argues that the writing's 'grammatical slipperiness' serves to 'focus attention as much on Tiresias's consciousness as on what he is conscious of' (p. 70).

sullying the hallowed image he has made; Eliot hallows the sullied figure he has imagined, as Oliver Goldsmith comes to her rescue, in however anaesthetized a form: 'When lovely woman stoops to folly and | Paces about her room again, alone' (253–4). The record she puts on the gramophone seems a mindless attempt to cancel the memory of the recent unfulfilling sexual encounter. Yet, in another reversal of Romantic irony's movement from the highfalutin to the antacid, Eliot allows the transition at this point to transform the previously 'Unreal City' (207) into a place of beauty.

Transition, deftly employed by the Romantics, and at the heart of Byron's self-divided critique of Romanticism, enables Eliot to leave behind the unlit 'stairs' down which his latter-day Corsair 'gropes his way' (248). Briefly, unforgettably, we are again with Ferdinand in *The Tempest*, a source covertly present in earlier references, but now openly acknowledged as a quotation in the line 'This music crept by me upon the waters' (257), and now as an openly conceded source of aesthetic power as it is in Shelley's 'With a Guitar. To Jane'. The Shelleyan poem is complex in its inflections; its octosyllabic couplets twist from 'joy' to 'pain' (7, 8) in the opening lines, partly because of the hint of an emotional scenario in which Shelley/Ariel is excluded from the happiness enjoyed by Ferdinand and Miranda, but partly, too, because it is the nature of art to 'Make the delighted spirit glow' (6) by exhibiting 'harmony' (4). Eliot uses the 'harmony' bequeathed by the quotation from *The Tempest* to enhance his sense of present-day possibilities, in a passage which may seem an interlude in an overall anti-masque, but which, in fact, alerts us to the many-sided nature of the poem's moods and tones. Here, Eliot finds the 'Unreal City' a place to be apostrophized ('O City city', 259) with something more than merely obvious irony. The poem shows a love of 'music', both extra-textual and metrical, that adds up to a recovery of aesthetic nerve: a pentameter dwells with qualified but real contentment on 'The pleasant whining of a mandoline' (261), before the metre adapts sensitively to 'a clatter and a chatter from within | Where fishmen lounge at noon' (262–3) (a transformation of the banalities and edged comments reported in the pub scene towards the close of 'A Game of Chess'); the writing then flowers into an exuberant savouring of verbal melody as it admires the 'Inexplicable splendour of Ionian white and gold' (265) in a way that recalls the evocation of the 'stately pleasure-dome' (2) in 'Kubla Khan'.

The tone quickly alters, but the passage is a Romantic poem in little, Wordsworthian in its sensitivity to the significance of the ordinary, Coleridgean in its admiration for 'Inexplicable splendour'. In 'What the Thunder said', Eliot also calls Coleridge's poem to mind at the height of the poetry's counter-Romantic version of the apocalyptic sublime. The muse who reappears as a 'raving slut' (III. 5) in Yeats's 'The Circus Animals' Desertion' briefly manifests herself as the 'woman' who 'fiddled whisper music on those strings'. This woman is spiritual sister across the decades to the 'woman wailing for her demon-lover' (16) and the 'damsel with a dulcimer' (37), paradoxically complementary sources of inspiration in 'Kubla Khan'. Eliot responded to the 'haunted' music of Coleridge's work and career, remarking of the Romantic poet in his Norton Lectures of 1932–3 that 'for a few years he had been visited by the Muse . . . and thenceforth was a haunted man; for anyone who has ever been visited by the Muse is thenceforth haunted'.[24] The 'whisper music' replays in a sinister minor key the 'music' which serves as prelude to the revelation of 'Inexplicable splendour' in 'The Fire Sermon'; it also offers a vignette of distracted, autotelic composition that might suggest artistic fiddling while Western civilization goes to ruin. The trajectory described as a whole, however, by 'What the Thunder said' owes much to an ambivalent reinvestment in Romantic millennial imaginings.[25] The poetry builds, that is, to an imagining of the purged or destroyed, coupled with suggestions or hints or, in Eliot's case, 'aethereal rumours' (415) of a subsequently rebuilt or regenerated world. However, whereas Coleridge's 'Religious Musings', Blake's *The Four Zoas,* and Shelley's *Prometheus Unbound* ground themselves on traditional Apocalypse narratives, according to which 'a new heaven and a new earth' (Revelation 21: 1) will come into being, Eliot's poem commits itself to no such vision of renewal. But the writing is impossible to imagine without the Romantic notion of the poem as, in Charles Taylor's words, 'the locus of manifestation'.[26] It is in the poem, and as the poetry works, that the poet's thought abides; the poem's meta-description, 'fragments . . . shored against my ruins', pre-empts ideological appropriation. But by attempting to set his lands in order, the speaker suggests a residual stay against confusion.

In the section, Eliot hallucinates gospel narrative in deeply affecting ways, and, in doing so, may remind one of Romanticism's revisionary workings. The Christian promise of resurrection, in particular, trails phantasmagoric clouds of uncertainty. If Gethsemane sharpens into visionary chiaroscuro in the 'torchlight red on sweaty faces' (322) and 'agony in stony places' (324), there is also a sense, in the hypnotic but baffled rhythms of the opening, that whatever has happened, happened long ago: 'We who were living are now dying | With a little patience' (329–30). The lines cry out to be read as a comment not only on post-Christian but also on post-Romantic culture. But it is the power of the poetry to restore a sense of the primitive and the sacred even as it seems to

---

[24] Eliot, *Use of Poetry and the Use of Criticism,* p. 69.
[25] See Morton D. Paley, *Apocalypse and Millennium in English Romantic Poetry* (Oxford: Clarendon Press, 1999).
[26] Charles Taylor, *Sources of the Self: The Making of the Modern Identity* (Cambridge: Cambridge University Press, 1989), p. 378.

lament their going. Questioning, the technique central to Wordsworth, Shelley, and Keats (as Susan Wolfson and others have shown[27]), means that the 'little patience' passes into larger interrogation: 'Who is the third who walks always beside you?' (359) begins the questioning process, after the bleak indicative declaration 'But there is no water' (358); 'But who is that on the other side of you?', the paragraph finishes, transmitting its energy to historical-cultural investigation in 'What is that sound high in the air' (366), a line stripped of punctuation, since the air is heavy with portentous answers. In fact, the lines, 'Falling towers . . . Unreal' (373–6), both rephrase and respond to, the millennial question *par excellence*, 'What is the city over the mountains' (371). In the lines following the account of the woman's 'whisper music', Eliot refers again to 'towers' (382), this time 'Tolling reminiscent bells, that kept the hours' (383), and to 'voices singing out of empty cisterns and exhausted wells' (384). These 'towers' now inhabit the poetry's *imaginaire*, as though drifting apart from the post-First World War cities of which, a few lines earlier, they seemed to be representatives. And true to the poem's sense of creating a space that is its own, an influential legacy of Romantic poetry, Eliot invites us to attend to intra-textual echo. Those 'reminiscent bells' recall, among other things, the modern-day *Inferno* of 'The Burial of the Dead', in which 'Saint Mary Woolnoth kept the hours | With a dead sound on the final stroke of nine' (67–8). Symbolist poetry is an influence here: one thinks of Rimbaud reworking phrases and images in 'Mémoire' with affecting, luminous intensity. But a further influence is the practice of Romantic poets: examples include Shelley's love of repeating words and phrases until they take on a semantic colouring unavailable in any dictionary, as when the 'unimaginable shapes' (4. 244) of the final act of *Prometheus Unbound* send us in pursuit of imagined 'shapes' (at, for example, 1. 202, or 2. 5. 108) in previous acts; or the 'dead sound' with which Keats repeats 'Forlorn' at the beginning of the final stanza of 'Ode to a Nightingale'. Such poetry intensifies our awareness of the fact and process of reading a poem, not simply in a self-regarding way, but in a fashion that alerts us to the poem as ineluctably its own guarantor, even as, hauntingly, its voices, in the case of *The Waste Land*, seem identifiable with those arising from 'empty cisterns and exhausted wells'. If the phrase speaks of tradition's bankruptcy, it articulates, too, the poem's dependence for its spiritual vision on nothing less than the capital accrued by previous cultures.

For the counter-Romantic who wrote *The Waste Land*, all things fall and can only be rebuilt if the new poetic architecture bears the scars of 'Falling towers', 'tumbled graves' (387) and emptiness. Moody argues that '*The Waste*

---

[27] See Susan J. Wolfson, *The Questioning Presence: Wordsworth, Keats, and the Interrogative Mode in Romantic Poetry* (Ithaca, NY: Cornell University Press, 1986).

Land put an end to English romanticism by taking absolutely seriously the feelings it had soothed.'[28] The comment underestimates the refusal simply to be soothed evinced by poets for whom 'the miseries of the world | Are misery' (Keats, *The Fall of Hyperion*, I. 148–9). Indeed, *The Waste Land*, however counter-Romantic its creator's poetics, gives a new start to English Romanticism by reminding the reader of the persistent obduracy of the longings and desires it dramatizes and analyses. Eliot's idiom may not be that of the Romantic poets, but this difference bears witness to the ongoing vitality of the verbal revolution wrought by the Preface to *Lyrical Ballads*.[29]

III

In the essay on Baudelaire, Eliot observes that the French poet 'gave new possibilities to poetry in a new stock of imagery of contemporary life', admiring particularly 'the elevation of such imagery to the *first intensity*—presenting it as it is, and yet making it represent something much more than itself'.[30] Such imagery presents the subjective as though it tallied with the objective. Eliot's analysis of its workings allows it to be related to, and distinguished from, Romantic poetics and poetry. The imagery used by Baudelaire and Eliot demonstrates and conjoins what Wordsworth in his analysis of lines from 'Resolution and Independence' calls 'the conferring, the abstracting, and the modifying powers of the Imagination' ('Preface to Poems (1815)', p. 633). Wordsworth links 'huge Stone' to 'Sea-beast' and attaches the composite image to 'this Man; not all alive nor dead'; Baudelaire, in lines from 'Le Vin des Chiffonniers' quoted by Eliot in his essay, finds 'Au cœur d'un vieux faubourg' an equally 'vieux chiffonnier', and links city 'mediately' and rag-picker 'immediately', to use Wordsworth's adverbs (p. 633), to 'un poète', searching for meaning among the metropolitan debris. It implies, this searching for imagery of the first intensity, a spiritually flayed response to the modern, and it is unsurprising that Eliot also praises Baudelaire for his belief in 'Sin in the permanent Christian sense', which he distinguishes from 'the modernist Protestantism of Byron and Shelley'.[31]

---

[28] Moody, p. 109.

[29] Eliot implicitly aligns his own post-Mallarméan attempt to 'purify the dialect of the tribe' ('Little Gidding', ii) with Wordsworth's (pre-Mallarméan) attempt when he refers in 'The Music of Poetry' to 'a time like ours, when a refreshment of poetic diction similar to that brought about by Wordsworth had been called for' (*On Poetry and Poets*, p. 35).

[30] Eliot, 'Baudelaire', pp. 425, 426.

[31] Ibid. 425–6 (for Eliot's quotations from 'Le Vin des Chiffonniers'), 427.

Chapter 5 will explore Stevens's response to the Romantics and their understanding of evil and suffering. Eliot's counter-Romanticism required him to underplay in his critical polemic the grasp displayed by poets such as Byron and Shelley of suffering and evil, a double-headed opponent of what the latter calls 'dreams of baseless good' ('Julian and Maddalo', 578) and the former dismisses yet yearns after as an 'unreach'd Paradise' (*Childe Harold's Pilgrimage*, IV. 122. 1096). But one of the legacies that Eliot inherited from Shelley was a sense of remorse, an emotion analysed and explored with great intensity by the 'modernist Protestant' poet W. B. Yeats.[32] In 'To Criticize the Critic', Eliot comments on a famous phrase of his ('a classicist in literature, a royalist in politics, and an Anglo-Catholic in religion') that it had followed him through life, 'as Shelley tells us his thoughts followed him: "And his own thoughts, along that rugged way, | Pursued, like raging hounds, their father and their prey" '.[33] It is a genial use of a serious moment, but the allusion (to *Adonais*, 278–9) reminds us that the figure pursued by his own thoughts who surfaces here and is rarely absent from Eliot's work owes much to Romantic characters such as Childe Harold and the Poet of *Alastor*. At moments in *The Family Reunion* Harry brings to mind Prometheus tortured by the Furies in Act 1, and the impact on him of their presence calls forth from Eliot a recognizably Shelleyan confession of inexpressibility, 'That apprehension deeper than all sense, | Deeper than the sense of smell, but like a smell | In that it is indescribable', and a Shelleyan image of 'a vapour dissolving | All other worlds, and me into it' (1. 2). The writing recalls the Janus-faced nature of imagery in Shelley, in which dissolution might describe loss of selfhood through erotic encounter, as in *Prometheus Unbound*, 2. 1, when Panthea speaks of her encounter with Prometheus, or destruction of self in an altogether more sinister way, as in the third act of the same work, where Jupiter gloats over recollections of Thetis's anguished outcry during sexual congress, 'all my being, | Like him whom the Numidian seps did thaw | Into a dew with poison, is dissolved' (3. 1. 39–41). Harry is terrified, yet curiously exultant; the Furies heighten his awareness of 'another world', and thus serve as stringent spiritual guardians; they point, by contrast, towards 'a door that opens at the end of a corridor, | Sunlight and singing'.

Doubles populate the Romantic imagination; inspiringly, they appear through a revolving door between the quotidian and 'another world'. More darkly, they rise up like projections of an inner dread. Bornstein, with the thorny issue of the poet's alleged anti-Semitism in mind, argues that 'A man anxious to deny forces within himself has an insatiable need of scapegoats, and Eliot maintained one of the most plentifully stocked demonologies of

---

[32] See Peter McDonald, 'Yeats and Remorse', *Proceedings of the British Academy*, 94 (1998), pp. 173–206.
[33] Eliot, 'To Criticize the Critic', in *To Criticize the Critic* (London: Faber, 1965), p. 15.

modern time.'³⁴ Certainly, the 'need for scapegoats' is evident in his 1932–3 Norton Lectures on the Romantics, and, indeed, in the labelling of Byron's and Shelley's ethical awareness as 'modern Protestantism'. The phrase ignores Byron's critique of Calvinism and Shelley's hinted mockery of the 'Protestant apprehension' in the Preface to *The Cenci* (p. 317). Yeats thought Shelley a man rather like Bornstein's Eliot, fighting self-projected shadows when out of phase; but no one grasped processes of projection more keenly than Shelley did. Yet, in his very misunderstandings and simplifications of Romanticism, Eliot contrives to widen a gap between his conscious, polemical superego and the imaginative secret planner at work in his poems, and to allow himself to continue working, at rewarding cross purposes, within, as well as at odds with, the possibilities opened up by Romantic poetry.

By the time of *Four Quartets*, his own Anglo-Catholic goal of impersonal order could be reached only through what he might think of as 'modernist Protestant' quest. Just as Shelley's work is peopled with doubles, so Eliot's poetry involves confrontations between the barely coherent self and its fractured mirrorings. Wordsworth is often thought of a sponsor of the egotistical sublime, but among his most significant bequests is what Frederick Garber, in his study of the poet, describes as the 'poetry of encounter'.³⁵ Coleridge's Mariner, in turn, compares his predicament to one 'that on a lonesome road | Doth walk in fear and dread' (446–7), who 'knows, a frightful fiend | Doth close behind him tread' (450–1), a fiendish projection which influences Eliot's description in 'The Dry Salvages' of 'the backward half-look | Over the shoulder, towards the primitive terror'.³⁶ A 'work of ... pure imagination' that licenses and questions its own imaginings, 'The Ancient Mariner' suggests that poets pay a heavy price for such a 'backward half-look'. The Coleridgean word for that price is 'agony', a 'woful agony, | Which forced me to begin my tale' (579–80), a term repeated in the following stanza where 'That agony returns' (583). It is striking that in 'The Dry Salvages', Eliot, straight after his allusion to 'The Ancient Mariner', refers to 'moments of agony', seeing them as semi-parodic yet potentially illuminating spots of time. 'People change, and smile: but the agony abides. | Time the destroyer is time the preserver,' he comments, half-echoing and inverting in the first line Shelley's 'The One remains, the many change and pass' (*Adonais*, 460) and adapting to 'Time' the double sense

---

³⁴ Bornstein, *Transformations*, p. 150. For a subtle and thought-provoking discussion of relevant issues, see Christopher Ricks, *T. S. Eliot and Prejudice* (1988; London: Faber, 1994). Ricks argues that Eliot's poems invite us 'to judge exactly how much easier it is to attack the prejudices of other people than our own' (p. 283).

³⁵ See Frederick Garber, *Wordsworth and the Poetry of Encounter* (Urbana: University of Illinois Press, 1971).

³⁶ Carlos Baker comments that the image appears 'exactly where a remembrance of "The Ancient Mariner" might most be expected to occur' (*Echoing Green*, p. 273).

of the west wind, in Shelley's ode, as both 'Destroyer and Preserver' (14). Involuntarily, almost, the poetry acknowledges the awareness shown by Coleridge and Shelley of 'agony' and of experience's equivocality. The poem, imbued with a post-Romantic sense of danger, seeks to 'apprehend | The point of intersection of the timeless | With time'. With its air of depicting an abstract spiritual geometry, the writing offers, in Bornstein's words, an 'unromantic solution to romantic problems'.[37] 'Apprehend' has about it the mind's eagerness fully to grasp, as when Shelley argues in *A Defence of Poetry* that 'to be a poet is to apprehend the true and the beautiful' (pp. 676–7), but 'The point' recedes from any attempt to take possession, an elusiveness that makes Eliot's meaning for him.

Yet the poetic yield of such writing, annulling itself in an act of religious humility, is ambiguous. More successful as a many-layered evocation of an 'intersection time' is the encounter with the 'familiar compound ghost' in 'Little Gidding'. In 'What Dante Means to Me', Eliot makes clear the influence of Shelley's account of Rousseau in *The Triumph of Life* on the passage in 'Little Gidding'. Eliot praises the Shelleyan passage as constituting 'some of the greatest and most Dantesque lines in English'.[38] Shelley uses *terza rima* to offer warning, confess error, and narrate catastrophe: ' "If thou canst, forbear | To join the dance, which I had well forborne!" | Said the grim Feature (of my thought aware). | | "I will unfold that which to this deep scorn | Led me and my companions"'. Eliot quotes the lines from a text ultimately deriving from Mary Shelley's version of the poem in *Posthumous Poems*, a text which differs significantly from modern editions: the comma after 'canst' (omitted by modern editors) turns 'forbear' into a command rather than part of the 'if' clause', and the full stop at the end of the tercet (a comma in modern editions) makes the admonition more authoritative. The passage reveals a Romantic updating of Dantescan confrontation with 'Life', and is the more unsparing for revealing Rousseau's attempt, half-belying his posthumous self-culpation, to lay blame for his downfall on the lack of 'purer nutriment' (202). This blame might involve criticism on Shelley's part, but it also shows dramatically a flaring up of smouldering spiritual pride. Indeed, the modernity of Shelley's passage lies in its visionary psychologizing, its development of a language for failure, and its ability to see, in the thwartings that mar an individual life, the revelation of a larger cultural failure. Whether the Narrator could have avoided Rousseau's failure is impossible to say, given the fact that the poem was never finished. But the poem shows that Romanticism could involve courageous quest, rather than self-regarding pursuit of illusion, and while Shelley's answers would

---

[37] Bornstein, *Transformations*, p. 161.
[38] Eliot, 'What Dante Means to Me', in *To Criticize the Critic*, p. 130.

never be Eliot's, the manner of his searching left a strong imprint on a passage which, as Harry Blamires has shown, seems, like much of *Four Quartets*, 'anxious . . . to reflect his indebtedness to the poets of the nineteenth century whose work had been put out of fashion by the poetic revolution he himself initiated'.[39]

Shelley and Dante both influence the ruthless diction applied to the vanities of a literary career, when the ghost sardonically promises, as a final gift, 'the rending pain of re-enactment | Of all that you have done, and been; the shame | Of motives late revealed, and the awareness | Of things ill done and done to others' harm | Which once you took for exercise of virtue'. Eliot's genitives plunge from one wince-inducing revelation to another. We might be in Yeats's *Purgatory*, in which Eliot felt that the Irish poet 'gives a masterly exposition of the emotions of an old man'.[40] Yet Eliot achieves a purgation of sorts in a way that Yeats's old man, condemned to endless recurrence, is denied, and the 'Little Gidding' passage concludes with a minimal hope, 'The day was breaking', which recalls Tennyson's 'Dark house' section (VII) in *In Memoriam*. Tennyson watches the emergence of a newly 'blank day' (12), on which later sections will write messages of glimmering hope.[41] Eliot's ghost leaves a 'disfigured' rather than a 'bald' street, but Eliot's figurations—involving allusions to many authors, including Keats and Shelley—prepare for the change imagined in later sections, when, it is asserted, 'faces and places, with the self which, as it could, loved them' 'become renewed, transfigured, in another pattern'.

It is tempting to think that, at some sub-textual level, the 'Little Gidding' *terza rima* passage is apologizing to the shade of Shelley for earlier words done to his harm. Certainly it shows the Romantic movement being 'renewed, transfigured, in another pattern'. The design is one in which secular griefs and ethical self-laceration serve as a means of entry into 'a pattern | Of timeless moments', in which the poem we read is itself 'an epitaph' that promises resurrection of older voices. 'We are born with the dead: | See, they return, and bring us with them.' The pattern-making might risk static poetic algebra, were it not both for the larger music of Eliot's sequence and for the nuances that vivify what might otherwise seem gestural. So, 'See, they return' alludes to Ezra Pound's 'The Return' ('See, they return; ah, see the tentative | Movements, and the slow feet, | The trouble in the pace and the uncertain | Wavering!'),[42] itself a poem about recall, the emergence into the present of past voices, and reminds

---

[39] Harry Blamires, *Word Unheard: A Guide through Eliot's 'Four Quartets'* (London: Methuen, 1969), p. 148.
[40] Eliot, 'Yeats' (1940), in *On Poetry and Poets*, p. 258.
[41] *The Poems of Tennyson*, ed. Christopher Ricks (London: Longmans, 1969).
[42] Ezra Pound, *Collected Shorter Poems* (London: Faber, 1984).

us, too, of the crucial visionary function performed by 'See' in Shelley's *Prometheus Unbound*. The *terza rima* passage has allowed previous voices to 'return': Keats, for example, is evoked by 'loitering' in the line 'I met one walking, loitering and hurried', the word conjuring up the knight-at-arms of 'La Belle Dame Sans Merci', discovered 'Alone and palely loitering'.[43] Blamires reads the allusion as bringing 'images that appropriately cancel out those of the *Burnt Norton* garden—"The sedge has withered from the lake | And no birds sing" '.[44] Allusion works here in a multiply 'compound' way, since the garden was itself found by passing through 'the door we never opened'. Once discovered by the poet's and the reader's imaginations, it can never be forgotten, and the effect of Eliot's allusions as they leave doors ajar to the eruption of echoic virtualities is comparable. In other words, the fate of Keats's knight, reprising in a minor key that of Shelley's Rousseau, is there for all time as an imaginative possibility that bears on Eliot's own 'exploration'; yet that exploration unavoidably follows its own course, searching for a way of harnessing Romantic despair to modern spiritual struggle, always positioned, as all poetic quests are, 'At the recurrent end of the unending'. Something similar happens with the leaves that gust into 'Little Gidding' from Shelley's 'Ode to the West Wind'; in that poem the 'leaves dead | Are driven, like ghosts from an enchanter fleeing' (2–3); in 'Little Gidding', 'the dead leaves still rattled on like tin'. Shelley's leaves play a prominent role in the Ode's symbolic drama of decay and renewal; Eliot allows them to serve as prelude to a coming back to life of one who, like Shelley and Yeats, 'left [his] body on a distant shore', but who will walk with the poet 'in a dead patrol'. The 'interminable' rhythms of the *terza rima* that is, in fact, only the simulacrum of *terza rima* suit perfectly the blendings and differentiations which distinguish Eliot's imitation of the encounter with Rousseau in *The Triumph of Life*. The movement of the initial five tercets is itself 'loitering and hurried', before 'pointed scrutiny' discerns 'The eyes of a familiar compound ghost | Both intimate and unidentifiable'. Eliot's language has a remarkable suggestiveness and economy; so the 'dead master' is one 'Whom I had known, forgotten, half recalled', the verbs enacting a de-familiarizing process of familiarity. In his assumed 'double part', Eliot is both 'here' and not here: he is at once Dante addressing Brunetto, Shelley confronting Rousseau, and himself seeing himself in relation to others, doubled by the ghost, hearing his own in 'another's voice'. If *The Waste Land* dramatizes something close to the 'mind of Europe', the passage in 'Little Gidding' enacts Eliot's career-long dialogue and quarrel with previous poets, especially Romantic poets, and reminds us that 'the mind of Europe—the mind of his own country— . . . is a mind which changes, and that this change is a development which abandons nothing *en route*'. And in the end

---

[43] See Blamires, *Word Unheard*, p. 143.   [44] Ibid.

the 'Little Gidding' passage retains its autonomy, not simply collapsing into a heap of literary allusions, again conforming to Eliot's view that in great poetry, such as Dante's Paolo and Francesca or Ulysses episodes, or Keats's 'Ode to a Nightingale', it is 'the intensity of the artistic process, the pressure, so to speak, under which the fusion takes place, that counts'.[45]

Bornstein is partly right to see *Four Quartets* as a poem that seems to 'divide against itself'.[46] The poem values imaginative experience, but seeks to discipline it in the light of Christian belief, as though it, too, might otherwise exist only as something 'Driven by daemonic, chthonic | Powers'. Yet those 'Powers', picked out for emphasis, have their full share of the poetic spotlight, and Eliot seems less haplessly self-divided than powerfully able to peer into the very hiding places of Romanticism's appeal, taking Romanticism to be one domain in which 'daemonic, chthonic | Powers' are allowed expression. Indeed, 'The Dry Salvages' argues against tidy periodicization; the past is always there to be 'revived'; it has 'another pattern, and ceases to be a mere sequence'. The poet in Eliot knows that the Romantics have not been safely put to bed, entombed as monumental irrelevances. So long as 'voiceless wailing', the 'sudden fury', and 'moments of happiness' break through the carapace of daily experience, so long will the words of poets such as Coleridge and Shelley, the poetry tacitly concedes, speak to us. Again, Wordsworth's privileged moments bear heavily on a passage such as the following from the close of 'The Dry Salvages':

> For most of us, there is only the unattended
> Moment, the moment in and out of time,
> The distraction fit, lost in a shaft of sunlight,
> The wild thyme unseen, or the winter lightning
> Or the waterfall, or music heard so deeply
> That it is not heard at all, but you are the music
> While the music lasts.

A Modernist updating of Wordsworth's idiom, the writing does not seek to authenticate its intuition of the 'unattended | Moment' through carefully recreated experiences in the Wordsworthian manner. Rather, it relies on local limpidities of phrase and rhythm to carry its meaning and feeling. The poem is itself 'the moment in and out of time', making of its movements realities to which it refers: the enjambment that enriches the straggling adjective 'unattended' with surprised and belated significance, so that 'unattended' now speaks of grace rather than of unawareness; the series of 'or's that recall Shelley's use of 'like' in 'Hymn to Intellectual Beauty', stringing chance 'moments'

---

[45] Eliot, 'Tradition and the Individual Talent', in *Selected Essays*, pp. 16, 19. Eliot writes: 'The ode of Keats contains a number of feelings which have nothing particular to do with the nightingale, but which the nightingale ... served to bring together' (p. 19).

[46] Bornstein, *Transformations*, p. 157.

along a silvery thread of emergent spiritual 'attention'; or, most self-reflexively, hard on the heels of the 'unseen' thyme, the 'music heard so deeply | That it is not heard at all, but you are the music | While the music lasts'. Keats never quite made his 'unheard melodies' (see 'Ode on a Grecian Urn', 11) as credible. For him they were part of a debated antithesis; for Eliot his 'music' is heard only 'While the music lasts', coming into being for the duration of a phrase.

The value placed by Eliot on the epiphanic moment in *Four Quartets* exemplifies his covert affinity with the Romantics, even as he seeks to redefine Wordsworth's valuation of 'spots of time' in *The Prelude*. For Wordsworth, such spots are of value for their 'deepest feeling that the mind | Is lord and master, and that outward sense | Is but the obedient servant of her will' (*The Prelude*, 1805, XI. 271–3), where the repetition of 'Is' reinforces the mind's mastery; for Eliot, epiphanies serve as haunting guarantees of a larger national and religious myth. But Eliot fulfils Wordsworth as much as he revises him when in 'East Coker' he asserts: 'Not the intense moment | Isolated, with no before and after, | But a lifetime burning in every moment'. Wordsworth's practice may sometimes suggest that there is only an 'after', merely a recollection and re-creation of extraordinary experience. Yet, when Bornstein argues that Wordsworth's spots of time 'strengthen us for our existence in time', whereas 'Eliot's moments catapult us out of time',[47] his judgement seems less than fair and underplays Eliot's complex commitment to time; after all, 'Only through time time is conquered'. Wordsworth re-creates in a different way the experience whose meaning we missed; he persuades the reader to live through the experiential stages until the spot of time in all its unparaphrasable directness and strangeness is summoned up. Eliot's intensities arise even more suddenly and inexplicably than Wordsworth's, as at the start of 'Little Gidding'. There, the chariot of Life in Shelley's *The Triumph of Life*, which emits 'a cold glare, intenser than the noon, | But icy cold' that 'obscured with   light | The Sun as he the stars' (77–8, 78–9), contributes to the poet's apprehension of 'A glare that is blindness in the early afternoon, | And glow more intense than blaze of branch, or brazier'. The sensory intensity, sharpened by the alliteration, is as strong as in Wordsworth. But Eliot has dispensed with narrative.

Eliot is, above all, at his most powerfully counter-Romantic in his fascination with the thisness of writing: 'My words echo | Thus, in your mind.' These lines at the start of 'Burnt Norton' interrupt and quicken what might have been merely pseudo-philosophical rumination. The words make us aware that in the poem we have opened a door into the rose garden by hearing of the fact that we did not; Eliot's words cast a spell over us as they echo in our minds. It is intriguing that the same passage's 'bowl of rose-leaves' is traced by Grover

---

[47] Ibid. 154.

Smith to Shelley's 'Music, when soft voices die'; as the same critic points out, the poem ends with lines that anticipate Eliot's self-conscious haunting of our imaginations: 'And so thy thoughts, when thou art gone, | Love itself shall slumber on' (7–8).[48] The ensuing question in 'Burnt Norton'—'Shall we follow?'—recalls the entrance into different states in Act 2 of *Prometheus Unbound*, where Asia and Panthea are urged by a chorus of 'Echoes' to 'follow, follow' (2. 1. 173). And the reader does, tracking the course of *Four Quartets'* counter-Romantic process of inspiration. Trying to describe where poems 'start from', Eliot had recourse to the words of a belated Romantic poet, Thomas Lovell Beddoes, and his 'bodiless childful of life in the gloom | Crying with frog voice, "what shall I be?"'.[49] If that is the quintessential Romantic and post-Romantic compositional question, Eliot also shows his affinity with a crucial Romantic drive in 'The Frontiers of Criticism'. He asserts: 'When the poem has been made, something new has happened, something that cannot be wholly explained by *anything that went before*. That, I believe, is what we mean by "creation".'[50] 'That which is creative must create itself' (p. 418), wrote Keats, and the two utterances suggest the nature of the correspondence between Eliot's work and the creative imperatives of Romantic poetry.

---

[48] Grover Smith, *T. S. Eliot's Poetry and Plays: A Study in Sources and Meaning* (Chicago: University of Chicago Press, 1956), p. 259; Shelley is quoted from Grover Smith.
[49] Eliot, 'The Three Voices of Poetry', in *On Poetry and Poets*, p. 98.
[50] Eliot, 'The Frontiers of Criticism', Ibid. 112.

4

'The Guts of the Living': Auden and Spender in the 1930s

I

'Auden told me that I should drop the "Shelley stunt". "The poet is far more like Mr. Everyman than like Kelley and Sheats." '[1] Spender's recollection makes it clear that Auden had little time for Romantic posturing. Auden's stated dislike of Shelley, in particular, was strong. Reviewing Herbert Read's *In Defence of Shelley*, he comments, 'Reading him, I feel that he never looked at or listened to anything, except ideas.' Like Eliot, Auden sought in poetry 'the objectively presented'.[2] At best, Shelley, for the reviewing Auden, was a mythic figure, one who, as his early poem 'Richard Jefferies' reveals, is never quite believed in. Jefferies was 'No Shelley to light up the firmament | And plunge to darkness like a shattered star' (3–4), and so much the better for him, the poem implies through its overblown mimicry.[3]

Yet Auden works as a complicatedly post-Romantic poet, and it is pertinent to note that whilst rubbishing 'Kelley and Sheats', he took in, with Spender, 'a wide view of the undulating countryside', a countryside depicted by Spender, taking revenge on Auden's apparent anti-Romanticism, as a landscape out of Constable or Wordsworth: 'The monumental trees, among green cornfields and dark hedges, were like old, thick, impregnable walls, with fissures and crevices between their dense-leaved boughs, like crannies between massive stones.'[4] To a remarkable degree, Auden invests post-Romantic disenchantment with mesmeric appeal. In a poem, 'The Road's Your Place', composed in the same month (May 1925) as 'Richard Jefferies', he follows in Wordsworth's footsteps as he remodels the woodcock- and boat-stealing episodes from *The Prelude*, Book i, to describe his sense of being, in the Romantic poet's phrase,

---

[1] Stephen Spender, *World Within World* (1951; London: Faber, 1977), p. 62.
[2] W. H. Auden, *The English Auden: Poems, Essays and Dramatic Writings, 1927–1938*, ed. Edward Mendelson (London: Faber, 1977); hereafter *EA*, p. 357.
[3] Quoted from Auden, *Juvenilia: Poems, 1922–1928*, ed. Katherine Bucknell (London: Faber, 1994).
[4] Spender, *World Within World*, p. 63.

'a trouble to the peace' (1850, i. 316) in the natural world.⁵ Auden's poem narrates a foiled quest for 'A tarn' (2). Wordsworth, having stolen the boat, is confronted by a 'grim shape' which 'Towered up between me and the stars' and bequeathed as its legacy 'a dim and undetermined sense | Of unknown modes of being' (1850, i. 381, 382, 392–3), where the line-ending allows the 'sense' its never-ending, illimitable glimpse of sublimity. Auden mimics Wordsworth's evocation of fear: 'all at once | Three crags rose up and overshadowed me | "What are you doing here, the road's your place" |—Between their bodies I could see my tarn— (12–15).⁶ The script is one of frustrated 'seeing', and a post-Freudian feeling of being 'overshadowed' by the rebuking parent pervades the poem as it does Wordsworth's. But Auden seems to subtract from the Wordsworthian original any hint of a vocation-strengthening pay-off. His poem ends on a downbeat, the poet self-mockingly cast as a shoe-shuffling, juvenile intruder sent packing by 'three tall angry hills', the adjectives making of the hills affronted and accusing adults or, in Bloomian terms, an ephebe's rejecting precursors: 'What could I do but shift my shoes awhile | Mutter and turn back to the road again | Watched out of sight by three tall angry hills' (16–18). Auden's 'turns' in the poem recall the river that, for Wordsworth, mirrors the way *The Prelude* has 'Turned and returned with intricate delay' (1850, ix. 8); yet, even in this early poem, he shies away from any notion of 'recompence' ('Tintern Abbey', 89).

At the same time, 'I could see my tarn,' the poet writes, and he was able to 'Mutter and turn back to the road again', to continue on his thwarted course. Guilt and frustration are to the fore in his early poems of separation from the natural, yet the wish for contact, fulfilled in the later 'In Praise of Limestone', is present. That later poem appears to rebuke Romantic extremism: its landscape is no place for 'The best and the worst' and makes 'uneasy' the poet who, in his Stevens-like commitment to an 'antimythological myth', might be seen as the existential heir to strains in Romanticism. But in its address to a 'Dear', its sense of the solace-giving 'murmur | Of underground streams', and, above

---

⁵ The 1850 reference is given here and in subsequent *Prelude* references in these early poems, as the 1805 version was not published until 1926. Thereafter, the 1805 version is used, unless otherwise indicated. The 1850 text is quoted from William Wordsworth, *The Prelude: The Four Texts (1798, 1799, 1805, 1850)*, ed. Jonathan Wordsworth (London: Penguin, 1995).

⁶ Quoted from Auden, *Juvenilia*; on page 95, Katherine Bucknell comments that '[A. S. T.] Fisher noted [in 'Auden's Juvenilia', *Notes and Queries*, 21 (1974), p. 371] that the three crags recall Wordsworth's description of the cliff which seemed to stride after him as he rowed his stolen boat . . . in the first book of *The Prelude*', and that the passage is 'the only excerpt from *The Prelude* that [Auden] included in his 1935 anthology *The Poet's Tongue*'. See Bucknell's introduction for a fine discussion of Auden's ambivalent view of Romanticism: 'he publicly derided Romanticism while at the same time privately aspiring to become a visionary poet' (p. xxxii).

all, in its modulations from stance to stance, the poem represents a genial, intermittently ironizing, but finally affirming sequel to 'Tintern Abbey'.[7] In its imagining of 'faultless love', it reminds us of Auden's career-long pursuit of that absolute, Romantic as well as Christian in inflection. The early work is often conscious of 'love' as an acute absence, an absence discernible in the accounts of landscapes.

Richard R. Bozorth suggests, in connection with 'Who stands, the crux left of the watershed', that 'Auden's favorite maneuver is to invert the Greater Romantic Lyric, making the reader survey a scene that bespeaks not imaginative community but difference'.[8] That Auden is working in the tradition of the Greater Romantic Lyric in 'Who stands' is a suggestive if simplifying idea. M. H. Abrams, whose coinage the term was, defines 'the Greater Romantic Lyric' as involving a 'repeated out-in-out process, in which mind confronts nature and their interplay constitutes the poem'.[9] Auden does not signal the presence of 'the mind' through straightforward use of the first-person pronoun, yet its troubled operation is pervasive. One might go further and say that the air of desolateness which hangs over Auden's reshaping of the Greater Romantic Lyric has to do with the apparent erasure of an aura: the poem cancels the Wordsworthian dream of communion, yet it confirms the Coleridgean dictum that 'we receive but what we give' ('Dejection: An Ode', 47). Indeed, Auden's form of 'imaginative community' is one that emphasizes difference. Whereas Wordsworth speaks of a belief that 'Nature never did betray | The heart that loved her' ('Tintern Abbey', 126–7), Auden suggests a landscape separate from, yet connected to, the speaker by a kind of mutual estrangement. Comically, in a late lyric 'Dame Kind' (quoted from *Collected Poems*), Auden suggests that there has been an original contract between Nature and humans—'She mayn't be all she might be', he says of Nature, 'but | She *is* our Mum', lines in which Auden parodies and honours what Wordsworth, writing no less outlandishly of 'the infant Babe' (*The Prelude*, 1805, II. 237), calls 'The gravitation and the filial bond | Of nature, that connect him with the world' (263–4).

Yet, from its first line, 'Who stands, the crux left of the watershed' baffles, throwing up 'cruxes' rather than solutions. The opening sounds for a moment

---

[7] Anthony Hecht comments on the way in which in the poem's sixtieth line 'a single addressee enters the poem, rather belatedly and, therefore, in a way reminiscent of Wordsworth's "Tintern Abbey"' (*The Hidden Law: The Poetry of W. H. Auden* (Cambridge, Mass.: Harvard University Press, 1993), p. 309. The poem is quoted from Auden, *Collected Poems*, ed. Edward Mendelson (London: Faber, 1991).

[8] ' "But Who Would Get It?": Auden and the Codes of Poetry and Desire', *ELH* 62/3 (1995), 709–27 (p. 722).

[9] M. H. Abrams, 'Structure and Style in the Greater Romantic Lyric' (1965), quoted from *Romanticism: Critical Concepts in Literary and Cultural Studies*, ed. O'Neill and Sandy, i. 198.

as though it were a question from a sentry, before we realize that 'Who stands' means 'whoever should stand'. Auden produces an atmospheric, yet diagnostic account of alienation. The first paragraph celebrates past heroism associated with lead mining and elegizes 'An industry already comatose, | Yet sparsely living'. The language is both objectively descriptive, as though an economic historian were holding the pen, and coloured by words such as 'comatose' or (especially in the aftermath of *The Waste Land*) 'sparsely living' which turn the scene into a symbol of social and psychological ruin. As ever, Auden is able to sound as if he understood the causes of a generation's sense of inadequacy, failure, and decline. At the same time, he is able to evoke the experience of doubt, dilemma, and loss of direction. The blank verse cuts out any Romantic or Tennysonian melliflousness, as, among other things, Auden manages covertly to thematize the position of the modern poet, somehow the wrong side of the poetic and historical 'watershed'. Wordsworth's ghost haunts the account of experiences involving 'fells impassable', but human heroism is itself subdued to the level of animal endurance, as the dead miner, in his coffin, 'Through long abandoned levels nosed his way | And in his final valley went to ground'. '[N]osed his way' makes the coffined miner at home, yet less than fully human; Auden himself commented to Isherwood that 'The shape of the coffin should justify nosed. The deliberate association of the process with animals is obvious.'[10] If there is oneness with nature here, it is of the bleakest kind.

The second antistrophic paragraph makes it clear that the landscape represents a way of living which it would be foolish for the 'stranger' to attempt to identify with or romanticize: 'Go home, now, stranger, proud of your young stock, | Stranger, turn back again, frustrate and vexed: | This land, cut off, will not communicate'. The syntax mimes the longing for 'communication' and the condition of being 'cut off'. Separation in the poem is a physical fact and a psycho-social condition. Turnings back are again imperatives that restrict, rather than returns that enrich. But the poem is alive with the need for contact, and in this respect it plays its own modernist variation on the theme of being 'cut off' explored by Coleridge in 'Dejection: An Ode'. Just as Coleridge can win from his sense of imaginative failure poetry of great power, so Auden's *dédoublement* allows him to suggest trespass and evoke spectral possibilities of renewal. Trespass informs the image in 'Beams from your car may cross a bedroom wall, | They wake no sleeper', where a thwarted post-Romantic longing gives 'wake no sleeper' an oddly positive inflection; the phrasing is not the same as 'do not wake any sleeper'. Possibilities of renewal suggest themselves tantalizingly in the mention of 'bark of elm | Where sap unbaffled rises, being Spring'. If 'the ignorant sea' and the 'sap unbaffled' remind us that nature is

---

[10] Quoted in Auden, *Juvenilia*, p. 219.

not invested with consciousness, and that 'Spring' is not a Shelleyan symbol, but a natural event, they inflict less damage on Romantic pretensions than they might seem to do: the Romantics are often aware of the gap between mind and nature, the natural and the symbolic, and recognize that language is often driven to make connections backed up only by its own rhetoric. Indeed, the close of the poem, with its arresting image of a creature 'scenting danger', shows the virtual unavoidability of Romantic tropes which project feelings on to the natural world. They show, too, that side of Auden which is in control of, and superior to, any extractable theme. 'Who stands' is, in the end, a performance, the verbal enactment of a brilliantly serious game.

In the poem, Auden comes into possession of his own poetic domain. In doing so, he dethrones Wordsworth, or at least what in a journal entry he refers to as 'Wordsworthian nature-worship, the nostalgia for the womb of Nature which cannot be re-entered by a consciousness increasingly independent but afraid'. Yet, as he also points out, such 'nature-worship' accompanies 'growing self-consciousness', neatly if not wholly wittingly putting his finger on a central tension in Wordsworth's own work (Rousseau is Auden's exemplar of the two tendencies (*EA*, p. 298)). Auden's poetic capacity to hold an audience, to enchant in the name of a bleakly diagnostic wisdom, is closely entwined with his promise of tough-minded disillusion. As John Bayley noted some decades ago, Auden 'is an emancipator of Romantic Symbolism, but it is in this tradition that his roots lie'. Bayley claims that 'Auden is a Symbolist of the common fate', and draws a sharp distinction between 'the vision itself that counts' and any theorizing or rationalizing as a result of which 'his poetry sags and loses momentum'.[11] This distinction valuably reminds the reader that the poetry of early Auden lives in and through moments of intense focus. So, when in 'Consider this and in our time', the poem responds to the aftermath of the Wall Street Crash with a swashbucklingly panoptic vision, it is the aesthetic *frisson* of so doing that enthrals, rather than any paraphrasable profundity of analysis.

It is perfectly respectable to present the poem as describing a sick society, among whose symptoms is the stratification into classes. Yet 'Consider' gleefully eludes earnest Marxist appropriation. Its life comes from a post-Romantic relish of the object, rediscovered to be numinous in the very act of emphasizing its ordinariness. 'Consider this', the poem opens, where 'this' is as empty or over-full of referentiality as is Wordsworth's 'Was it for this?', the germ of *The Prelude* (1805, I. 271). The speaker's portentous imperative implies that he has assumed the mantle of poet-prophet with responsibility for 'our time': but the poem makes its points without passing blame. Auden, a post-Blakean mental

---

[11] John Bayley, *The Romantic Survival* (1957; London: Chatto & Windus, 1969), pp. 156, 157.

traveller, notes the 'cigarette-end smouldering on a border | At the first garden party of the year'. The cigarette 'smouldering on a border' behaves like a symbol, inviting interpretation that concentrates on 'smouldering' tensions within a society internally divided by that most Audenesque of images, the 'border'. Yet such an interpretation, valid in its way, is in danger, as Bayley saw, of burdening Auden's poetry with an over-ponderous freight of meaning. The poem, in fact, makes of social collapse an imaginative romance, one in which we are able, with the poet, to relish the depiction of the inner emptiness of the privileged, 'Supplied with feelings by an efficient band'. There, the language coolly and coldly mimics the inadequacy of those who need to be 'Supplied with feelings', a phrase which makes strange any Romantic idea that 'feelings' are an innate human possession. It also suggests the potential for social discontent in those shut out of 'the plate-glass windows of the Sport Hotel', 'Sitting in kitchens in the stormy fens'. In a stanza from *Childe Harold's Pilgrimage,* canto III, Byron asserts that the motive for creation is to 'live | A being more intense'. 'Even as I do now' (6. 46–7, 49), he caps the assertion. The lines are applicable to Auden's procedure in 'Consider', in which he and his readers 'live | A being more intense' through a poetry that is at once parable art and escape art, to confuse the categories he invoked in 1935.

When Freud's notion of the death-wish, Thanatos, reappears as the 'supreme Antagonist', the shift into home-made myth half recalls the vatic seriousness of Yeats's 'The Second Coming', and, behind it, the Zoas who stalk the pages of Blake's prophetic books. But the writing strikes a sardonically high-spirited note that is very much Auden's own. Auden uses his personification with conspiratorial knowingness: 'You talk to your admirers every day | By silted harbours, derelict works, | In strangled orchards'. Again, landscape undergoes post-Romantic alchemy as it shapes itself into an emblem. The adjectives slide from the literal to the figurative: 'silted harbours' has a geographical accuracy, whereas 'strangled orchards'—invoking the idea of 'strangulation'—brings into play an unspecific but suggestive violence, a violence especially suggestive of a repressive silencing. What is new in Auden's work is its ability to position itself with self-aware impassivity between seriousness and play. So, the stealthy, irresistible inroads made by the Antagonist result in 'A polar peril, a prodigious alarm', an extremist idiom that savours its alliterative *élan* and views with some gusto the apocalyptic scenario. This is not to gainsay the insight which allows Auden to posit a connection between 'immeasurable neurotic dread' and social disintegration, or to construct a line such as 'The convolutions of your simple wish', in which a lifetime's psycho-drama is caught up in and by an iambic pentameter. But it is to note the remarkably self-possessed tone of the poem, whose great virtue is that Auden is able both to enter into the feelings and activities of a supposedly doomed class, idling with them as they enjoy 'The leisurely conversation in the bar | Within a stone's throw of the sunlit water', and to dramatize energies of collapse and potential change. Occasionally a local technique recalls Romantic practice, as when Auden refers to the proleptically 'ruined boys', using an epithet in a way that brings to mind Keats's line in *Isabella*, 'So rode the brothers and their murder'd man' (209), praised by Leigh Hunt for its 'fine daring anticipation'.[12] 'Murder'd' and 'ruined' both suggest the latent, insidious presence in the here-and-now of a seemingly fated futurity. Generally, the poem updates and overhauls Romantic imaginings of disaster and revolution; it gives its faith to no modern-day guru, no Godwin or Paine reshaped as Marx or Freud, but it borrows Freudian and Marxist insights to construct a miniature fantasy that finishes by evoking the impulse towards and the futility of escapist flight, 'humming down arterial roads'. The poem's post-Romantic mode of vision suggests imaginative power in the presence of panic, chaos, and disintegration.

In his Thirties work, as he seeks to retain imaginative autonomy and not to write propaganda, Auden takes his poetic bearings, in part, from Romantic precursors. For all his detestation of Shelley, his work bears the impress of the Romantic poet's influence. As Carlos Baker has observed, Auden's assertion in *The Poet's Tongue* (1935) that 'Poetry is not concerned with telling people what to do, but with extending our knowledge of good and evil' (*EA*, p. 329) is a position with which 'the mature Shelley of 1818–1822 would certainly have agreed', and, as Baker also remarks, the final section of 'In Memory of W. B. Yeats' comes close to summarizing 'the *Weltenschauung* of *Prometheus Unbound*, even though Auden's idiom is markedly different from that of Shelley.'[13] Auden's 'idiom' is, indeed, 'different' as he defamiliarizes the conventions of elegy; yet it betrays a direct borrowing from Byron, as Jerome McGann has shown. Auden prays that 'In the deserts of the heart | Let the healing fountain start', a prayer that is fractionally less confident, for all the force of its trochaic jussive constructions, than the Byronic line which Auden is rehearsing, from the end of the 'Stanzas to [Augusta]': 'In the desert a fountain is springing' (45).[14]

Certainly, the elegy's opening eschews (until the mock-sublimity of the section's closing two lines) the high-flown apostrophes that characterize the marmoreal beginning of *Adonais*. Yet, when Auden writes, in the poem's first section, 'By mourning tongues | The death of the poet was kept from his poems', he recalls Shelley's latter-day mannerist evocation of the posthumous

---

[12] Leigh Hunt, *The Autobiography of Leigh Hunt*, 3 vols. (London: Smith, Elder & Co., 1850), ii. 207.

[13] Baker, *Echoing Green*, pp. 350, 351.

[14] The echo is pointed out by Jerome J. McGann, *Fiery Dust: Byron's Poetic Development* (Chicago: University of Chicago Press, 1968), p. 93.

existence briefly sustained by Keats's creations; even less substantial than poems, 'The quick Dreams, | The passion-wingèd Ministers of thought' (73–4) plant the first seeds of a transcendent resurrection. Keats's death is overcome by the life of his poems, a life borne witness to and shaped by Shelley's own 'mourning tongue'. Shelley's image for poetic legacy in 'a young heart' (393)— 'the dead live there | And move like winds of light on dark and stormy air' (396–7)—has a turbulent Manichean energy; the 'winds of light' seem both to enter the 'dark and stormy air' breathed by the heart in its 'mortal lair' (393) and to arrive as themselves part of a figurative meteorological package that includes 'light' and 'stormy air'. The result is to convey the incessant struggle at the heart of creativity and creative response. Auden, himself modifying the words of his elegiac predecessors, including Shelley, remarks laconically: 'The words of a dead man | Are modified in the guts of the living.' Auden's lines, with their calculatedly flat rhythms, play down anything *cantabile* in this section; but the modification of a dead man's words 'in the guts of the living' (rather than simply in their minds or memories) implies the very kind of absorption and takeover which this chapter and, indeed, book has been describing. All poets, after their creations have gone from them, whether through physical death or merely through publication, experience *sparagmos*, a scattering: 'Scatter, as from an unextinguished hearth | Ashes and sparks, my words among mankind' (66–7), cries Shelley, close to the end of 'Ode on the West Wind'; Auden comments on the dead Yeats, 'Now he is scattered among a hundred cities | And wholly given over to unfamiliar affections', the passive verbs announcing the poet's powerlessness to control his work's reception, a powerlessness which Shelley ecstatically embraces.

'In Memory of W. B. Yeats' moves beyond the flat, the wry, and the sardonic in its second and third sections. It ends with a recovery of the value to be found in an 'unconstraining voice' that persuades us 'to rejoice', a rhyme that shows the poetry recovering its nerve, even as there are no illusions about the continued presence in life of 'human unsuccess'. The very metre of this third section, composed in 'trochaic tetrameter quatrains', may well be intended to 'recall' Blake's 'The Tyger', as Hecht asserts.[15] Enlisting Blake's sense of an energy radiant 'In the forests of the night' and Yeats's invocations of tragic joy, Auden asks his representative poet to 'follow right | To the bottom of the night', possibly 'recollecting the song of the Echoes' in *Prometheus Unbound*, as Baker suggests, and certainly, as the same critic proposes, following the trajectory of Shelley's lyrical drama, which requires a journey 'Through the grey, void abysm, | Down down' (2. 3. 72–3).[16] At one level, Auden may rebuke Romantic delusions about poetry's significance when he writes in the second

---

[15] Hecht, *Hidden Law*, p. 148. [16] See Baker, *Echoing Green*, p. 351.

section, 'poetry makes nothing happen'; yet, in the same breath, he aligns himself with Shelley's opposition to propagandist poetry in *A Defence of Poetry*.[17] Moreover, adroitly exploiting the stress system of his subdued alexandrine, so that the first syllables of 'poetry', 'nothing', and 'happen' all coincide with the metre's accentual demands, he slyly introduces the notion that poetry occupies an imaginative Utopia, a no-place where 'nothings'—the nothings of poetic invention—take on a local habitation and a name. Poetry 'survives', a verb that sees off 'executives', attaches itself to 'the valley of its saying', an image that recalls Wordsworth's poem-like river that 'sent a voice | That flowed along my dreams' (*The Prelude*, 1805, I. 275–6), and emerges as 'A way of happening, a mouth'.

'A way of happening', poetry becomes a means of interrogating history without being subsumed by it; Auden's reaction against too grandiose a claim for poetry is apparent in the minimalism of 'a mouth'. But the 'mouth' is the source of a river as well as a reduced version of the 'voice' central to Romantic poetics,[18] and demanding its due in Auden's retrospective critique in 'September 1, 1939' of 'a low dishonest decade', where he uses his 'voice' to discredit debased Romanticism, among other things:

> All I have is a voice
> To undo the folded lie,
> The romantic lie in the brain
> Of the sensual man-in-the-street
> And the lie of Authority
> Whose buildings grope the sky.

This 'romantic lie' is less the lie of Romanticism than the self-enclosed, need-driven fantasy of 'the sensual man-in-the-street'. In its opposition to 'Authority', graphically depicted as sexually molesting 'the sky', as well as haplessly 'groping for answers',[19] and the poverty of everyday consciousness, the line 'All I have is a voice' looks haltingly modest; in fact, it represents a tentative but tenacious commitment to the notion of poetic vocation: Auden may not be an unacknowledged legislator, but his voice descends, however much it alters its inflections, from Blake's 'voice of the Bard', itself subject (in the poem in which it appears, 'Introduction', *Songs of Experience*) to uncertainty and bafflement. Like the close of the elegy for Yeats, 'September 1, 1939' finds its way towards a prayer-like wish to 'Show an affirming flame', a line which might supply a motto

---

[17] Anthony Hecht writes: 'In claiming that poetry makes nothing happen, Auden must have had in mind the extravagant claims made in poetry's behalf by some of the Romantics, by Shelley in particular' (*Hidden Law*, p. 144).

[18] See ibid. 147 for the suggestion that 'mouth' contains as one of its meanings 'the delta of the submerged river image that issues into the general sea'.

[19] Ibid. 166.

for Romantic poetry's central project. But the 'affirming flame' flickers against a shadowy background. Like Yeats before him (see Introduction, p. 7), Auden may reverse the imagery used by Shelley in 'Hymn to Intellectual Beauty', where intellectual beauty nourishes human thought 'Like darkness to a dying flame' (version A, 45), yet his awareness of doubleness is comparable to Shelley's and to that of other Romantics. Shelleyan affirmation burns against a backdrop of sceptical doubt and uncertainty about whether reality will bear out human desire. Audenesque affirmation is born out of a sense that, like others, he is 'composed . . . | Of Eros and of dust, | Beleaguered by the same | Negation and despair'. Wordsworth, too, concedes an equivalent composite nature when he concludes the woodcock-stealing episode in the 1850 version of *The Prelude* with a mingling of humility and exultation: 'Dust as we are, the immortal spirit grows | Like harmony in music' (I. 340–1). There, the writing does not oppose our dust-ridden nature to the capacities possessed by 'the immortal spirit'. Wordsworth's syntax implies that the capacity for growth of the spirit depends on and is entwined with the fact that we are 'Dust', an essential bass-note, it would seem, in any 'harmony' we produce. And in its sense of being 'Beleaguered' by 'Negation and despair', Auden's poem descends from Wordsworth's 'Tintern Abbey', with its longing to escape 'the burthen of the mystery' (39).

Auden's perspective, at and beyond the decade's end, consciously returned to the Romantic era for parallels and contrasts. The author of *The Enchafèd Flood* speaks of 'The Polemical Situation of Romanticism' as though it were a recurrent human battle in which, so far as the poet is concerned, there is a seemingly inevitable conflict with 'the poetic tradition and the attitudes of the preceding generation' as well as with 'the beliefs and attitudes of his society in which he lives which are hostile to his conception of art'. Auden then quotes five illustrative passages from Blake to illustrate the Romantic writer's grasp of the need for 'battle . . . on two fronts'.[20] Blake is admired for his 'usual unerring insight', which is not to say that Auden subscribes to Blake's beliefs.[21] But the passage shows Auden understanding the present in terms drawn from Romanticism, as he does in significant passages from the octosyllabic couplets of his *New Year Letter*, which proposes a connection between the present age and Wordsworth's: 'Like his, our lives have been coeval | With a political upheaval.'[22] Auden implies that Wordsworth's movement from 'weaving a platonic dream | Round a provisional regime | That

---

[20] Auden, *The Enchafèd Flood; or, The Romantic Iconography of the Sea* (1951; London: Faber, 1985), pp. 46–7. The Blakean passages are his account of Cowper telling him that he is 'mad as a refuge from unbelief—from Bacon, Newton and Locke'; 'Mock on, Mock on Voltaire, Rousseau'; his account of 'the bounded' as 'loathed by its possessor' (from 'There is No Natural Religion [b]', Erdman, p. 2); his parody of the Lord's Prayer; and a two-line squib attacking Newton.

[21] Auden, *Enchafèd Flood*, p. 51.

[22] Quoted from Auden, *Collected Poems*, ed. Mendelson. 1991).

sloganized the Rights of Man' to disillusioned reaction, 'Left by Napoleon in the lurch, | Supporting the Established Church', has an affinity with the journey enjoined on those who saw in Revolutionary Russia a fulfilment of Marxist hopes:

> We hoped; we waited for the day
> The State would wither clean away,
> Expecting the Millennium
> That theory promised us would come:
> It didn't.

For once, Auden's erratic use of the colon fulfils admirably and wittily its grammatical role, to 'deliver the goods', which, in this case, is the fact that the goods were not delivered.

Unsurprisingly, Auden recognized the validity and role for modern poetry of comedy and 'light verse'. In an essay on 'Light Verse' (1938), he offers an account of modern poetry that places emphasis on the division that sprang up in the Romantic period between poet and audience, once the 'patronage system broke down' (*EA*, p. 365). On Auden's reading, one reprised in his *Letter to Lord Byron*, poets from the Romantics onwards

> turned away from the life of their time to the contemplation of their own emotions and the creation of imaginary worlds, Wordsworth to Nature, Keats and Mallarmé to a world of pure poetry, Shelley to a future Golden Age . . . Instead of the poet regarding himself as an entertainer, he becomes the prophet, 'the unacknowledged legislator of the world', or the Dandy who sits in the café, 'proud that he is less base than the passers-by, saying to himself as he contemplates the smoke of his cigar: "What does it matter to me what becomes of my perceptions?"' (*EA*, p. 366)

This account feels trenchant rather than profound, but in its comic brio it exhibits one way in which Auden manages the Romantic legacy: through his distilled aphoristic style, he himself adopts the persona of the Dandy he describes, while maintaining a sense that poets should stay in touch with 'the life of their times'. Auden's own influence as a mediator between the Romantics and more recent poetry is especially evident in his appreciation of what Byronic comedy could offer. The comic in a more elliptical, parodic vein pervades his Thirties poems. His attitude to poetry itself can smack of the brilliant schoolboy running rings round his stodgy elders, mimicking with perfect gravity their more earnest accents. He has an incipient post-colonial awareness in his understanding of the workings of power, and the 'Six Odes' that make up Book 3 of *The Orators* are works of poker-faced parody.[23] The

---

[23] For more on *The Orators* and the proto-Muldoonian way in which 'one can hear each voice listening to itself and turning hollow', see ch. 4 (written by Gareth Reeves) in Michael O'Neill and Gareth Reeves, *Auden, MacNeice, Spender: The Thirties Poetry* (Basingstoke: Macmillan, 1992); quotation on p. 90.

linguistic gestures of power rehearse themselves with deadly seriousness; yet the writing ebulliently mocks imperialist attitudes: 'The youngest drummer | Knows all the peace-time stories like the oldest soldier, | Though frontier-conscious, || About the tall white gods who landed from their open boat.' 'Nations themselves *are* narrations,' Edward Said reports a critic as saying,[24] and Auden's Thirties poetry brims with the overt and covert stories that England tells about itself.

The gnomic, menacing, paid on both sides tone of the early Thirties work, was a hard act to sustain. Byron offered Auden a less duplicitous, though equally flexible, way back to some kind of common discourse. 'No egoist can become a mature writer until he has learnt to recognise and to accept, a little ruefully perhaps, his egoism': so Auden wrote of Byron in a Thirties essay that sees the Noble Lord's irony as saving him from his Satanism.[25] In a later essay, 'Don Juan', Auden dismisses the Byron who 'tried to write Poetry with a capital P' (his words), but he is full of insightful admiration for *Don Juan*: 'Serious poetry requires that the poet treats words as if they were persons', he says in a suggestive antithesis, 'but comic poetry demands that he treats them as things and few, if any, English poets have rivaled Byron's ability to put words through the hoops.'[26]

Auden himself comes close to such an ability. In the clerihew, 'Lord Byron | Once succumbed to a Siren: | His flesh was weak, | Hers Greek' (quoted from *Collected Poems*), the words reveal a scandalously deadpan refusal to behave like persons. *Letter to Lord Byron* compliments, by imitating, Byron's virtuosity in *Don Juan*, which, Auden tells us, he has read 'on the boat to Reykjavik | Except when eating or asleep or sick'. The deflation achieved by that clinching rhyme shows that Auden has learned from Byron's handling of *ottava rima*, though he deftly averts comparison by choosing 'Rhyme-royal' as his stanza form, in case he 'should come a cropper'. What has gone is the portentous poet of the early Thirties, and the poem implicitly says, as Paul Muldoon has his 'Wystan' assert in '7, Middagh Street', 'I will not go back as *Auden*'.[27] If Byron debunks epic proprieties, ' Hail, Muse! *et cetera*' (*Don Juan*, III. 1. 1), Auden satirizes Thirties Utopianism: 'Hail to the New World! Hail to those who'll love | Its antiseptic objects, feel at home' is how one stanza starts; the next begins: 'Preserve me from the Shape of Things to Be'. Like Byron in *Don Juan*, Auden is able to write a public poetry, a poetry that has its often journalistic finger on the pulse, as when he brings Byron's hero into the contemporary

---

[24] Edward Said, *Culture and Imperialism* (London: Chatto, 1993), p. xiii.
[25] Auden, 'George Gordon Byron', in *Prose and Travel Books in Prose and Verse*, i: *1926–1938*, ed. Edward Mendelson (London: Faber, 1996), p. 489.
[26] Auden, *The Dyer's Hand and Other Essays* (London: Faber, 1963), p. 399.
[27] Muldoon's poetry is quoted from his *Poems, 1968–1998* (London: Faber, 2001).

social whirl: 'I see his face in every magazine', and goes on to mimic one of Byron's slyest rhymes: ' "Don Juan at lunch with one of Cochran's ladies" . . . "Don Juan, who's just been wintering in Cadiz, | Caught at the wheel of his maroon Mercedes." ' The source is *Don Juan*, canto II, in which the master's mate is saved from being eaten 'by a small present made to him at Cadiz, | By general subscription of the ladies' (st. 81, 647–8).

Auden admires in Byron 'A style whose meaning does not need a spanner', saying that his predecessor 'is the master of the airy manner'. In *Letters from Iceland* (co-written with Louis MacNeice), where the poem first appeared, Auden wrote: 'I bought a Byron with me to Iceland, and I suddenly thought I might write him a chatty letter in light verse about anything I could think of, Europe, literature, myself. He's the right person I think, because he was a townee, a European, and disliked Wordsworth and that kind of approach to nature, and I find that very sympathetic.'[28] The note helps explain why the poem is a fascinating episode in the reception of Romanticism. Long before Jerome McGann and followers, Auden was suspicious of aspects of so-called Romantic Ideology. Standing Wordsworth's sonnet to Milton on its head, he writes, 'Byron, thou should'st be living at this hour!', and he tells the Romantic poet that he's 'glad to find I've your authority | For finding Wordsworth a most bleak old bore': an insult the more biting for choosing an adjective at the centre of one of Wordsworth's great spots of time, when he recalls 'the bleak music of that old stone wall' (*The Prelude*, 1805, XI. 379). Byron despised Wordsworth, to quote various insults from the Dedication to *Don Juan*, for 'his place in the Excise' (46), for the dull pretentiousness of his *Excursion*'s 'vasty version | Of his new system to perplex the sages' (27–8), and for his egotistical belief, with the other Lake poets, that 'Poesy has wreaths for [him] alone' (38). Auden dislikes Wordsworth, at least for the purposes of his comic *tour de force*, as a poet whose cult of nature allows his readers' potential radicalism to be safely siphoned off: 'His well seems inexhaustible, a gusher | That saves old England from the fate of Russia.' 'Gusher' implies windiness and emotional effusiveness, and the rhyme with 'Russia' suggests that the poetry serves as a safety-valve permitting the siphoning off of feelings which might, otherwise, insist on political expression.

Not that Auden writes from the perspective of the paid-up Marxist. As often, he occupies a space between rival views and diagnostically distanced from them. So, for all his admiration of Byron as 'Neither a preacher, ninny, bore, nor Brownie', Auden examines the phenomenon of Byronism; he is even prepared to imagine, if only in other people's quotation marks, an updated ' "Lord Byron at the head of his storm-troopers" ': 'Suggestions have

---

[28] Auden, *Prose and Travel Books*, i. 280.

been made', he writes, 'that 'the Teutonic | Führer-Prinzip would have appealed to you | As being the true heir to the Byronic.' Auden goes on to, in effect, absolve Byron of this charge, asserting, in terms Michael Foot will re-echo, 'Injustice you had always hatred for', even if this praise is coupled with the comment, 'And we can hardly blame you, if you missed | Injustice just outside your lordship's door'. Auden himself misses Byron's concern with the fate of the frame-breakers in his maiden speech and poems such as 'An Ode to the Framers of the Frame Bill'. Yet, if his stanzas do not embrace all that there is to be said about Byron's politics, they display a vigilant, canny refusal to be drawn in any uncritical way into the Romantic poet's glamorous orbit.

As well as permitting him to analyse the politics of Byronism, Auden's poem gives him room in which to describe his witty but complex views on the role of art and the artist since Romanticism: in particular, the fate of aestheticism or 'the Poet's Party', the aftermath of which has left 'the sobering few', such as, one assumes, Auden himself, 'trying hard to think of something new'. Auden's ironies are sharp-edged and continually in close proximity to ethical convictions: it is vital to him, for example, that 'Art's subject is the human clay', a position that brings him close to Byron's complex sympathy for 'our helpless clay' (*Don Juan,* I. 63. 499). Ultimately the nearest Auden comes to a defence of poetry in the poem is his claim that it helps in understanding what he calls 'The Trap', whose origins are psychological or political: the artist 'seems to like it, couldn't do without it, | And only wants to tell us all about it'. Indeed, Auden's post-Thirties work often reveals him to be a clear-sighted, urbanely if sometimes sadly self-aware poet of 'The Trap', alert to contradictions, yet capable of reason, wisdom, and tolerance.

II

Louis MacNeice wrote in 'Eliot and the Adolescent':

The paradox of *my* generation, who were aged about eighteen in 1926, is that while (again like most adolescents?) we were romantics, i.e. anarchic, over-emotional and set on trailing our coats, the date of our birth had deprived us of the stock, i.e. the Nineteenth Century, 'romantic' orientation. A year before I read Eliot my favourite long poem was *Prometheus Unbound* but this had already cloyed; Shelley's enthusiasms were beginning to seem naïve to a child of the Twentieth Century, even to a child who had only fleeting contacts with its over-industrialized, over-commercialized, over-urbanized, over-standardized, over-specialized nuclei. What we wanted was 'realism' but —so the paradox goes on—we wanted it for romantic reasons. We wanted to play

Hamlet in the shadow of the gas-works. And this was the opening we found—or thought we found—in Eliot.[29]

Eliot as the predecessor who allowed poets such as the early Auden, Spender, and MacNeice to 'play Hamlet in the shadow of the gas-works' helps us to grasp the concept of a ' "realism" ' embraced 'for romantic reasons'. Spender's attachment to the word 'real' in his early poems bears witness to 'romantic' energies of sensed separation and longed-for healing. As if responding to the Eliotic evocation of the post-Baudelairean 'Unreal City', he declares in one poem ('Rolled over on Europe'), 'Only my body is real' and 'Only this rose | My friend laid on my breast, and these few lines | Written from home, are real'.[30] The rhythms, constantly at odds with a nominal iambic pulse, emphasise the wish to be in touch with the 'real'. Moreover, the 'real' lodges itself in subjective identity and in the act of writing. In these respects, Spender implicitly defines his poetic self against Eliot's, since Eliot—though capable in poems such as 'Prufrock' of 'considerable realism'—sustains serious doubts about the possibility of finding the 'real' in a dimension that is secular.[31] In his book-length study of Eliot (1975), in which Spender makes the argument just posited, he glosses lines from *Four Quartets* in this way: 'To live in reality, *dans le vrai*, for more than moments, is almost intolerable. Reality is that moment in time which, for the person experiencing it, stands outside time.' Admittedly this is a retrospective comment about a poem written after Spender's Thirties poetry, yet it makes explicit his admiration for a poet whom he conceives of in the same work as a 'visionary' but 'also realistic', and, in opposition to Matthew Arnold (as Eliot and Spender see the matter), 'in his poetry nothing but a poet'.[32]

A post-Romantic lineage makes itself felt. Of the 'visionary' poetry in 'What the Thunder said', Spender writes that in it 'The "I" has become the depersonalized witness of the world which has become it', as though consciousness and world were, in some terrible fulfilment of Romantic dreams, unified, and he invokes as a parallel 'the process Keats imagined in *Hyperion* and *The Fall of Hyperion*' when the poet becomes Apollo.[33] Spender, too, imagines 'extremes' in his Thirties work; but, like Hart Crane, he takes Eliot's vision of 'doom' as a point of departure for a different, more affirmative outlook.[34] Yet affirmation is a less ideologically shrill matter for Spender than it is sometimes represented as being.

---

[29] Louis MacNeice, *Selected Literary Criticism*, ed. Alan Heuser (Oxford: Clarendon Press, 1987), p. 149.
[30] Stephen Spender, *New Collected Poems*, ed. Michael Brett (London: Faber, 2004).
[31] Spender, *Eliot* (1975; London: Fontana, 1986), p. 41. Spender sees 'a certain hollowness at the centre' of *The Waste Land*, 'the hollowness of describing civilization in terms of the temporal city, when the true quest is for the eternal city, the *Civitas Dei*' (p. 118).
[32] Ibid. 161, 10.   [33] Ibid. 113.   [34] Ibid. 114, 116.

Poem after poem in his early work wrestles with the dilemma of being a poet who wishes to be a writer who can do something 'that matters', to quote from 'Who live under the shadow of a war'. Indeed, in his self-consciousness about his poetry, Spender joins hands with many of his Romantic precursors. 'Moving through the silent crowd' recalls Blake's *Songs*, especially 'London', in the contrast it establishes between the apparent simplicity of its ballad-like movement and the tangled depth of its perceptions. Spender's 'I' in this poem is a descendant of the Blakean speaker who wanders through London, and who is able, or cursed, to 'mark in every face I meet | Marks of weakness, marks of woe' (3–4). Whereas Blake emphasizes the system that shapes and finds its echo in 'mindforg'd manacles', Spender, noting the 'unemployed' (his later title) 'who idle in the road', combines subdued social protest with an investigation of his own near-narcissistic involvement. 'I have the sense of falling light', he asserts at the end of stanza 1, a knowingly belated Romantic gesture that extracts from the scene his own subjective 'sense'. Such a sense is the guilt-ridden prize won by the poet from his phantom-like movement through 'the silent crowd'. Spender presents the unemployed as 'silent' and even silenced, effectively beyond his understanding; as they 'greet friends with a shrug of shoulder | And turn their empty pockets out, | The cynical gestures of the poor', there may be some degree of social observation at work, but the categorizing impulse evident in the last line betrays the poet as wholly and self-consciously excluded from 'the poor'. By contrast, Blake is able not just to see, but more vividly to 'hear' 'How the Chimney sweepers cry | Every blackning Church appalls' (8, 9–10), where 'How' implies knowledge of an interlocking process of oppression and hypocrisy. This is not, however, to criticize Spender, who in his last stanza performs a poetic self-analysis of dizzying intricacy that shows his poem's unique form of authenticity:

> I'm jealous of the weeping hours
> They stare through with such hungry eyes.
> I'm haunted by these images,
> I'm haunted by their emptiness.

The triple use of the first person makes clear that this is a poem about the poet's understanding of what he is up to as he tries to comment on social injustice. It emerges that he feels the unemployed have access to a reality of suffering and deprivation that makes him 'jealous'. It transpires, too that he has been 'haunted' by 'images' of 'hungry eyes', a statement carrying with it the implicit admission that such haunting is a corruptly privatizing response. But the final line, conceding that the poet is 'haunted' by the 'emptiness' of his 'images', saves the poem by sacrificing it. The lure of representation is annulled, and the poem's hoarded 'hauntings' are subjected to critique.

'The majority of artists today are forced to remain individualists in the sense of the individualist who expresses nothing except his feeling for his own individuality, his isolation.' This remark from Spender's 1933 essay 'Poetry and Revolution' might define the post-Romantic individualism at work in 'Moving through the silent crowd', an individualism not incompatible with the hope that 'by making clear the causes of our present frustration they [artists] may prepare the way for a new and better world'.[35] It is as though Spender were tussling in poem and essay with Shelley's remark, to which he refers more than once, that 'Poets are the unacknowledged legislators of the World' (p. 701). He comments in *World Within World* that while at Oxford he traded his sense that the poet was 'a kind of shadowy prophet behind the throne of power, Shelley's unacknowledged legislator of mankind' for a new (and arguably no less Shelleyan) view of poetry as 'a use of language which revealed external actuality as symbolic inner consciousness'.[36] Yet his poetry battles to make 'symbolic inner consciousness' a place where social change can be imagined. At times the relationship between 'external actuality' and 'symbolic inner consciousness' is that of a brusque clash, as is the case in the Petrarchan sonnet 'Without that once clear aim, the path of flight'. The poem laments the loss of 'that once clear aim, the path of flight', a path that could be thought to run through and from Romantic poetry, and concludes with a residual post-Romantic trust in the efficacy of 'This writing': 'The city builds its horror in my brain, | This writing is my only wings away.' Spender, in effect, says with the Poet of *Alastor,* in a passage excerpted in Spender's selection of Shelley's poetry, ' "Vision and Love!" | . . . I have beheld | The path of thy departure' (366–8). As occurs in the work of the Romantics, Spender's appeal to 'This writing' salvages meaning from cultural wreckage: one thinks, for example, of Keats's appeal in *The Fall of Hyperion* to 'This warm scribe my hand'. In other poems Spender takes up the challenge of inventing a revolutionary poetics for the modern age: celebrating pylons as offering 'the quick perspective of the future', but elegizing, against his sense that 'quick' means 'living' as well as 'fast', 'our emerald country'; attempting to transfuse into the hyper-modern image of the aeroplane (or 'air-liner') a concept of beauty topping that of the natural, but responding, too, to a latent suspicion that no ultimate elevation beyond 'the landscape of hysteria' is possible.

In 'Not palaces, an era's crown', the last poem in his 1933 *Poems,* Spender writes in stress-packed lines a poetry that is deliberately that of the will, one that strenuously rejects aesthetic or sensuous pleasures. Yet the poem's syntax bespeaks Spender's fascination with the 'palaces' and 'architectural gold-leaved

---

[35] Spender, *The Thirties and After: Poetry, Politics, People, 1933–75* (London: Fontana/Collins, 1978), p. 53.

[36] Spender, *World Within World,* p. 95. See also *Thirties and After,* p. 221, where he remarks (in a journal entry for 16 Oct. 1965) that 'American poets, far more than English ones, cling to the idea that the poet is "unacknowledged legislator"'.

flower' which he takes five lines to tell us he does not build—or rather he tells us that he builds 'Not' from these things. The workings of the poem briefly recall Shelley's dallying in the third section of 'Ode to the West Wind' with 'old palaces and towers, | Quivering within the wave's intenser day, || All overgrown with azure moss and flowers | So sweet, the sense faints picturing them!' (33–6). Shelley allows for the powerful tug of the relics left by an unjust ancien regime, especially as they are reclaimed and even redefined by the mirroring water, or the 'azure moss and flowers'. The sense's fainting can only, for Shelley, be a temporary interlude, much as, for Spender, 'stamping the words with emphasis', 'The spirit drinking timelessness' is in flight from the will's true task: namely, to advance 'Our goal which we compel: Man shall be man'. For Shelley, however, natural reclamation is at one with the imagining of change. For Spender, the rejection of the senses' 'gardens' and 'singing feasts', which serve as synecdoches of a quasi-Romantic Orientalism, exacts a weightier cost, as his language recognizes, reserving its most felicitous effects for the sensuous pleasures from which it is exiling itself. Again, a Shelleyan parallel illuminates Spender's practice. 'Man shall be man' recalls the close of Act 3 of *Prometheus Unbound*, included in Spender's selection from Shelley:

> The loathsome mask has fallen, the man remains
> Sceptreless, free, uncircumscribed, but man
> Equal, unclassed, tribeless, and nationless,
> Exempt from awe, worship, degree, the king
> Over himself; just, gentle, wise: but man
> Passionless?—no ... [37]

These lines, notoriously difficult to edit, are printed as Spender prints them. They serve as a possible source of, and certainly a suggestive parallel with, Spender's 'Man shall be man', a 'programme' glossed further in his poem's terse second paragraph as 'Death to the killers, bringing light to life'. 'Death to the killers' may be more aggressive than Shelley's own complex feelings about violent overthrow in his lyrical drama; the idea of such overthrow seems explicitly to be condemned by Prometheus' remorse after hearing his curse repeated by the Phantasm of Jupiter ('I wish no living thing to suffer pain', 1. 305), but it finds its way back into the poem's figurative networks, pervading the volcanic imagery of Act 2 and the first scene in Act 3, where Demogorgon drags Jupiter down with him. If 'light to life', the last words of Spender's poem, returns to the opening of John's gospel ('In him was life; and the life was the light of men', 1: 4), it also seeks foundational support from Shelley's 'Life of Life!' lyric in *Prometheus Unbound*, 2. 5. 48.

But to compare Shelley's lyric with Shelley's poem is to recognize that in 'Not palaces' Spender risks dividing his imagination in two, with figurative life

---

[37] Quoted from Spender (ed.), *A Choice of Shelley's Verse* (London: Faber, 1971).

and light on one side and honest plain-speaking commitment on the other. By contrast, Shelley is able to use his figurative language, which summons up a unity that effortlessly doubles, divides, and rejoins itself, to evoke a transfiguration of the ordinary that corresponds to his poem's desire for change. Herbert Read was both on to an important kinship and in danger of too quickly mistaking the nature of Spender's achievement when in a review of *Poems* (1933), he wrote: 'perhaps the book's most notable quality is its social consciousness, and the perfect fusion of this often too intractable material with the poetic idiom. Another Shelley speaks in these lines.'[38] 'Not palaces' wins its considerable poetic victory by foregrounding the 'intractable' nature for poetry of 'social consciousness' and the impossibility of a 'perfect fusion' between its 'material' and 'the poetic idiom'. In his 'In railway halls, on pavements near the traffic', Spender rejects the 'consolation' offered by the 'curving beauty of that line | Traced on our graphs through history'. Once more, he shapes a productive tension between his practice and that of his forebears: 'that line' is both a lineage constituting a poetic tradition and the very line employed by Spender in his poem. Spender rejects sentimentality and poetic transcendence in his treatment of the poor, but his protestations—'No, I shall weave no tracery of pen-ornament | To make them birds upon my singing-tree'—seem to know that they are backfiring, bringing to mind the impact on the reader of the opening of Keats's 'Ode on Melancholy'. There, Keats's triply negative imperative, 'No, no, go not to Lethe' (1), tells of the hold over his imagination of Lethe and its consolations. Similarly, Spender's 'No, I shall weave no tracery' concedes the inability of the poet not to weave a 'tracery of pen-ornament'. But again, Spender succeeds in writing a poem by voicing doubts about poetry in a way that the Romantics inaugurate.

Spender's view of poetic legacy is not always so self-cancellingly at odds with itself. Indeed, the ancestral voices of Romanticism figure largely in his final collection, *Dolphins* (1994). Coleridge's account of the 'primary imagination . . . as a repetition in the finite mind of the eternal act of creation in the infinite "I AM"' (*Biographia Literaria*, i. ch. 13) affects the short-lined celebration of 'Dolphins':

>The dolphins write such
>Ideograms:
>With power to wake
>Me prisoned in
>My human speech
>They sign:
>'I AM!'

---

[38] Herbert Read, *Adelphi*, 5 (Feb. 1933), p. 379.

Jehovah's self-definition underpins both passages, yet the context of Spender's poem, concerned with escape from the prison of 'human speech', suggests that the later writer has Coleridge in mind: the dolphins deliver a speech-rebuking, yet poetry-generating reminder of a symbolic language to be found beyond human speech, but known only through human speech: only human speech can allow us to think of dolphins writing 'Ideograms' or of signing '"I AM!"'. In 'Poètes Maudits' from the same volume, Spender produces a tense, affecting, and intently detached account of the poet Rimbaud, who forms a major link between the Romantics and early twentieth-century poetry in English. The poem's fineness lies in its multiplicity of perspectives on Rimbaud's and Verlaine's poems and careers; but it is able to note an ecstatic high point relevant to the present volume, in which Rimbaud is 'Visionary, Prophet, Magus of | One unreal final ultimate | Of Hell or Heaven, a new Love where | Poem knew poem as truth'. The language, there, balances scepticism against visionary recognition; after all, the 'ultimate', though 'final', is 'unreal', yet that 'unreality' participates in the aspirations of a latter-day visionary Romanticism.

Spender signs a more heartfelt truce with the Romantic tradition in 'Worldsworth'. As in the earlier 'One More New Botched Beginning', where the past breaks into the present as 'doors | Burst open suddenly by gusts | That seek to blow the heart out', Spender draws consciously on the Wordsworthian tradition of involuntary memory storming back to engross the present. His short lines again hold at arm's length the potentially overpowering pentameters of the Romantic tradition and ensure that the particulars of memory stand out sharply. But the poem concludes with an epiphanic moment in which Spender simultaneously connects his past self, his parents, and a poetic tradition that seeks to marry word and world:

> Our parents,
> Seated in deck chairs on the lawn,
> Read to each other poems
>
> — The murmuring reached my bed—
>
> Rhythms I knew called Wordsworth
> Spreading through mountains, vales,
> To fill, I thought, the world.
>
> '*Worldsworth*', I thought, this peace
> Of voices intermingling—
> 'Worldsworth', to me, a vow.

The writing is superbly in control of its theme of 'voices intermingling': not just the poet's and his parents', but also those of Spender and Wordsworth. The twice-repeated 'I thought' prevents the world-filling rhythms from seeming emptily vatic. Yet it also suggest the significance of subjective 'thought', an idea reinforced by the highly Wordsworthian final phrase, 'to me, a vow'. The phrase reactivates the power of the close of the 'Ode: Intimations of Immortality': 'To me the meanest flower that blows can give | Thoughts that do often lie too deep for tears' (205–6), where 'To me' is at once modestly self-limiting and proudly in need of no external endorsement. And it recalls Wordsworth's experience in *The Prelude*, 1805, Book IV, when, after the manifestation of the 'sweetness of a common dawn' (337), he asserts, 'I made no vows, but vows | Were then made for me; bond unknown to me | Was given, that I should be, else sinning greatly, | A dedicated Spirit' (341–4). Wordsworth is unabashed in his sense of being 'A dedicated Spirit'; Spender half-mocks his boyish wish to connect the 'peace | Of voices intermingling' with a vision of the worth of the world. But the tenacity with which he rehearses Romantic values in his work, accompanied by a capacity for intelligent detachment, is responsible for some impressive and neglected poetry, including his extraordinary post-Blakean vision in 'Rejoice in the Abyss' of the aftermath of a London bombing in which he 'saw | The dead of all time float on one calm tide | Among the foam of stars | Over the town', and in which 'The streets were filled with London prophets, . . . | Who cried in cockney fanatic voices: | "In the midst of life is death!" ' The message of the poem, the need to ' "Rejoice in the abyss" ', to accept 'emptiness | As the centre of your building and your love', is only seemingly at odds with a Blakean emphasis on love and forgiveness. For Spender, what must be recognized is that 'regenerations', in Blakean terms, depend on the capacity to accommodate 'the all-tremendous unfathomable Non Ens | Of Death' (*Jerusalem*, 98. 34, 33–4).

In his finest poems, then, Spender finds a neo-Romantic idiom capable of confronting the major issues of his time. In 'I think continually of those who were truly great', he deals with the very subject of the current chapter, poetic legacy. The poem succeeds in combining 'pen-ornament' with 'social consciousness' by focusing on 'those who were truly great', where the past tense has an unavoidably elegiac tinge. Summoning up heroic figures from the past (as occurs elsewhere in the 1933 volume in poems such as 'Beethoven's Death Mask') to suggest continued possibilities for 'the flowering of the spirit', the poem admits its dependence on previous traditions. It is a poem of aspiration, of hope, and necessarily, as in the Romantics, of need. As in Shelley's poetry, the command to 'See' serves in the final section as a clarion call to visionary sight, and as in Shelley, there is much that is affecting about the fact that the reader is deliberately made to strain to see 'how these names are fêted by the waving grass', a challenge to the visualizing sense compounded by the following lines. When Spender invokes 'the soul's history', he implies his hope that it will offer a counterweight to the realities of actual 'history' which the youthful

Shelley described memorably as a 'record of crimes & miseries'.[39] Just as Shelley exempts his 'sacred few' (128) from the chaos depicted in *The Triumph of Life*, so Spender's 'truly great' seem only to live for a limited span and to spurn the earth with something close to Gnostic contempt: 'Born of the sun, they travelled a short while towards the sun, | And left the vivid air signed with their honour.' Spender's final sign-writing image reminds us, however, that the 'air' is an image for the sustaining of the Romantic tradition; he—like the other poets discussed in this book—has 'left the vivid air signed with [his] honour' by virtue of his creative relationships with Romantic poetry.

[39] Percy Bysshe Shelley, *The Letters of Percy Bysshe Shelley*, ed. Frederick L. Jones, 2 vols. (Oxford: Clarendon Press, 1964), i. 340.

5

'The Death of Satan': Stevens's 'Esthétique du Mal', Evil, and the Romantic Imagination

I

Wallace Stevens is too fine and strange a poet to be put to the work of serving simply as one of the great critics (in his verse) of High Romantic poetry. Yet, if one accepts George Steiner's dicta that 'All serious art, music and literature is a critical act' and that 'The best readings of art are art', it seems right to explore Stevens's deep if oblique response to the achievement and dilemmas bequeathed by the Romantics.[1] My main text here is his poem 'Esthétique du Mal', first published in the *Kenyon Review* in 1944. Not only is it a poem published in a time of war under whose coming shadow Thirties poetry had been written by Auden, Spender, and others; it is also a poem (like much Romantic poetry) concerned with war. Like Blake's famous lyric at the head of *Milton*, Stevens's poem involves itself in 'Mental Fight' ('And did those feet . . .?', 13) about the function of poetry. It was catalysed into being by a letter that Stevens read in the Spring issue of the same periodical: a letter, in Stevens's words, 'about the relation between poetry and what he called pain' (the correspondent had found 'the poetry in the *Kenyon Review* lamentable in many ways because it is cut off from pain').[2] Stevens goes on, 'Whatever he might mean, it might be interesting to try to do an esthétique du mal.'[3] 'Mal' encompasses, in its post-Baudelairean inflections, 'evil' and 'pain', while refusing to be reduced to either. Indeed, as Eleanor Cook points out, 'The word "mal" is untranslatable in some ways, thus providing in little an allegory about pain.'[4]

---

[1] George Steiner, *Real Presences: Is There Anything in What We Say?* (1989; London: Faber, 1991), pp. 11, 17.
[2] Stevens is quoted from *Letters of Wallace Stevens* (hereafter this edition is referred to as *Letters*), p. 468. The correspondent in the *Kenyon Review* is quoted from Eleanor Cook, *Poetry, Word-Play, and Word-War in Wallace Stevens* (Princeton: Princeton University Press, 1988); hereafter referred to as 'Cook', p. 192.
[3] *Letters*, p. 468.   [4] Cook, p. 190.

Among the pains allegorized by the poem is that suffered by the imagination as it watches itself take verbal pleasure in the representation of suffering. In his poem 'History as Poetry', Geoffrey Hill has a sardonic phrase for what is involved in such representation: Hill refers to 'The tongue's atrocities', indicting poetry for making capital out of history's innumerable 'atrocities'.[5] In 'Esthétique du Mal' Stevens falls short of straightforward indictment as he investigates the nature of an 'esthétique', an aesthetic or a poetics, of evil and pain. Certainly, though, his meditations imply a great deal about ways in which his Romantic forebears handle the question posed in his essay 'Imagination as Value': 'Is evil normal or abnormal?'[6] For, strangely, given its arabesques and its preciosities, its pleasure in making the visible more than a little hard to see, Stevens's poetry hungers after what he calls 'the normal': 'when we speak of perceiving the normal', he writes in the same essay, 'we have in mind the instinctive integrations which are the reason for living ... the chief problems of any artist, as of any man, are the problems of the normal.' Yet celebration of the 'normal' in Stevens does not involve any overlooking of 'the solitude and misery and terror of the world'.[7] Nor does he forget that 'the normal' is itself a construction, one that may depend on the author's removal from 'the ancient troughs of blood', to borrow a phrase from Geoffrey Hill's 'Ovid in the Third Reich'. Such is an implication of these lines from the opening section of Stevens's poem: 'He could describe | The terror of the sound because the sound | Was ancient.' 'Could' and 'because' entwine causally in an explanation of how one can speak only because 'terror' is now silent.

As Lucy Beckett has shown, Stevens's 'subject' in 'Esthétique du Mal' 'is one of Keats's subjects, the problem of how the poet is to justify his existence and his art in a world in which he perceives pain and misery and knows that these things are not be ignored'.[8] In particular, she connects Stevens's concern with this 'problem' to *The Fall of Hyperion*. Arguably, Keats anguishes in ways that Stevens contrives to hold at arm's length. For Keats's Moneta, telling the poet-dreamer to 'Think of the earth', 'Only the dreamer venoms all his days, | Bearing more woe than all his Sins deserve' (i. 175–6). For Stevens in section XV of 'Esthétique du Mal', 'The greatest poverty is not to live | In a physical world, to feel that one's desire | Is too difficult to tell from despair'. Keats condemns 'dreaming', though the rub is that he does so in a poem subtitled 'A Dream'. Stevens recommends living 'in a physical world' in a poem that rewards itself for imagining so doing with 'the metaphysical changes that occur, | Merely in living as and where we live'. For both, the imagination, defined by Stevens in 'Imagination as Value' as 'the power of the mind over the possibilities of things', may not wish solely to shock the

---

[5] Quoted from Geoffrey Hill, *Collected Poems* (Harmondsworth: Penguin, 1985).
[6] Stevens, *Necessary Angel*, p. 154.   [7] Ibid. 154–5, 156, 154.
[8] Lucy Beckett, *Wallace Stevens* (Cambridge: Cambridge University Press, 1968), p. 11.

virtuous philosopher, but certainly wants to get behind his guard. For both, 'the good of the imagination may be evil and its evil good', to quote Stevens again from 'Imagination as Value'.[9]

The wish to believe a 'poet is a sage; | A humanist, physician to all men' (I. 189–90) impresses the reader; but it is only one voice in *The Fall of Hyperion*, even if it be the voice of the poem's superego. Closer to its id is the instinct to make poetic capital out of ethical unease, to compact desire and despair, as in the description of Moneta's face, where Keats confronts something like a personification of art in its role as keeper of the secrets of 'high tragedy' (I. 277). Driven beyond 'the miseries of the world' (I. 148), Keats imagines a sublime pain, a pain sublimated, in that 'wan face, | Not pin'd by human sorrows, but bright blanch'd | By an immortal sickness which kills not' (I. 256–8). Oxymoron-slowed enjambments ('deathwards progressing | To no death was that visage', I. 260–1) are expressive of tranced stasis, and move us in no direction other than the poet's quasi-incestuous overture towards his maternal muse, his longing to know 'what things the hollow brain | Behind enwombed' (I. 276–7). In Stevens's case, alliteration lures us towards the very eliding of 'desire' and 'despair' against which he counsels. Keats may recommend health; he has, however, effectively to plead guilty to Moneta's charge, 'A fever of thyself' (I. 169), for the poem to hold our attention. Stevens worries, too, about possible complicity with the imagination in a state of 'fever'. 'Esthétique du Mal' as a consequence seeks (or feigns to seek) withdrawal from 'the false engagements of the mind' (IV), and asserts the possibility of a new poetry. Such a poetry, 'the thesis scrivened in delight, | The reverberating psalm, the right chorale' (XV), assumes the possibility of there being 'a race | Completely physical in a physical world'. Stevens, though, wants us to hear dissonant notes: 'Completely physical' has the air of fantasy, while the appositionally linked 'thesis', 'psalm', and 'chorale' protest their emergence into actuality too stridently to be convincing.

Both Keats and Stevens might agree with M. H. Abrams's view that, for the Romantics, 'essential evil is equated with the aggregate of what drives things apart'.[10] But the Romantics find that 'the dark italics', a phrase from section XV of 'Esthétique du Mal', compel their imagination. Stevens's wording is itself the more compelling for lacking specificity; the definite article implies that '*the* dark italics' are always with us, and there is a suggestion that these 'dark italics'—presumably composed by or bearing witness to 'mal'—refuse to conform to any ethical rules associated with the 'roman' typeface of 'the normal'. For the Romantics, the intrusion of 'dark italics' can prove both a problem and

---

[9] Stevens, *Necessary Angel*, p. 136.
[10] M. H. Abrams, *Natural Supernaturalism: Tradition and Revolution in Romantic Literature* (New York: Norton, 1971), p. 294.

an artistic opportunity. 'Our sweetest songs are those that tell of saddest thought' ('To a Skylark', 90), Shelley tells his superhumanly joyous skylark. For other Romantics, happiness does not exactly write white, but is often known retrospectively as an absence pointed up by present unhappiness. In 'Dejection: An Ode', Coleridge should feel as well as see how beautiful things are, but it is his poem's 'saving grace'—to borrow Richard Chase's comment on Whitman's 'Crossing Brooklyn Ferry'—that he does not. Chase has in mind the dark side of the Whitmanian moon to which we turn in section 6: 'It is not upon you alone the dark patches fall. | The dark threw its patches down upon me also ... | I am he', Whitman, in effect, boasts, 'who knew what it was to be evil. | I too knitted the old knot of contrariety', his free verse growing confessional and serpentine, not least in the shruggingly accepting movement into the use of a past tense.[11] For Whitman this recognition is an admission of long withheld but common knowledge ('I'm saying nothing you didn't in your heart of hearts know', he indicates when referring to that 'old knot'). It sets off the return to celebration in the final rhapsodic litany of invocations.

If Whitman glances at the Wordsworth who 'Sick, wearied out with contrarieties, | Yielded up moral questions in despair' (*Prelude*, 1805, x. 898–9), only to find solace in nature, Dorothy, and poetry, he points up a difference between himself and his English forebear. In Whitman acceptance of evil leaks eerily into, appears to be part of, his conviction of the goodness of being, a goodness borne witness to by the poet in the Adamic act of naming. To name evil, for Whitman, is to transubstantiate it into good. Wordsworth seems always to be shaping a theodicy, continually to 'trust' with Tennyson 'that somehow good | Will be the final goal of ill', even though, as with Tennyson, it is the shaping and human drama of the need to trust rather than the theological design that make an impact.[12] In Wordsworth, the drive is towards a discovery of the 'Abundant recompence' that comes in the wake of, and is, indeed, made possible by, 'loss' ('Tintern Abbey', 89, 88). Loss and grief serve as providential catalysts of his imagination. Wordsworth is the poet of 'There was a time', of 'celestial light' glimpsed beyond a monosyllabic curtain of words betokening loss: 'The things which I have seen I now can see no more' ('Ode: Intimations of Immortality', 1, 4, 9). Or he is the poet who claims that 'deep distress hath humanized my Soul' ('Elegiac Stanzas, Suggested by a Picture of Peele Castle', 36), as though he were less than fully human when not experiencing deep distress. Or he is the poet of the illimitable that includes and swallows up darkness and

---

[11] Richard Chase, from *Walt Whitman Remembered* (1955), in *Walt Whitman: A Critical Anthology*, ed. Francis Murphy (Harmondsworth: Penguin, 1969), p. 344; Whitman is quoted from Walt Whitman, *Leaves of Grass*, intro. by Gay Wilson Allen (New York: The New American Library, 1958).

[12] Alfred, Lord Tennyson, 'In Memoriam', LIV. 1–2, quoted from *Poems of Tennyson*.

fear. So, 'Winds thwarting winds, bewildered and forlorn' take their place in—and yet cry out against—a glimpsed synthesis that breaks even the bounds of its own inclusiveness. As Wordsworth descends the Alpine gorge, simile passing into self-generating metaphor allows him to figure the scenery as being 'like workings of one mind, the features | Of the same face, blossoms upon one tree, | Characters of the great Apocalypse, | The types and symbols of Eternity, | Of first and last, and midst, and without end' (*The Prelude*, 1805, VI. 560, 568–72). Milton's God sponsors this, but he is now occluded behind the veil of Wordsworth's creation, as the poet hymns his own startlingly fresh discovery of ultimate reality, of an 'Eternity' that depends on imaginative recognition—and includes, as a perpetual possibility, those thwarted and forlorn winds.

At the close of 'Esthétique du Mal', in lines discussed in a different context in Chapter 1, Stevens at once backs away from and move towards confident assertion, expressing a subdued delight in our seeming capacity to receive far more than we give, but making clear that such receivings are dependent on our 'living as' as well as 'where we live':

> One might have thought of sight, but who could think
> Of what it sees, for all the ill it sees?
> Speech found the ear, for all the evil sound,
> But the dark italics it could not propound.
> And out of what one sees and hears and out
> Of what one feels, who could have thought to make
> So many selves, so many sensuous worlds,
> As if the air, the mid-day air, was swarming
> With the metaphysical changes that occur,
> Merely in living as and where we live.

Nothing more clearly illustrates Stevens's instinct to qualify, to give himself to utterance that plays with, rather than settles for, ultimate meaning. The verse builds forcefully, the more so as its syntactical momentum is slowed by qualifications to which the writing will not finally yield. Especially in the choice of 'was' where one might expect 'were' in the line, 'As if the air, the mid-day air, was swarming', we hear, as Helen Vendler puts it, 'the affirmation beneath the hypothesis'.[13] But, more accurately, we are in touch with a poetry for which 'hypothesis' and 'affirmation' are inseparable. Those 'dark italics' that 'Speech' 'could not propound' indicate Stevens's sense of a Iago-like residue of recalcitrant darkness in the human soul. But the wave of the poetry's rhetoric, driven on by an unexpected and not wholly logical 'And' in the phrase 'And out of what one sees', flows past this obstacle. 'Rhetoric' is meant to suggest that there

---

[13] Helen Vendler, *On Extended Wings: Wallace Stevens' Longer Poems* (Cambridge, Mass.: Harvard University Press, 1969), p. 33.

is something consciously wrought about Stevens's stumbling upon the imagination's capacity to respond to and bring about 'changes'. The selving and shape-changing of the writing may, indeed, imply that the 'dark italics' are in the midst of all, generating their opposites as wished-for recompense. Stevens's repeated use of 'one' seeks to usher the sublime ego of the post-Romantic poet to the poem's margins, and to prepare the way for the embrace of uncommonly common experience signalled by 'we' in the final line.

The reader may be taken by that last line—'living as and where we live'—to the Wordsworth who describes in *The Prelude* how at the onset of the French Revolution all those who were accustomed to dream or desire

> Were called upon to exercise their skill
> Not in Utopia, subterraneous Fields,
> Or some secreted Island, Heaven knows where,
> But in the very world which is the world
> Of all of us, the place in which, in the end,
> We find our happiness, or not at all.
>   (1805 x. 722–7)

The writing inhabits the view it describes, the voice falling with weight and authority on the argument-clinching 'very' and 'in the end'; and yet, with the finest and most poignant of ironies, Wordsworth implies that this anticipation of Stevens's attachment to the 'normal', this offering brought to the humanist's altar, sadly but ultimately involves a state of delusion. He delivers such an implication through the work's narrative design (by this late stage we have already seen the consequences of this-worldly reformist hope) and by ever so slightly mimicking the delighted tone of those who feel justified in redirecting Utopian instincts towards 'the very world which is the world | Of all of us'. That Wordsworth includes himself in 'us' means that irony is self-directed.

Shelley's sense that Wordsworth offers here a covert critique of the Utopian prompted him to refer with his own irony to the passage (published in *The Friend*, 26 October 1809, and in Wordsworth's 1815 *Poems* as 'French Revolution, As It Appeared to Enthusiasts at its Commencement'). In a late letter, the younger poet favours discontent with, over acceptance of, the 'normal':

Perhaps all discontent with the *less* (to use a Platonic sophism) supposes the sense of a just claim to the *greater*, & that we admirers of Faust are in the right road to Paradise. —Such a supposition is not more absurd, and certainly less demoniacal than that of Wordsworth—where he says—

> This earth
> Which is the world of all of us, and where
> *We find our happiness or not at all.*

As if after sixty years of suffering here, we were to be roasted alive for a million more in Hell, or charitably annihilated by a coup de grace of the bungler, who brought us into existence at first.[14]

This fascinatingly mixed response to Wordsworth suggests Shelley's own complicated response to the problem of evil and suffering. Shelley did not know the passage in Book VI of *The Prelude* (1805), when Wordsworth pins his allegiance, movingly, to the compensatory vision of 'infinitude' (539) and 'something evermore about to be' (542) made possible by 'hope that can never die' (540); a vision hard to distinguish from the strain in Shelley that identifies hope with creativity, the need, in the face of Jupiter's potential return, 'to hope, till Hope creates | From its own wreck the thing it contemplates' (*Prometheus Unbound*, 4. 573–4). Shelley criticizes Christianity for its deferral of hope to another world, a deferral cynically exploited by oppressive political regimes; yet his refusal ever to be contented by what it is leads him to a not dissimilar stance.

To say this is not to try to entrap Shelley in contradictions, or sorrow over a web in which he entangles himself, but to delight, rather, in the dialectical intelligence and awareness at work in so much of his finest poetry. In 'Julian and Maddalo', for example, a work obsessed by the question of how suffering a rises, should be endured, and can (or cannot) be exorcized, Julian speaks out of Shelley's Platonically sophistical side when he says, 'We know | That we have power over ourselves to do | And suffer—what, we know not till we try; | But something nobler than to live and die' (184–7). But 'noble' as this rider's accents may sound, as his imagination, to adapt Stevens, presses back against the pressure of reality, Maddalo threatens to unhorse him with his affectionately scornful, 'You talk Utopia' (179), and his unanswerable assertion that 'poetry'—far from being the record of the happiest and best moments of the happiest and best minds—is inseparable from 'wrong': 'Most wretched men | Are cradled into poetry by wrong; | They learn in suffering what they teach in song' (544–6). Maddalo's assertion is 'unanswerable' because—to its enduring credit—the poem finds no way out of the labyrinth into which the Maniac's suffering monologue conducts us. No mere emblem or case study, the Maniac speaks of some 'dreadful ill' (525), which his tortured relationship with language tells us is 'unspeakable' (526), and concludes by wishing, like a poet turning against his utterance, for his words to be buried, entombed, sealed over (see 508–10). Some sympathetic but seemingly ineffectual lines show Julian imagining a psychotherapeutic solution, a talking cure that would involve 'An entrance to the caverns of his mind' (573), but this was 'all | Accomplished not' (577–8). Is it merely, despite Julian, simply to be entered in

---

[14] Shelley, *Letters*, ii. 406–7.

the catalogue of 'dreams of baseless good' (578)? Does Shelley, indeed, affect us more as a poet who laments 'the contagion of the world's slow stain' (*Adonais*, 356) than as a conjuror through words of 'beautiful idealisms of moral excellence' (Preface to *Prometheus Unbound*, p. 232)?

One might put the matter another way, and say with Stevens, in lines from which the title of the present chapter is drawn, that 'The death of Satan was a tragedy | For the imagination' ('Esthétique du Mal', VIII), in Shelley's case and in the case of the other canonical Romantics, less because their imaginations were impoverished by the loss of the archetypal embodiment of evil in the Christian scheme than because this loss left an absence which could still give rise to tragic imaginings. Those tragic imaginings include the awareness of how our best desires (such as those expressed by Julian in regard to the Maniac) may be unfulfillable. So, *Prometheus Unbound* may, in its fourth act, take the form of a humanist answer to Dante's paradisal visions, an answer that deconstructs old myths and catches itself in the process of creating new ones. But Shelley's preference for Prometheus over Satan does not diminish the potentially tragic nature of the hero's fight against forces within and without (embodied in the Furies' temptations in Act 1). Though Satan's faults and wrongs engender in the mind a 'pernicious casuistry', much as Beatrice in *The Cenci* provokes in the audience a 'restless and anatomizing casuistry', Prometheus, too, participates in the potentially tragic (pp. 230, 317). Act 1 is a tragedy that ends with Prometheus, all passion spent, realizing the sombre implications latent in the optimistic view articulated by Julian that 'it is our will | That thus enchains us to permitted ill' (170–1). In the Shelleyan universe human beings are at once responsible for moral evil and placed in situations where it is almost impossible not to be complicit with it. A state of being and something done, evil is both noun and verb, to borrow Nicci Gerrard's terms in an *Observer* article about Myra Hindley:'Evil is a noun, something like dirt inside us. . . . evil is like a verb: something you do, not something you are.'[15] Shelley, in treating evil, is by turns exploratory and analytical: exploratory when he has his Third Fury taunt Prometheus about the way in which the Furies (embodiments of evil impulses) 'can obscure not | The soul which burns within' (1. 484–5), but threaten to 'dwell' (placed menacingly at a line-ending) 'Beside it' (1. 485–6); analytical in the Fury's speech at line 618, where the language takes abstractions and twists them into a scourge-like rope of knotted contradictions: 'The good want power, but to weep barren tears. | The powerful goodness want, worse need for them' (1. 625–6).

Act 2 will explore how forces other than those of will lead out of tragedy; Prometheus' willed resistance bears witness to a view of evil as essentially

---

[15] Nicci Gerrard, 'The Face of Human Evil', *The Observer*, 17 Nov. 2002, p. 14.

'mind-created' in Melvin M. Rader's phrase.[16] Yet Prometheus gives way to Asia, his female counterpart, at once embodiment of love and sceptical quester, testing Demogorgon with conundrums about the origins of evil; it is the unanswerability rather than answerability of her questions ('a voice | Is wanting, the deep truth', we learn, 'is imageless', 2. 4. 115–16) that catalyses the 'destined hour' (2. 4. 128). At this point Shelley's poem ceases to be anything remotely like, if it ever was, an intellectual allegory; it becomes, through its own workings, a mirror of the processes of desire and hope, which in the absence of philosophical certainty take centre-stage. It is from such processes rather than from settled conviction that the Utopian imaginings of Acts 3 and 4 derive. When, for example, the Spirit of the Hour asserts, 'All things had put their evil nature off' (3. 4. 77), the image ghosting the line is that of a discarded mask, as though evil were a mere garment; this is the side of the poem that plays with the notion that 'evil' is a respelling of 'veil': 'veil by veil, evil and error fall', in Prometheus' speech in 3. 3 (62). Evil as a discardable veil, though, is the optimistic aspect of a vision which also sees evil as only too durable, only too easily re-wearable. What can be put off can be put on, as Shelley's poetry, with its variations on the theme of potentiality, continually reminds us. For example, there is friction at the close of Act 3 between the longing to scale 'unascended Heaven' (3. 4. 203) and the recognition of 'chance, and death, and mutability' (3. 4. 201) as 'clogs' (3. 4. 202) on such aspiration.

II

Yeats depicts Shelley in *A Vision* as a poet 'who can never see anything that opposes him as it really is'. His Utopian aspirations 'for the future of mankind' compensate, Yeats suggests, in illusory ways for his disappointments: 'He lacked the Vision of Evil', Yeats writes, the definite article raising the stakes, 'could not conceive of the world as a continual conflict' (unlike the author of the critique, the subtext runs, who knew that poetry comes from self-quarrelling), 'so, though great poet he certainly was, he was not of the greatest kind'. Dante 'suffering injustice and the love of Beatrice, found divine

---

[16] Melvin M. Rader, 'Shelley's Theory of Evil', in *Shelley: A Collection of Critical Essays*, ed. George M. Ridenour (Englewood Cliffs, NJ: Prentice-Hall, 1965), p. 106. Rader's important essay argues that in *Prometheus Unbound* Shelley 'distinguishes ... between two types of evil: one sort is ineradicable and objectively grounded; the other sort is subjective but deeply based' (p. 105). For good discussion of Prometheus' initial 'manichaeanism' in the lyrical drama, see Richard Cronin, *Shelley's Poetic Thoughts* (London: Macmillan, 1981), p. 140.

justice and the heavenly Beatrice, but the justice of *Prometheus Unbound* is a vague propagandist emotion, and the women that await its coming are but clouds'.[17] Stevens in section III of 'Esthetique du Mal' evokes and bids farewell to Dante's world-view: 'His firm stanzas hang like hives in hell | Or what hell was, since now both heaven and hell | Are one, and here, O terra infidel'. *Terra firma* gives way to 'terra infidel', and one wonders whether, for Stevens, Romantic humanism as well as the Christian doctrine of incarnation is responsible for the transition: 'The fault lies with an over-human god, | Who by sympathy has made himself a man | And is not to be distinguished, when we cry | | Because we suffer.' This reaction against what Blake calls the 'human form divine' concludes with the wry ventriloquizing of the hope that 'pain, no longer satanic mimicry, | Could be borne, as if we were sure to find our way'. Stevens's 'as ifs' make it hard to know whether his own sureness is being subjected to 'mimicry' here.

But unsureness is what saves Romantic poetry from what, since Arnold, Eliot, and Babbitt, has always been the shrewdest sword thrust through its armour. Did not the Romantics, after all, side with Rousseau, for whom men were born free, not stained by original sin, but trailing clouds of glory? Yet 'evil' is the more powerful in Romantic poetry for serving as a spur to imaginings of spiritual sustenance. Where would the Romantics be without evil, the 'hateful siege | Of contraries'?[18] When Coleridge flagellates himself at the end of 'The Eolian Harp' as 'A sinful and most miserable man' (62), his emphasis has often been heard as part of an overstated religious fervour that he feels obliged to assume. Certainly, he defers to his wife's reproving look and his own promptings of guilt over the heterodox speculations of the preceding section, in which 'animated nature' (44) is surmised to be 'organic Harps diversely fram'd' (45). Diversity ultimately resolving into harmony is one way in which the Romantics are often tempted to figure the co-presence in experience of good and evil—and is more marked in an earlier draft of the poem in which the harps are 'so aptly hung' (40) that even 'Shrill Discords' (42) would be harmonized. At a deeper level, though, Coleridge's recognition of inherent sinfulness prompts, his poem half-invites us to think, the previous flights of fanciful speculation. The very idea of the universe as a symphony of contrapuntal harmonies depends on there being a dissonant, irreconcilable note, that struck by the fear of ineradicable sinfulness. In its inexplicable absence of connection with the rest of the poem, the line in question from 'The Eolian Harp' (62) mimics the unanswerability of the traditional theological poser, *unde malum?*

---

[17] Yeats, *A Vision*, p. 144.

[18] John Milton, *Paradise Lost*, IX. 121–2, in Milton, *Poetical Works*, ed. Douglas Bush (London: Oxford University Press, 1969).

For all his theological grapplings and aspirations, Coleridge is never able to discard wholly the knowledge that 'Evil exists'.[19] The knowledge dogs the footsteps of Coleridge's imaginary walk in 'This Lime-Tree Bower My Prison', ghosting the poem's chiaroscuro patterning of imagery, its descent into 'that still roaring dell' (9) and emergence 'Beneath the wide wide Heaven' (21). The blank verse enacts the turning towards that 'wide wide Heaven', a rehearsal in turn of the journey taken by 'gentle-hearted Charles' (28), who has been 'winning [his] way | With sad yet patient soul, through evil and pain | And strange calamity' (30–2). 'Deep joy' (38) and intuitive perception of a presence in nature reward Charles's steadfastness, and the luminous final section fills with a grace in which Coleridge receives what he has given; in turn, he can bless even the rook (68–73). The often-noted subliminal recollection of *Macbeth* (III. iii. 51ff.) haunts, yet is allayed by, Coleridge's vision of 'the mighty Orb's dilated glory' (72). Round the corner awaits 'The Rime of the Ancient Mariner', in which the 'wide wide Heaven' gives way to the 'wide wide sea' (233, 598), and in which prayer and poetic spells can only heighten the sense of evil as both nightmare and conundrum. By contrast with the subversive Blake of *The Marriage of Heaven and Hell*, for whom 'Good is the passive that obeys Reason' and 'Evil is the active springing from Energy' (p. 34), 'evil' in 'The Ancient Mariner' is inexplicable, untraceable to the will, and deeply lodged within the human. Coleridge, as Seamus Perry has shrewdly observed, can advance yet not advance such a view, since it is a view that can be ascribed to a deeply fallible narrator (Catholic and given to thinking in terms of sin and redemption).[20] However one tackles the poem's cruxes, it stays with the reader as offering both a heartfelt but somehow unreassuring moral and a terrifying and somehow ungraspable experience.[21]

To recur to M. H. Abrams's *Natural Supernaturalism*, the point needs to be made that the Romantics took evil very seriously indeed. Abrams is at his most eloquent on this. After an energetic catalogue of the manifold sufferings treated by Wordsworth's poems, sufferings from which, as he gleefully points out, Arnold 'averted his ken', Abrams writes: 'As for what is called "the problem of evil" ... that ... was precisely the central and pervasive concern of the major Romantic philosophers. Finding no longer tenable the justification of earthly

---

[19] Quoted, respectively, from 'Appendix 1' in *Coleridge: Poetical Works*, and from *Opus Maximum*, ed. Thomas McFarland with Nicholas Halmi, vol. 15 of *The Collected Works of Samuel Taylor Coleridge* (Princeton: Princeton University Press, 2002), p. 238.

[20] See Perry, *Coleridge and the Uses of Division*, p. 286. Perry remarks wittily that 'One of the few theological positions that we can confidently declare Coleridge to have shunned was Catholicism' (p. 286); yet, in a poem in which all fixities dissolve, it is arguable that Coleridge's anti-Catholic prejudice undergoes transformation.

[21] For further discussion, see my chapter 'Poetry of the Romantic Period: Coleridge and Keats', in *A Companion to Romance from Classical to Contemporary*, ed. Corinne Saunders (Oxford: Blackwell, 2004), 305–20.

suffering as a divine plan for sorting out those beings who will be translated to a better world, they undertook to justify the experience of suffering within the limits of experience itself.' And he goes on: 'A critic's charge that Romantic writers neglected the problem of evil is probably only a way of saying that he does not approve of their solution to the problem'.[22] 'Solution' may be too strong for what the Romantics do offer. In *Hellas*, refusing to attempt to disentangle 'the Gordian knot of the origin of evil', Shelley writes: 'That there is a true solution of the riddle, and that in our present state that solution is unattainable by us, are propositions which may be regarded as equally certain'. There is, in those words, a confession and an apologia: Shelley, confessing the limits of knowledge, asserts the poet's function of attaching 'himself to those ideas which exalt and ennoble humanity' (p. 585). Evil, for Shelley, is a stone in the midst of all, which incites his imagination into dervish-like displays of whirling energy; what Jerrold E. Hogle calls 'process' in the work is the poet's attempt to unfix the fixities into which imaginative relations petrify.[23]

'Esthétique du Mal' mounts its own investigations, yet they recall those of the Romantics, as paraphrase, with all its attendant reductiveness, brings out. The poem consists of fifteen sections. In the first, the poem's 'he' reflects on Vesuvius and the sublime, and, after entering into a trance of verbal self-awareness in which 'pain' vanishes as it is asserted ('Pain killing pain on the very point of pain'), he collects himself to assert that 'Pain is human', a form of meaning, a human experience and category. Naples in 1944 is a theatre of war in the present, as well as being a site in the past of the proximity of horror (volcanic destruction) and natural beauty. In the second section, 'pain' is seen as 'indifferent to the sky', yet gains dignity from that separateness. In the third, already discussed, Stevens attacks Christianity's 'over-human god' who has 'weakened our fate'. In the fourth the notion of 'The genius of misfortune' emerges: a genius that might be glossed as the single-minded capacity to be and perceive 'evil'; it is a form of imaginative genius in which 'In desperate hallow, rugged gesture, fault | Falls out on everything'. This parodically or desperately 'hallow' or holy vision assonantally unifies all that it sees, makes of it—rather as Byron does in *Childe Harold's Pilgrimage*, cantos III and IV—evidence of a pervasive fall. Section V begins to imagine a proper language for 'all true sympathizers'—presumably with pain and suffering — but its rejection of 'the inventions of sorrow or the sob | Beyond invention' is at best desired rather than attained (this is not an adverse criticism, since the section invokes rather than claims). Section VI switches to parable, the sun pecked at by a 'big bird', possibly the imagination suffering the

---

[22] Abrams, *Natural Supernaturalism*, p. 444.
[23] In Jerrold E. Hogle, *Shelley's Process: Radical Transference and the Development of this Major Works* (New York: Oxford University Press, 1988).

'imperfection' visited upon it by 'The genius of misfortune', even as it 'becomes less gross' while experiencing deviant but fascinating 'lapses', 'glitters', and 'divinations of serene | Indulgence'. In section VII Stevens composes an elegy for a dead soldier. Criticized by Helen Vendler for its aestheticizing of suffering ('How red the rose that is the soldier's wound'), the writing imagines a solution to death, a 'deathless rest'; it feels like a calculatedly 'serene | Indulgence'.[24]

As if in reaction, VIII begins by asserting that 'The death of Satan was a tragedy | For the imagination', presumably because the imagination has lost a myth and an appropriate heroic or epic style. This section bears directly on the Romantics, in its allusion to Shelleyan 'vacancy' (in *Alastor* and 'Mont Blanc') and assertion that 'The tragedy . . . may have begun, | Again, in the imagination's new beginning': it is duplicitous (again) in its implications: we have not lost tragedy (this is good); new imaginative beginnings are tainted with tragedy (this is more sorrowful). Section IX sustains the attempt to imagine 'Another chant, an incantation, as in | Another and later genesis'; section X tells us that the poem's 'he' 'had studied the nostalgias', the homesickness for 'the most grossly maternal' being dealt with here, before passing into the nostalgia that 'he | Should understand', undercutting the complacency of detached intellectual command. Section XI, to be discussed in more detail later, proposes, finds wanting, and thrives on linguistic responses to suffering. Section XII dwells on the need to dispose the world in categories and speculates on the possibility of 'a third world without knowledge . . . in which the will makes no | Demands' and 'accepts whatever is as true, | Including pain' (possibly Keats's 'To Autumn' comes close to embodying such a third world in Romantic poetry). Section XIII returns to tragedy and sees the Oedipal conflict as central to the idea, and yet views the idea itself as 'fragmentary . . . | Within the universal whole' (one thinks of Coleridge's attempted final position in 'The Rime of the Ancient Mariner'). Obscurely the recognition of tragedy tames it, masters it, unperplexes it, leaves us with a catharsis that Stevens sardonically identifies with 'politest helplessness'; the phrase pulling the rug from beneath the solace it attempts to offer. Section XIV turns to the political revolutionary, the 'lunatic of one idea' (Shelley in *Prometheus Unbound* from one perspective), a form of the sublime that involves crazed, misdirected energies and offers futile deliverance from the ever present fact of pain. To conclude, section XV urges acceptance: 'The greatest poverty is not to live | In a physical world, to feel that one's desire | Is too difficult to tell from despair': a condition to which Shelley and Byron come perilously close at moments (one thinks, for example, of Byron's infatuated attempt to escape his infatuation with 'The unreach'd Paradise of

---

[24] Vendler speaks of the section's 'slackened poetry' in *On Extended Wings*, p. 209.

our despair').²⁵ It finishes with a question that abandons the question mark, since it has become assertion, an assertion in which Stevens celebrates the recompense of imaginative attention to the 'normal', and in which evil is granted a secondary, minor role. Or at least, that is the idea. In fact, as in 'Tintern Abbey', where the overcoming of the 'burthen of the mystery' (39) persuades readers such as Keats that they had never fully understood before the 'burden' or the 'Mystery', Stevens's affirmation of 'So many selves, so many sensuous worlds' (already discussed) fights hard to prevent 'the dark italics' from seeping through the passage.²⁶

Eleanor Cook defines Stevens's understanding of evil in 'Esthétique du Mal' in these terms: 'he sets about undoing the dialectic of evil versus good, *mal* versus *bon*, where the good is understood in transcendent, notably Christian, terms. What he works toward is a dialectic of evil versus the normal, of evil versus the good understood as normal, everyday, earthly good.'²⁷ But, as her own acute reading of the poem reveals, 'works toward' bears considerable emphasis. At the poem's heart is what Harold Bloom, quoting phrases from section XI, calls the ' "man of bitter appetite," accepting only the Nietzschean lordship of "the gaiety of language" '.²⁸ Even here, however, Stevens does not so much accept as assert bitterly and with conflicted irony. In the passage Stevens persists with his attempt to disentangle himself from 'sleek ensolacings' (a phrase from the end of the previous section). He does so by capturing himself in the act of self-admiration for supposedly disentangling himself from 'sleek ensolacings'. Section XI starts with the air of a poet summarily summing up, wheeling on that most ponderous of small words, 'Life', and asserting that it is 'a bitter aspic', thus contradicting the idea floated in section X that 'life | Itself was innocent'. 'Aspic', a 'savoury meat jelly used as garnish' (*OED*), has a 'bitter taste'. Stevens wants us to hear the tone of a man passing a final judgement and yet engaged in phrase-making, caught at a distance from what he talks about, 'Life'—much as, in consciously aesthetic mode, he begins the poem 'reading paragraphs | On the sublime' (I): a phrase that conveys its irony through the deadpan enjambment that alights on the 'sublime' after those prosaic 'paragraphs'.

To stay with that opening for a little longer (since it establishes a way of working subsequently intensified or 'exacerbated', to use Stevens's own word in section XI), the next lines amusingly capture a tension that refuses to be sent packing by humour. 'Vesuvius had groaned | For a month. It was pleasant to

---

[25] Byron, *Childe Harold's Pilgrimage*, IV. 122. 1096.
[26] For Keats on the 'burden of the Mystery', see his letter of 3 May 1818, in Oxford Authors, p. 397.
[27] Cook, p. 191.
[28] Harold Bloom, *Wallace Stevens: The Poems of Our Climate* (Ithaca, NY: Cornell University Press, 1977), p. 234.

be sitting there, | While the sultriest fulgurations, flickering, | Cast corners in the glass.' The verse is too coolly self-aware to be convicted of fiddling while the magma erupts. Stevens is not exactly revelling in the 'sublime'; indeed, his use of 'pleasant' ('pointedly not a sublime term', as Cook observes) has about it a saving banality that anticipates the extraordinary affirmation of the ordinary at the end.[29] At the same time, its savouring of effects—the 'flickering' in a mirror of those 'sultriest fulgurations'—implies language's too easy triumph over the pains of experience. The writing is, in effect, a parody of Shelley's radiant assertion in *A Defence of Poetry* that 'Poetry turns all things to loveliness ... It transmutes all that it touches, and every form moving within the radiance of its presence is changed by wondrous sympathy to an incarnation of the spirit which it breathes' (p. 698). Stevens worries at this issue in section XI: 'We are not | At the centre of a diamond' plays its negation against the bitter positive with which the section opens, and recalls the comment (in the section dealing with 'the death of Satan' as 'a tragedy | For the imagination') that 'negation was eccentric'. Satan has been knocked off his unpriceable pivot, and his departure ushers in two vignettes of human suffering. In the first, 'The paratroopers fall and as they fall | They mow the lawn.' Tragedy repeats itself as surrealist farce, yet the echoes of Marvell suggest how the vignettes might take on elegiac colouring.[30] In the second, 'A vessel sinks in waves | Of people, as big bell-billows from its bell | Bell-bellow in the village steeple.' By now, tragedy has become a matter of vowel sounds; the triple 'farewell' with which this paragraph closes might, among other things, bid 'farewell' to the comparatively first-order shipwrecks of Coleridge and Byron (in *Don Juan*, II). If Byron laughs grimly at the plight of the shipwrecked, he does so that he may not weep: the plight of those in the open boat is at once mediated through asides, comparisons (with those living on annuities, stanza 65) and contrasts (the digestion of woodcocks, stanza 67), and conveyed to us with cinematic realism. Byron accommodates hints of blasphemy (the scene is overlooked and superintended, albeit in simile, by 'one whose hate is masked but to assail', l. 388) within a story that has the logic and inconsequence of existential event. Stevens finds that his preference for second-order reflection and symbolic meditation turns in on itself here.

For at this point, Stevens breaks off to announce, 'Natives of poverty, children of malheur, | The gaiety of language is our seigneur'. 'Gaiety' has a Nietzschean ferocity, a hard bravado that seeks to outface our lack of meaning (poverty) and our subjection to 'malheur'. Bitterly the poem turns on the one clear value to surface from its explorations, as the gaiety of language consumes itself: 'A man of bitter appetite despises | A well-made scene', Stevens writes, and not only do the previous fictions undo themselves as so many confections, but

[29] Cook, p. 195.   [30] For these echoes, see ibid. 207.

so, too, does the process of undoing. Even the dismissal of 'sleek ensolacings' convicts itself, in the section's closing lines, of self-regard: 'The tongue caresses these exacerbations.' Stevens confronts the temptation that awaits the post-Romantic imagination feeding scrupulously yet corruptly on its own scruples. To the degree, though, that it shakes off the habitual, that enemy of the Romantic imagination, Stevens's lines defeat, in Shelley's words in *A Defence of Poetry*, 'the curse which binds us to be subjected to the accident of surrounding impressions' (p. 698), and they remind us of that imagination's mobile, redefining, and many-faceted dealings with good and evil, and of its intricate 'passion for yes' ('Esthétique du Mal', VIII).

6

'Shining in Modest Glory': Post-Romantic Strains in Kavanagh, Heaney, Mahon, Carson, and Others

I

This chapter will sketch a general picture of the use made of Romantic poetry by mainly Northern Irish poets (Kavanagh is a borderline exception). It will then look in more detail at Patrick Kavanagh's and Seamus Heaney's and, to a lesser degree, Derek Mahon's and Ciaran Carson's poetry. A point of departure might be James Joyce laying in to 'romanticism' (with a small 'r'): 'in realism you are down to facts on which the world is based: that sudden reality which smashes romanticism into a pulp. What makes most people's lives unhappy is some disappointed romanticism, some unrealizable or misconceived ideal.'[1] To the degree that Romantic poetry embodies the pursuit of an 'unrealizable or misconceived ideal', it tends to provoke opposition in contemporary Northern Irish poets, aware, among other things, of the political havoc caused by abstract idealism. John Montague, for instance, forcing himself in 'Tim' to 'drink | from the trough of reality', declares in *The Rough Field* that 'No Wordsworthian dream enchants me here | With glint of glacial corrie, totemic mountain'.[2] Still, Romantic poetry, as inaugurated by *Lyrical Ballads*, itself seeks to 'chuse incidents and situations from common life', albeit with a 'certain colouring of imagination', and by means of 'a selection of language really used by men' (Preface to *Lyrical Ballads* (1802), pp. 596–7). Moreover, who is more alert to the ways in which the 'ideals' may be 'misconceived' than poets such as Keats and Shelley? With some justice, Aidan Day contends that *Alastor* can be read as 'a demonstration of the solipsistic emptiness of an inward-looking spiritual orientation', even if it is the case that Shelley has an 'inward' sympathy with the Poet's need to image 'to himself the Being whom he loves' (Preface to *Alastor*, p. 92).[3]

---

[1] Joyce to Arthur Power, quoted from James Joyce, *Ulysses*, ed. Jeri Johnson (Oxford: Oxford University Press, 1993), pp. xxiii–xxiv.
[2] John Montague, *Collected Poems* (Loughcrew: Gallery Press, 1995).
[3] Aidan Day, *Romanticism* (London: Routledge, 1996) p. 160.

The capacity of Romantic poetry to enact and criticize longing and desire is part of its fascinating doubleness: as a movement which implies that art is at once autonomous and shaped by historical circumstance, which licenses transcendental questing while valuing the meanest flower that blows, and which gives a new status to the self even as it frequently investigates the self's relationship with society, Romanticism affords subsequent poets an important model. To adapt Basil Bunting on Pound's *Cantos*, the Romantic poets are like the Alps and take some getting round.[4] Northern Irish poets, in particular, have found it valuable to wrestle with the angel of Romantic poetry. They may rebel against the apparent bardic self-importance of a Wordsworth, but the ancestral features are observable in the younger faces. Tom Paulin, for instance, shares something of the early Auden's scepticism about the political meanings of Romantic individualism (' "Lord Byron at the head of his stormtroopers!" '), and he is happy to endorse Hazlitt's adverse judgements on Shelley and Coleridge.[5] Yet the close of 'Inishkeel Parish Church' compresses into itself a Romantic-influenced glimpse of freedom, 'an enormous sight of the sea, | A silent water beyond society'.[6] If Larkin, with his 'enormous yes' or his undeceived gaze through high windows, is more immediately to the fore here, Shelley's Julian (in 'Julian and Maddalo'), a lover of 'waste | And solitary places' (14–15), is in the background, as is Wordsworth's 'Ode: Intimations of Immortality', with its rollingly expansive metaphor of the 'immortal sea' (166) discerned by the soul 'in a season of calm weather' (164).[7]

Again, for all the resistance quoted above, Montague's *The Rough Field* shows the lure of Wordsworthian impulses and poetic practices as it dramatizes and enacts circlings, leadings-on, and near returns. As Robert F. Garratt argues, 'Montague protests too much.' Garratt goes on to point out how 'References to a Wordsworthian preoccupation with memory, with childhood experiences, and with the role of the imagination are sprinkled throughout various sections of *The Rough Field*'.[8] However, it is noteworthy that Montague's phrasing in the lines quoted above echoes, not Wordsworth, but Yeats: the

---

[4] 'There they are, you will have to go a long way round | if you want to avoid them', writes Bunting in 'On the Fly-Leaf of Pound's *Cantos*', in Basil Bunting, *Collected Poems* (Oxford: Oxford University Press, 1978).

[5] Auden's 'Letter to Lord Byron', quoted from Tom Paulin (ed.), *The Faber Book of Political Verse* (London: Faber, 1986). For Paulin's agreement with Hazlitt's critical views of Coleridge and Shelley, see his *The Day-Star of Liberty: William Hazlitt's Radical Style* (London: Faber, 1998).

[6] Quoted from Paul Muldoon (ed.), *The Faber Book of Contemporary Irish Poetry* (London: Faber, 1986).

[7] Larkin's 'enormous yes' comes from 'For Sidney Bechet'. I also allude to the end of 'High Windows'. The edition used is Philip Larkin, *Collected Poems*, ed. with intro. by Anthony Thwaite (London: The Marvell Press and Faber, 1988).

[8] Robert F. Garratt, *Modern Irish Poetry: Tradition and Continuity from Yeats to Heaney* (Berkeley: University of California Press, 1986), p. 217.

Yeats who in a gesture of disenchantment with dream asserts in 'The Circus Animals' Desertion', 'It was the dream itself enchanted me'. In an act of simultaneous repression and evocation, Montague repudiates Wordsworth but brings to light the hold over his imagination of Yeats's phrasing, and replays his great if problematic Irish forebear's drama of self-reflexive poetic 'enchantment', a drama that has its origins, in turn, in Yeats's complex debt to the Romantic tradition.

II

But there is another story to be told about Romanticism and Irish poetry apart from a narrative centred on Yeats. In his late sonnets, Patrick Kavanagh produces a maverick post-Romantic poetry that discovers the beauty of the quotidian, hybridizes the comic and the pastoral, and imbues its workings with a dashingly reckless confessional brio. 'It took me many years to learn or relearn not to care. The heart of a song singing it, or a poem writing it is not caring': Patrick Kavanagh's commitment expressed in 'Self-Portrait' to 'not caring' cares greatly about the need 'not to care'.[9] If he echoes T. S. Eliot's plea, 'Teach us to care and not to care' from *Ash-Wednesday* I, Kavanagh is the reverse of hieratic or solemn in his dedication to 'not caring'. Yet, for a body of work that advertises itself as 'uncaring', Patrick Kavanagh's poems about poetry in *Come Dance with Kitty Stobling*, published in 1960, seem self-preoccupied: preoccupied both with the poet's former and present selves and with their own modes of being. Circumspectly yet generously praised by Seamus Heaney for their 'pure self-possession' and 'grievously earned simplicity', qualities that point up their source in a Romantic concern with poetry's complex autonomy, these poems ricochet between extremes of mood and artistic impact.[10]

In 'The One', the third of a group of poems referred to as 'three coloured sonnets' on their journal publication in *Nonplus* (1959),[11] Kavanagh captures that 'simplicity of return' which 'Self-Portrait' opposes to the 'simplicity of going away' and regards as offering the 'ultimate in sophistication'.[12] Any invocation of 'simplicity' since *Lyrical Ballads* cannot elude the example of Wordsworth's practice and poetics. The first line of 'The One', 'Green, blue,

---

[9] Patrick Kavanagh, *A Poet's Country: Selected Prose*, ed. Antoinette Quinn (Dublin: Lilliput, 2003), p. 313.
[10] Heaney, *Finders Keepers*, p. 144.
[11] Kavanagh's poems are quoted from his *Collected Poems*, ed. Antoinette Quinn (London: Allen Lane, 2004); the prose quotation is from this edition, p. 287.
[12] Kavanagh, 'Self-Portrait', in *A Poet's Country*, p. 313.

yellow and red—', has about it a spondaic calm that is misleading (excitement will take over), yet definitive. The voice utters the colours as though speaking a laconic rosary chant. When the line concludes with 'red', it paves the way for the 'God' who begins the next line: 'God is down in the swamps and marshes'. Straightaway the poem's off-centre divinity off-rhymes with 'red', entering the poem with a natural at-homeness among 'the swamps and marshes' that makes possible his epiphanic reappearance in the rhyme position of the sonnet's penultimate line. A catalogue of sober colouring, and the Wordsworthian link is evident in the pleasure taken in the natural and ordinary, the first line is at the same time a subdued mantra. It gathers to itself the force of the closing lines of 'Canal Bank Walk': 'For this soul needs to be honoured with a new dress woven | From green and blue things and arguments that cannot be proven'. That loose-limbed, assertive couplet describes a 'need'; the opening of 'The One' takes for granted that the need can be satisfied by 'green and blue things and arguments that cannot be proven'; it enacts what the earlier poem (the first in the 1960 volume) asserts.[13]

'Green', the poem's first word, may seem to have nationalist annotations, but this Kavanagh is the poet who in 'Self-Portrait' asserts that 'Irishness is a form of anti-art'.[14] Any link between nationalism and his brand of Romanticism is snapped asunder. The poem's 'Green', preceding the list of primary colours, has a quasi-Marvellian inflection, indicative of freshness, recovered innocence, naturalness. The naturalness of movement comes through quite un-Marvellian and quite deliberate syntactical slapdashness, though. Kavanagh's green, blue, yellow, and red thought of God is not set in a shade, but among the 'swamps and marshes'. It communicates as a barely punctuated flow of associations, so that connections wander with indolent ease: both 'God' and 'the flowering of our catharsis' are 'Sensational as April and almost incred- | ible'. 'Sensational' mixes journalistic slang and philosophical empiricism: the poem's sensationalism, its trust in the senses, leads directly to its intuition of a God who is kin to the lower-case 'god of imagination waking | In a Mucker fog' at the close of 'Kerr's Ass'. As such, Kavanagh's God is both object and agent of perception, just as the 'flowering of our catharsis' is a subjective state that precedes discovery of the significance possessed by 'raving flowers'. Among the poem's subtexts is obsession with the mind's relationship with reality; the latter is granted an apparent superiority, but it is a superiority that can be granted only by the mind.

The writing delights in the chances of rhyme: 'catharsis', the purgation of fear and terror, 'flowers' out of the mention of the God-filled 'marshes'. The colour 'red' sponsors a druggily slow-mo sense that God's presence is 'incred- |ible',

[13] See Kavanagh, *Collected Poems*, p. 294.
[14] See Kavanagh, *A Poet's Country*, p. 309.

where the enjambment flaunts its disregard of form without lapsing into cummingsesque or Nash-like smart-aleckry. There is *sprezzatura* in the way in which the poetry seems no more than a moment's thought in many details. Wordsworth may be one Romantic ancestor behind the poem, even as Shelley's *Adonais* ('The One remains, the many change and pass', 460) seems to underpin Kavanagh's appeal to 'the One and the Endless'. But a third Romantic poet, albeit in anti-Romantic mood, behind the poem is Byron. In 'From Monaghan to the Grand Canal', Kavanagh asserts in relation to his practice in these late poems: 'One of the good ways of getting out of all this respectability is the judicious use of slang and of outrageous rhyming. Auden in a radio lecture a year or so ago mentioned this and made a special reference to Byron's *Don Juan*. The new and outrageous rhymes are not to be confused with the slickeries of Ogden Nash. I draw attention to my rhyming of bridges with outrageous.'[15] Paul Muldoon, one realizes, was not the first twentieth-century Irish poet to be drawn to the example of Byron, and there is an affecting link between Kavanagh's late *ne plus ultra*, so-far-down-that-the-only-way-is-up-persona and Byron's aristocratic insouciance in his comic epic. Like Byron, to adapt Keats on the 'beauties' in Shakespeare's sonnets, Kavanagh is full of fine things said with all the air of unintentionality.[16] One might point to the way in which the rhyme-generated 'catharsis' brings into play two things: first, the idea of thatre, picked up in the following quatrain's reference to 'A humble scene', and the subsequent celebration of 'anonymous performers'; second, the suggestion of preceding tragedy, a suggestion spelt out more explicitly in other poems of this period, but here allowed merely to register.

In her magisterial study of Kavanagh's poetry, Antoinette Quinn detects a strain of 'preachy insistence' in lines at the poem's centre, those beginning 'The raving flowers'. Yes, Kavanagh can overstate the importance of the unimportant, but 'preachy insistence' is not quite accurate for the unpunctuated slide from unimportance to transcendence made here.[17] Rather, there is a lift of surprise as the 'backward place' turns out to rhyme with and be the local habitation of 'the face | Of the One and the Endless'. In 'raving flowers' Kavanagh repeats the trick of colloquial double meaning that he employs in 'every blooming thing' at the end of 'Inniskeen Road: July Evening': they are 'raving' as one might say that someone is raving mad, and yet their raving serves to disclose the quasi-Plotinian 'One and the Endless'. But whereas the earlier poem cursed and celebrated the poet's fate, the remarkable thing about 'The One' is that Kavanagh empties the poem of arrogant subjectivity—not through any

---

[15] Ibid. 279. [16] See Oxford Authors, p. 368.
[17] Antoinette Quinn, *Patrick Kavanagh: Born-Again Romantic* (Dublin: Gill & Macmillan, 1991), p. 420.

Objectivist programme denying the existence of ideas save in things, but through the dismissal of his own significance in the line 'Where no one important ever looked'. If arrogant subjectivity is sent packing, trust in the self's best impulses, impulses that delight in the mundane, is affirmed as the writing makes it newly important that he has looked at how 'the raving flowers looked'. 'Important' is one of Kavanagh's 'important' words: one recalls how at the conclusion of 'Epic', 'Homer's ghost came whispering to my mind | He said: I made the *Iliad* from such | A local row. Gods make their own importance.' It may be that here and in 'The One' Kavanagh has given his own inflection to Auden's use of the word in 'Musée des Beaux Arts': 'the ploughman may | Have heard the splash, the forsaken cry. | But for him it was not an important failure'. Indeed, Auden's conversational manner, its quasi-Byronic ability to use 'Almost any kind of the crude material of life', meant much to Kavanagh, as is apparent from his 'Auden and the Creative Mind'.[18] Auden's poem, however, is about the way we turn to our affairs, since we were not the one dead, about the contingent nature of disaster. Kavanagh in 'Epic' uses 'importance' to intimate how 'importance' is conferred by the imagination. The use of 'importance' at the poem's end after 'important' in the same work's first line is, therefore, not symptomatic of 'a slight failure of nerve'.[19] Indeed, the final sentence holds its nerve, repeating a key word in the expectation that the reader will see how the poem has made its own 'importance'.

In 'The One', 'importance' itself begins to seem impertinent, laughably beside the point. After all, the toils of 'The profoundest of mortals' have been 'baulked' of knowledge of 'The Mind'. 'Baulked' loiters at its line-ending, and the reader feels that the poem itself is baulked at this point, not sure where to go next, as it lapses into a somnolent, post-octave caesura. As Antoinette Quinn observes, 'Naming restores [the poem's] *elan*';[20] it kickstarts the idling engine as Kavanagh enumerates some of the 'raving flowers', paying oblique homage, one feels, as he can afford to in this self-confident or 'uncaring' mood, to the Wordsworth who places the primrose at the centre of the moral drama of *Peter Bell* and who compares his Lucy to a violet: paying homage, but refusing to embrace any Wordsworthian faith in nature, playfully, instead, spinning out his words as if inventing what he describes. So, the 'violet' glides into the 'violent wild iris', 'violent' holding at bay even as it evokes another, more recent forebear, W. B. Yeats: it unleashes a 'violence' that is innocent in its implications, untainted by the conscious complicity with darker political forces which the word suggests in a Yeatsian poem such as 'Ancestral Houses'. The lines gain in force when brought into juxtaposition with an argument

---

[18] Kavanagh, *A Poet's Country*, p. 219.
[19] Paul Muldoon, *To Ireland, I* (Oxford: Oxford University Press, 2000), p. 68.
[20] Quinn, *Patrick Kavanagh*, p. 420.

explicitly developed later in the volume in 'Question to Life', which starts 'Surely you would not ask me to have known | Only the passion of primrose banks in May | Which are merely a point of departure for the play'. The image of 'the play' repeats the idea of 'performance' in 'The One', an idea which gives a necessarily rehearsed dimension to Kavangah's ad lib desire to 'pray unselfconsciously with overflowing speech' (as 'Canal Bank Walk' has it, in lines at the paradoxical heart of his late poetic). Nothing is more self-conscious, though the self-consciousness is worn lightly, than the wish to 'pray unselfconsciously'. The play in 'Question to Life' turns out, though, when 'all is said and done' (an allusion to the more tragically and desolately inclined career review made by Yeats in 'The Circus Animals' Desertion'), to involve the need to 'be reposed and praise, praise, praise | The way it happened and the way it is'. Again, 'The One' enacts an injunction contained in a poem from the same volume, since it finds its own fashion of praising 'The way it happened and the way it is'.

What strikes the reader seeking to parse or paraphrase the sestet of 'The One' is the daringly relaxed avoidance of complete syntactical coherence. The verse behaves as though 'anonymous performers' were appositionally linked to 'an important occasion', as though the anonymity of the performance added up to an 'important occasion'. Quinn shrewdly notes that 'Naming is abandoned' at this point,[21] and in consonance with this shift of attention from the particular, one has, to make the phrases appositional, to move from the recurrently general (these flowers were often the catalyst of revelation) to the collectively singular: it all comprised 'An important occasion', where 'occasion' may draw to itself the idea of causation. 'Important,' which seemed to be sent packing, is now reinstated, and the 'occasion' celebrated begins to seem less any past event of vision than the poem's recovery in its own present tense of a moment when the poet, to adapt Wordsworth's terms, said to his soul, 'I recognise thy glory' (*The Prelude*, 1805, VI. 532). 'The Muse at her toilet' means to be down-at-heel Popeian pastiche, but lurches, somewhat disconcertingly, in the direction of the near-scatological; is this very non-U Muse visiting the outhouse WC, or is she a sort of rustic Belinda, preparing her dress and arranging her verbal vestments? One ends up preferring the latter, but the verse will not quite let one exorcize the possibility of the former. Among Kavanagh's most angelic words an earthiness plays as, with a sly wit, 'toilet' offers itself as wholly rhyme-begotten by the need for a chime with 'violet'; the phrase 'The Muse at her toilet' catches Kavanagh's Muse in a state of inelegant but insouciant dishevelment. Yet the continual if irregular anapaestic pulse prepares us for the final, rapturous claim, where the word 'beautiful' is repeated three times. The line demands to be read

[21] Ibid.

as buoyantly anapaestic: that is, as an iamb followed by three anapaests, so that the reader stresses the opening syllable of the adjectives and the final word of the line, 'God'. Kavanagh repeats the word, not with the anxiety that drives Keats to repeat 'happy' in the third stanza of 'Ode on a Grecian Urn', but with a renewed awareness of the 'profoundest' meaning of the word: a meaning which for Kavanagh has to do with the fact that beauty inheres in the local, in 'a cut-away bog', and irradiates the lives of 'local farmers'. That said, 'prepared to inform the local farmers' sounds amusingly like someone summoning up courage, and there is a hint of wryness as well as ecstasy in the poem's close. The wryness comes, in part, from the deliberate clash of registers: 'prepared to inform' might feature in a policeman's notebook or a municipal injunction, yet 'beautiful, beautiful, beautiful God' risks toppling over into banal rhapsodizing. Such is Kavanagh's control in these late poems, however, that the poetry wins from the clash a recognition that the Muse's informing message is based solely on poetic vision; the ponderousness of 'prepared to inform' laughs at poetry's self-importance, but does so sympathetically; 'beautiful, beautiful, beautiful God' dares to dally with a word ('beauty') at the heart of all art, and breathes into the most shopworn of adjectives a lilting, playful quality of affirmation. Romanticism, at least in its more rapturous incarnation, is indeed 'born again' at such a moment; yet Kavanagh's words tether themselves to the earthbound.

'Certainly praise: let the song mount again and again,' writes Auden in Rilkean mode in sonnet XIII of 'In Time of War'. The line is itself not without a flicker of irony at the expense of commitment to praise, all of Auden's best unillusioned tone present in that concessive adverb and the deliberately overstated repetition. Auden sets against this imperative another command: 'But hear the morning's injured weeping, and know why.' 'History opposes its grief to our buoyant song,' the poem continues, schematizing a quarrel out of which much post-1900 poetry that owes a debt to Romanticism is made. The quarrel is one dealt with and at least imaginatively resolved in different ways by works such as *The Prelude, Prometheus Unbound,* and *Don Juan:* each poem is conscious of political difficulties, but each is alive to the 'buoyant' rewards of poetry. Kavanagh's implicit poetic in his late, self-reflexive pieces may seem disinclined to give 'History' the status of master discourse or even worthy adversary. But in 'Winter', another sonnet, he both dismisses it from his presence and puzzles over it, turning it into a private possession. If the ego was extraordinarily absent in 'The One', in 'Winter' it is disconcertingly all-pervasive. The poem flirts with solipsism. Reality is perceived in terms that take us back to the consuming preoccupations of the perceiver. The poem personifies Winter, first, as an alien from outer space who 'had landed', then as a critic of his own poetry, the landscape forming a 'bare tree sonnet' 'as he

[Winter] scanned it'. 'Winter' itself, with its loose long lines, resists easy scansion, a fact that turns the line into a joke at the expense of the reader who would attempt to 'scan it'. Yet the poem takes its life from a comment from someone else; it is what 'someone mentioned' that catalyses the poem. 'Christmas, someone mentioned, is almost upon us', a conversational line suffused with adult awareness and tiredness; we are worlds away from the sacramental, intent inwardness of Kavanagh's earlier celebration of childhood's openness to the miraculousness of life in 'A Christmas Childhood'. When Kavanagh quoted this poem in 'Violence and Literature' to illustrate his remark that 'I am not enamoured of that life drama that goes out not with a bang but a whimper; indeed I find myself constantly regretting that I took no part in World War I', the first line read: 'Christmas someone remarked is almost upon us'.[22] In this comma-less version, the voice does not drop and muse as it recalls someone's words; in this version, those words sound like a pointed 'remark' rather than the casual or 'uncaring' 'mention' of the received reading.

It is that casualness that brings us into intimate contact with a 'life drama' of compelling force. Kavanagh's prose gloss alerts us to the poet's search for significance and to the poem's undercurrent of 'regret'. The poet depicts himself 'looking out my window', an image for desired connection with something outside the self. What is staring back at him is, as already suggested, a projection of his own wintriness embodied as a mindscape. But this mindscape in which Winter appears 'Complete with the grey cloak and the bare tree sonnet' (where the definite articles have an Audenesque ring of authority) serves as an image for both the self and the non-self; the 'gravel in the yard' that is said to be 'pensive' and 'annoyed to be crunched', as well as 'people with problems in their faces,' force themselves on the poet's and poem's attention. The last two lines of the octave assert the familiar stance of 'uncaring': 'Yet I with such solemnity around me refused to be bunched, | In fact was inclined to give the go-by to bars.' It is revealing that these lines use inversion and a seemingly sloppy and snook-cocking syntax to allow for a double reading. The first reading is: 'I refused to be bunched (that is, associated with) such solemnity'; the second, less overt, reading is: 'Despite the fact that there is such solemnity around me I refuse to be 'bunched', narrowed in upon myself.' Feeling 'inclined' one way in Kavanagh often speaks of an alertness to lean the other way, as when in 'Epic' he 'inclined | To lose my faith in Ballyrush and Gortin | Till Homer's ghost came whispering to my mind'. 'To give the go-by to bars', one assumes, means not drowning his sorrows and ranting with polemical anger, as in the years before the born-again conversion experience.

[22] Kavanagh, *A Poet's Country,* p. 254.

The sestet suggests a lifting up of non-alcoholic spirits, using the device of quickened commitment present at the start of the closing stanza of Keats's 'Ode to Psyche': 'Yes, I will be thy priest, and build a fane | In some untrodden region of my mind' (50–1), Keats declares, by his own eyes inspired. 'Yes, there were things in that winter arrival that made me | Feel younger, less of a failure,' writes Kavanagh, mounting a more downbeat affirmation. Kavanagh is at his most laid-back as with sardonic generosity he gives the benefit of doubt to 'things in that winter arrival'. This sestet is affirmation at its most achingly qualified. For one thing, affirmation is quietly but decisively a matter of the past; 'there were things'; 'it was actually earlier | Than many people thought', where the colloquial 'actually earlier' catches just that note of willed optimism never far from the use in speech of 'actually'; the phrase pulses with tacit longing as it makes its assertion. For another, the list of 'possibilities' is so morally even-handed that it sounds like a send-up, especially when history returns with a vengeance in the final 'or', almost as an accidental afterthought, catalysed by the most glancing of rhymes between 'earlier' and 'scare me, or': the last line, 'Taking part in a world war, joining up at the start of hostilities', is an intriguing option from the list of 'possibilities'; 'hostilities', as a rhyme companion for 'possibilities' casts an ironic glance at the open-ended hopefulness of the earlier noun. For all Kavanagh's explicit assertion in 'Violence and Literature' that he 'mentioned' in the poem his regret that he 'took no part in World War I', it is difficult to exclude the thought that the line alludes to the neutrality of the Irish Free State in the Second World War. Involving yourself in life, for Kavanagh, can be a matter of epiphanic praise, but in the downbeat ending of this poem, it seems like a double-edged business. The last line, long and trailing rather than clinching, has the poet imagining himself 'joining up at the start of hostilities'; it is less involvement in 'aggression' that Kavanagh momentarily desires than the experience of feeling at one with a collective mood, even as 'at the start' cannot but suggest the inevitability of disillusion. The appositional syntax of the poem's last sentence blurs together various private and public 'possibilities', some evidently positive, some less clearly so, all bearing witness to the poet's complex feelings about his 'own fantastic caution'.[23] That phrase implies regret, but 'fantastic' reattributes to the poet's 'caution' something of the sheer miraculousness of the 'Fantastic light' celebrated in 'Lines Written on a Seat on the Grand Canal, Dublin'. Fantasy seems to be embraced as fantasy in the phrase 'for South African adventure', as though Kavanagh were boyishly seeing himself as a hero in a Rider Haggard yarn; in the way it is sandwiched between the more private hopes expressed 'For love' and 'for fathering a baby', it leaps out as kicking against a life suffused with personal disappointments. The poem looks out

---

[23] Kavanagh, *A Poet's Country*, p. 255.

of its verbal window at various 'possibilities'; its achievement, in doing so, is to remind the reader that poetry may be a form of living by other means: a privileged, or a potential, or, possibly, merely an illusory space. It is a conclusion threaded through with the hopes and anxieties of a poet writing in the post-Romantic tradition. If 'The One' serves as a manifesto for a poetry delighting in the importance of the quotidian and casual, 'Winter' is less upbeat; here, all the fun and value lies in the way you say a thing—even if that thing is edged with regret and indeterminacy.

III

In the uses made by contemporary Northern Irish poets of the Romantic inheritance, Romanticism's own splits and divisions are multiplied and refracted. A tension at the heart of Romanticism concerns the role of imaginative 'colouring', to borrow Wordsworth's word, already quoted. The idea of a 'plain sense of things', in Wallace Stevens's phrase, is, ultimately, a notion impossible to divorce from a Romantic context. In 'The Plain Sense of Things', Stevens offers a post-Romantic elegy for High Romanticism ('The great structure has become a minor house'), but he implies the continuing relevance of the Romantic through his insistence that the 'absence of imagination had | Itself to be imagined'. Earlier poems by Stevens such as 'Tea at the Palaz of Hoon' and 'The Snow Man' are opposite sides of a coin minted by Wordsworth and Coleridge, most prodigally in their lyric exchanges of 1802. 'Tea at the Palaz of Hoon' affirms an inventive scenario in, and as a result of, which 'I was myself the compass of that sea'. 'The Snow Man' seeks to imagine 'Nothing that is not there and the nothing that is'. In his 1998 selected poems, Heaney sets side by side his own equivalents to these poems: 'Thatcher', in which the thatcher, a surrogate for as well as anti-self of the poet, leaves onlookers 'gaping at his Midas touch', and 'The Peninsula', a poem of emptied vision, which begins, 'When you have nothing more to say', and ends with a glimpse of 'things founded clean on their own shapes'.[24] This latter vision may seem the opposite of Romantic imaginings; but if it is an opposite, it is one brought into being by a dialectical turn against Romanticism.

In fact, the Romantics often prize otherness, discovered in the wrestle for primacy between language and experience. Even Shelley, aware of the mind's propensity to project feeling, begins his lyric cry of dejection with delighted, if strangely emotionless, notations of the external: 'I see the waves upon the

---

[24] Quoted from Heaney, *Opened Ground: Poems, 1966–1996* (London: Faber, 1998), as are all Heaney's poems in this book, unless otherwise indicated.

shore | Like light dissolved in star-showers, thrown' ('Stanzas Written in Dejection', 12–13). There, Shelley mimes an uninvolved seeing, but he betrays his imaginative involvement with the scene through a simile that expresses a yearning for a vision of connectedness. That kind of dramatic struggle stiffens the linguistic sinews of Romantic poetry, and it reappears in the work of Seamus Heaney, who moves towards a poetry that (as Heaney describes Blake's practice in 'The Sick Rose') offers 'an open invitation into its meaning rather than an assertion of it'.[25]

In 'Glanmore Sonnets', Heaney echoes Wordsworth's *The Prelude* at the start of the second sonnet:

> Sensings, mountings from the hiding places,
> Words entering almost the sense of touch,
> Ferreting themselves out of their dark hutch . . .

The lines plait references to Books I and XI of *The Prelude* (quoted from the 1805 version): Book i's 'Trances of thought and mountings of the mind' (20) and Book xi's 'hiding-places of my power' (335).[26] Both Wordsworthian passages deal with inspiration, and Heaney's poem follows suit, celebrating his own imaginative 'mountings from the hiding places'. But if Wordsworthian 'sense' uses empirical perception as the springboard for visionary intuition—of, for example, 'unknown modes of being' (*The Prelude*, 1805, I. 420)—Heaney's 'Sensings' combine the physical and the imaginative. His words enter 'almost the sense of touch', a reclamation of the sensuous that is forcibly corroborated by the third line's image of words 'Ferreting themselves out of their dark hutch'. In a further twist, however, 'Ferreting themselves' combines the startlingly literal (the words turn into ferrets) and the intellectually metaphorical (the words tug into existence a new sense of their own workings), a twist that shows how false it is to simplify Heaney solely into a celebrant of the physical. A Wordsworthian connection, in all its complexity, is proudly trumpeted here. In the sequence's third sonnet, however, Heaney turns self-consciously on such dreams of literary affinity, puncturing a faltering comparison between himself and his wife and

---

[25] Heaney, 'The Fire i'the Flint: Reflections on the Poetry of Gerard Manley Hopkins', in *Preoccupations: Selected Prose, 1968–1978* (London: Faber, 1980), hereafter cited as *P* in main body of the text, p. 83.

[26] For discussion of Heaney's response to Wordsworth, see Neil Corcoran, *Seamus Heaney* (London: Faber, 1986); Michael R. Molino, 'Heaney's "Singing School": A Portrait of the Artist', *Journal of Irish Literature*, 16/3 (1987), 12–17; Michael Parker, *Seamus Heaney: The Makings of the Poet* (Basingstoke: Macmillan, 1993); Helen Vendler, *Seamus Heaney* (London: Faber, 1998); Simon Dentith, 'Heaney and Walcott: Two Poems', *Critical Survey*, 11/3 (1999), 92–9; and Hugh Haughton, 'Power and Hiding Places: Wordsworth and Seamus Heaney', in *The Monstrous Debt*, ed. Davies and Turley, pp. 61–100. See also Heaney's selection of Wordsworth's poems (with a suggestive introduction) in *The Essential Wordsworth* (New York: Ecco, 1988). For a fine, wide-ranging discussion of the overall topic dealt with in this chapter, see Patricia Horton's unpublished Ph.D. thesis (Queen's University of Belfast, 1996), 'Romantic Intersections: Romanticism and Contemporary Northern Irish Poetry'.

'Dorothy and William' as his wife 'interrupts: | "You're not going to compare us two...?"'

One might generalize from the interplay between these two sonnets and argue that the longing for Romantic authority pervades Heaney's work, as does the ironic opposition to that longing. Other poets intensify such opposition. Chapter 7 will explore in detail how Paul Muldoon's 'Madoc: A Mystery' (1990) plays beguiling games with Coleridge's and Southey's Pantisocratic dreams. In one poem, for instance, he invokes Lacan as the presiding philosophical spirit in a conjuring up and dismissal of Coleridge's 'The Eolian Harp': 'The wraith pokes its tongue in Southey's ear—| 'Rhythm in all thought, and joyance everywhere'— | before leaving only a singe on the air.' In keeping with Muldoon's two-faced ironies, the Coleridgean affirmation at once mocks Southey and is, in turn, subjected to mockery. A few pages later in '[Quine]', as if to deflate the poetic inspiration figured in the Romantic poem, Muldoon grants his Coleridge—on the day of his death—only a vision of 'scrub | and salt-flats' in conjunction with 'A tinkle on an Aeolian harp'. This 'tinkle' introduces a relationship with the natural that is hardly numinous:

> July 25th, 1834. A tinkle on an Aeolian harp
> across the scrub
>
> and salt-flats.
> Coleridge props himself up under a canopy of gnats
>
> and returns their call to a pair of chickadees;
> 'Quiddities. Quiddities. Quiddities'.

The repetition of 'Quiddities' in this bathetic context annuls its sense; any Aristotelian respect for reality it conveys is ironized by Muldoon's elegant incongruities of phrasing and rhyme.

Irony is often, in fact, a feature of Northern Irish poetry's relationship with Romanticism. Given historical differences and cultural dissonance, it could scarcely be absent. But pinpointing irony's presence and activity can be difficult. Ciaran Carson interweaves phrases from Keats's 'Ode to a Nightingale' in 'The Irish for No'.[27] Here Carson sets sectarian atrocities against Keatsian sensuous luxuriance, and shows an alertness to the resulting cultural (and physical) 'Mish-mash. Hotch-potch'. Neil Corcoran reads the Keatsian echoes as bound up with allusions to Heaney in such a way as to discredit both poets: 'in the dark of contemporary social and political attrition', Corcoran writes, 'Carson finds Heaney's poetic of late Romantic expansiveness wanting'. It is a seemingly plausible reading in the light of passages such as the following:

> The stars clustered thick as blackberries. They opened the door into the dark.
> *The murmurous haunt of flies on summer eves.* Empty jam-jars.
> Mish-mash. Hotch-potch.

---

[27] Quoted from Ciaran Carson, *The Irish for No* (1987; Newcastle upon Tyne: Bloodaxe, 1988).

Early Heaney ('Blackberry-Picking' and 'Door into the Dark') is at once evoked and quashed here. Yet whether Heaney himself uncomplicatedly espouses a 'poetic of late Romantic expansiveness' in, say, 'Blackberry-Picking' is questionable; that poem faces up to the processes of rotting and souring clear-sightedly held at bay in, for example, Keats's 'To Autumn'. Corcoran is, in fact, more complexly persuasive when, earlier in his analysis, he argues that Carson's use of Keats's poem works 'almost uninterpretably'. For one thing, to quote the Ode is to recall an ideal of aesthetic finish; to the degree that Carson aims at shaping his lines, such a recollection draws the Belfast poet into artistic complicity with his Romantic forebear. For another, the intertextual play to which such '*bricolage* of reference', as Corcoran describes it, gives rise releases Carson's imagination to engage in free, though quietly tense, association.²⁸

Carson's poem opens with the question at the close of Keats's 'Ode to a Nightingale': '*Was it a vision, or a waking dream?*' The effect of this quotation, comfortably swallowed in the maw of a long line borrowed from C. K. Williams, is at once mocking, since what follows is an overheard quarrel, and a point of entry into Carson's decidedly post-Romantic, post-modern poetic world. Yet his hallucinatory jumble of narrative hints draws a kind of ersatz dignity from the Keatsian affiliation; this affiliation reappears later when we learn that 'The casements | Were wide open' and that 'We were debating, | Bacchus and the pards and me', and when Keats's own doubting but empowering statement, '*I cannot see what flowers are at my feet*', is brought into play. Such intertextuality, unresolvable in thematic terms, demands for its understanding a mock-heroic, labile poetics of quotation that allows for the precursor texts to be honoured even as they are being subverted. In this poem the Keatsian quotations bear on, even as they are undone by, the poem's grim allusions to atrocity. Carson's own style has enough commerce with surreal associationism for his initial borrowing of Keats's final question to take on self-reflexive relevance. The Keatsian quotations are not simply juxtaposed with an undercutting demotic idiom; they slide and seep into the new world of the poem, as when Carson writes, 'So the harbour slips away to perilous seas as things remain unsolved.' The poem's own relationship with Keatsian Romanticism seems itself to be 'unsolved', to be, in the poem's last words, 'debating whether *yes* is *no*'.²⁹

'Debating whether *yes* is *no*' might describe a common and sophisticated response made by Northern Irish poets to the intricate affirmations of Romantic poetry: a kind of post-Romantic irony, adding to Romantic irony's ability

---

²⁸ Neil Corcoran, 'One Step Forward, Two Steps Back: Ciaran Carson's *The Irish for No*', in *The Chosen Ground: Essays on the Contemporary Poetry of Northern Ireland*, ed. Neil Corcoran (Dufour: Seren, 1992), pp. 215, 214.

²⁹ See also Mary Fitzgerald-Hoyt, 'Grounding Keats's Nightingale: Ciaran Carson's *The Irish for No*', *Canadian Journal of Irish Studies*, 19/2 (1993), 76–80.

to assert and undercut in the name of creative freedom the awareness that any such freedom is caught up in the coils of textual associations. So, at the end of 'A Lighthouse in Maine', Derek Mahon happens on a lighthouse 'shining | In modest glory like || The soul of Adonais'.[30] For the Shelleyan splendour recalled there, Mahon's cunningly down-at-heel three-line stanzas contrive a low-key epiphany. Though 'The soul of Adonais' seems deliberately incongruous, the kind of incongruity that would occur to a literary sensibility, the sense of discovery—as the famous phrase resonates in a line to itself after a stanza break—is strong. Mahon is saying that the lighthouse has as much right to attention as 'The soul of Adonais', even as he complicates any notion of unmediated contact with the object by virtue of his poetic activity. 'Modest glory' may be a diminished version of Shelley's 'white radiance of Eternity' (463), but it is present, in the here-and-now, invoked in a spirit of anti-transcendental commitment to the earthly. As Mahon has said earlier in the poem,

> The north light
> That strikes its frame
>
> Houses is not
> The light of heaven
> But that of this world.

Even here, though, any hint of anti-Romantic polemic checks itself in that last phrase's glancing recollection of 'the very world which is the world | Of all of us, the place in which, in the end, | We find our happiness, or not at all' (*The Prelude*, 1805, x. 725–7). Generally, this looking back to and backing off from the Romantics, played out in many poems, illuminates the dilemma and achievement of poets from Northern Ireland. The Shelleyan vision of poets in *A Defence of Poetry* as 'the unacknowledged legislators of the World' (p. 701) may arouse an instinctive defensiveness in these poets; yet they can never wholly abandon this vision in their search for images and rhythms adequate to the condition of contemporary history.

IV

Writing about his translation of *Beowulf*, Seamus Heaney focuses, in particular, on what he calls 'the liminal situation of the literary translator, the one standing at the frontier of a resonant original, in awe of its primacy, utterly persuaded, and yet called upon to utter a different yet equally persuasive version of it in his

---

[30] Quoted from Derek Mahon, *Selected Poems* (1990; London: Penguin in association with Oxford University Press, 1993).

or her own words'.³¹ In Heaney's own relationship with English Romantic poetry, especially that of Wordsworth, there is something of this liminality, except for the fact that Heaney's relationship is that of the inventor, often in search of corroboration. As already suggested, Heaney's dealings with Wordsworth are pervasive. In his essay 'The Makings of a Music' he contrasts Wordsworth's music with Yeats's. Wordsworth's music reveals, according to Heaney, 'a wise passiveness, a surrender to energies that spring within the centre of the mind'; Yeats's verse suggests 'the music of energy reined down, of the mastered beast stirring' (*P*, pp. 63, 73).

Heaney is describing two kinds of Romanticism, neither of which is straightforwardly available to him because he grew up, as he puts it in 'Singing School', with a colonized sense of having 'no rights on | The English lyric'. Intriguingly, that poem has as an epigraph four and a half lines from *The Prelude* beginning (in Heaney's quotation), '*Fair seedtime had my soul, and I grew up | Fostered alike by beauty and by fear*' (1805, I. 305–6). After this epigraph suggestive of affinity and contrast, the poem proper opens with a wryly assertive nod towards the Patrick Kavanagh of 'Epic': 'Well, as Kavanagh said, we have lived | In important places.' The poem confirms, albeit ambivalently, that initial note of assertion about the poet's links with a home-grown tradition represented by Kavanagh. Heaney brings out the lived experience of growing up in a place where, among other things, 'the leather strap | Went epileptic in the Big Study' and the poet as a young man was harassed by policemen 'pointing | The muzzle of a Sten gun in my eye'. That is what it is really like, the poet seems to be saying, to be 'Fostered . . . by fear', and, in a sense, Wordsworth serves as an ironized reference point.

If the poet's 'act | Of stealth'—apparently, the throwing of biscuits over the school fence one night in September 1951—recalls the boat-stealing episode in The *Prelude*, Book I, Heaney turns his back on the inwardness celebrated by Wordsworth. Heaney pointedly truncates his original, the boat-stealing being for Wordsworth an 'act of stealth | And troubled pleasure' (I. 388–9). 'Troubled', as often in Wordsworth, hints at an imaginative disturbance that is ultimately affirmative, and he concludes the episode with a darkly empowering vision of 'huge and mighty Forms that do not live | Like living men' (I. 425–6), described as 'the trouble of my dreams' (I. 427). Heaney, by contrast, eschews any 'dim and undetermined sense | Of unknown modes of being' (The *Prelude*, 1805, I. 419–20) (here, at any rate) for a more socially constrained consciousness of the 'ministry of fear'. Later, in the sequence's final poem, 'Exposure', Heaney will lay claim to a tentatively lyrical state of poetic autonomy, a state that has exacted sacrifices, but is alive to possibilities. What

---

³¹ Heaney, 'The Drag of the Golden Chain', *Times Literary Supplement*, 12 Nov. 1999, p. 14.

weighs with Heaney is his 'responsible *tristia*', as, very much the post-Romantic, he, like the birches, is 'Inheriting the last light'. Unable to 'come on meteorite', he is no trumpeter of a prophecy, merely a cautious stroller 'through damp leaves, | Husks, the spent flukes of autumn'. Politically and personally, Heaney has taken cover, even as he risks exposure; feeling 'Every wind that blows', he does not command any Shelley-like wind to scatter his words among mankind. Yet, for all the poem's sense of loss—the poet has missed 'The comet's pulsing rose'—it does more in that just-quoted line, the last in the work, than recall 'The diamond absolutes'. It re-creates them by virtue of a phrase that, tapping Shelleyan and Yeatsian symbolic energies, makes present what has been missed.

Heaney, then, at the end of 'Singing School' reaffirms a precarious sense of continuity with Romantic lyric self-belief. The Wordsworthian music heard in 'The Makings of a Music' accords more with Heaney's early exploration of what Neil Corcoran calls 'an enlargement of consciousness ... enacted in some interchange between mind and nature'.[32] In poems such as 'Personal Helicon,' Heaney writes a poetry that meshes surrender to childhood experience with subsequent adult awareness. In addition, he is capable of a metapoetic dimension. So, that poem concludes:

> Now, to pry into roots, to finger slime,
> To stare, big-eyed Narcissus, into some spring
> Is beneath all adult dignity. I rhyme
> To see myself, to set the darkness echoing.

It would be absurd to find Wordsworth everywhere in such passages. The wit of 'big-eyed Narcissus' is hardly characteristic of the Romantic poet (who is not without his own forms of humour), while the poem of Wordsworth most brought to mind by the final sentence—*The Prelude*—studiously avoids 'rhyme'. But Heaney has, very adroitly, and yet without too knowing a self-consciousness, succeeded in making his poem at once 'personal' and in touch with tradition, with the springs of Helicon. The poem enacts its relationship with tradition in lines such as—and especially—'Others had echoes, gave back your own call | With a clean new music in it'. At the self-referential level, this formulation suggests how Heaney would like to relate to his precursors.

Behind the poem's end one can also hear an echo of Wordsworth's lines about echoing, which Heaney meditates on in 'The Makings of a Music'. The Wordsworthian lines are these: 'My own voice cheered me, and, far more, the mind's | Internal echo of the imperfect sound; | To both I listened, drawing from them both | A cheerful confidence in things to come' (*The Prelude*, 1805, I. 64–7; quoted from Heaney's essay). Heaney comments: 'even though he is

---

[32] Corcoran, *Seamus Heaney*, p. 47.

listening to the sound of his own voice, he realizes that this spoken music is just a shadow of the unheard melody, "the mind's internal echo"' (*P*, p. 63). Wordsworth is mediated here through Keats's 'Ode on a Grecian Urn', where Keats appears at his most aesthetically attuned to language and its limits: an appropriate mediation, considering that one finds, sketched in Heaney's prose, a hint of the poetically self-aware turn inwards of the end of 'Personal Helicon', which adds to Wordsworthian listening an act of seeing the self, brought about in and by the process of poetic composition ('I rhyme | To see myself'). Such self-seeing is both qualified appositionally and extended by the subsequent move 'to set the darkness echoing'. Heaney's stance at the close is more ambiguous than Wordsworth's in the just-quoted lines about 'the mind's | Internal echo'. Wordsworth's 'cheerful confidence in things to come' has given way to a less evidently 'cheerful' desire to set the darkness echoing. And yet Heaney actively wishes to 'set' going a process that will bring him into contact with a 'darkness' that might be within and outside the self, but lies beyond the conscious will. In this balance between the active and passive, Wordsworth's example and influence are detectable.

But if *The Prelude*'s interplay between self and world has shaped Heaney's poetic procedures, one senses that, with Wallace Stevens, in a passage quoted more briefly in Chapter 1, he would wish to claim that 'while . . . I come down from the past, the past is my own and not something marked Coleridge, Wordsworth, etc. . . . My reality-imagination complex is entirely my own even though I see it in others.'[33] Yet full independence shows at moments of maximum assimilation. By the time of *The Government of the Tongue*, Heaney has internalized Wordsworth to the point where he is able to draw, in his criticism, with ingenuity and insight on the self-referring dimension of the Boy of Winander section from *The Prelude*. The passage, in part, describes the poet as a young boy mimicking the cry of the owls until he is rewarded for his pains by their answering call. In Heaney's essay on Sylvia Plath, the passage is used to illustrate three stages of poetic development: the initial pleasure in managing to 'get it right', the second stage of eliciting 'actual cries' when 'scale-practising' passes into a living 'poetry of relation', and a third stage in which 'the workings of the active universe, to use another phrase from *The Prelude*, are echoed far inside him'. Wordsworth's lines reinforce Heaney's self-image as a poet driven by the quest for 'direct contact . . . with the image-cellar, the dream-bank, the word-hoard, the truth-cave—whatever place', as he puts it, making peace with a troublingly magnificent precursor, that 'a poem like Yeats's "Long-Legged Fly" emerges from'.[34] One can regard Heaney as seeing

---

[33] Stevens, *Letters*, p. 792.

[34] Heaney, 'The Indefatigable Hoof-Taps: Sylvia Plath', in *The Government of the Tongue* (1988; London: Faber, 1989); hereafter *GT* in main body of the text, pp. 154, 159, 163.

his career conforming to the three stages he draws from the Boy of Winander passage: early work, mid-career work such as the 'Glanmore Sonnets' in which the poet takes stock and asks 'What is my apology for poetry?', and finally more recent work that seeks 'to try to make space ... for the marvellous as well as for the murderous', in Heaney's words from his Nobel Prize acceptance speech, printed as 'Crediting Poetry' in *Opened Ground* (p. 458).

It is typical of Heaney's wary even-handedness that this attempt is heralded in a dialectically contrary way by aspects of *Field Work*, a volume angry, as 'Oysters' has it, that 'my trust could not repose | In the clear light, like poetry or freedom | Leaning in from the sea'. Even in 'Crediting Poetry' the 'marvellous' does not oust its alliterative partner and ideological opponent, 'the murderous'. Still, nothing is more Romantic in Heaney than his struggle to credit poetry with absolute value in itself and a kind of collateral ethical value. Shelley's already quoted claim in *A Defence of Poetry* that 'Poets are the unacknowledged legislators of the World' haunts Heaney's thinking on this subject. His 'The Unacknowledged Legislator's Dream', the first piece in the second part of *North* (1975), appears to reject the Romantic poet's claim. (Though the poem appears to be a prose-poem, the margins are not always justified on the right-hand side, so I shall indicate its 'line-breaks'.) The speaker begins with a reference to Archimedes' assertion that 'he could move the world if he could | find the right place to position his lever'.[35] Appropriately, Shelley quotes the original of this assertion as epigraphs to *Queen Mab* and *Laon and Cythna*, two revolutionary works. In Heaney's piece, the speaker dreams of undermining 'the masonry | of state and statute', but ends up in a prison cell. Yet the close veers between self-mockery (hubristic dreams have been put in their place) and the threat or promise of further action ('I jump on the concrete flags to | test them'). The final sentence sets up a challenge to the reader—'Were those your eyes just now at the hatch?'—that takes one back to Shelley. *A Defence of Poetry*'s account of how poetry changes lives, not by communicating the writer's 'conceptions of right and wrong' (p. 682), but by mobilizing the reader's imagination, is not far from Heaney's position in an essay such as 'The Interesting Case of Nero, Chekhov's Cognac and a Knocker'. Here Heaney argues that through poetry the tongue, 'ungoverned', 'gains access to a condition' that, 'while not being practically effective, is not necessarily inefficacious' (*GT*, p. xxii). Heaney stresses poetry's offer of release from the poet's 'predicaments', an emphasis that aligns itself with Shelley's wish to 'familiarize the highly refined imagination' of his readers with 'beautiful idealisms of moral excellence' (*GT*, pp. xxii; Shelley, p. 232). Certainly the two poets share the conviction that direct familiarization of the reader's (and poet's) imagination with 'beautiful idealisms', where that phrase

---

[35] Quoted from Heaney, *North* (London: Faber, 1975).

implies no sentimental escapism but the mind's finest hopes, is a central and 'potentially redemptive' part of the poet's task (*GT*, p. xxii). For all their differences, both Shelley and Heaney seek to imagine states in which 'hope and history rhyme', as the Irish poet puts it in section IV of 'Voices from Lemnos'. It is in *Seeing Things*, in particular, that one of Shelley's Promethean legacies, the envisioning of spiritual realities, comes to the fore. As often, Heaney consciously has Yeats in mind; but Shelley is one of Yeats's singing masters. When in 'Squarings', xxii, Heaney asks a series of queries about the whereabouts of 'spirit', and concludes, 'Set questions for the ghost of W.B.', it is possible to glimpse, in the background, the poetic cosmos of spirit echoes in *Prometheus Unbound*.

But it is Wordsworth who provides the steadiest Romantic focus for Heaney's thinking about the rival claims of poetry and politics, thinking that has animated much of his finest poetry. In 'Frontiers of Writing', a lecture delivered in 1993, he recalls an earlier essay 'Place and Displacement', in which he 'found an English literary parallel which nicely illuminated the typical case of the poet from the minority in Ulster'. This parallel was Wordsworth, dislocated and alienated after his country had gone to war upon Revolutionary France. Heaney finds heartening the very thing that some recent critics have found reason to fault: Wordsworth's turn to and use of poetry to describe 'a consciousness coming together through the effort of articulating its conflict and crises'.[36] This formulation might describe much of Heaney's own efforts to articulate conflict yet in doing so to heal trauma.

For Stan Smith, such healing follows a path from Wordsworthian predicament to Keatsian negative capability. Smith is responding shrewdly to the idiom of Heaney's 1984 'Place and Displacement' lecture (delivered as a Pete Laver Lecture at the Wordsworth Summer Conference in Grasmere), in which Heaney describes poetic development in this way: the writer is 'displaced from a confidence in a single position by his disposition to be affected by all positions, negatively rather than positively capable'.[37] But to pursue Heaney's debt to Romanticism in terms of switched allegiances would be to oversimplify. Wordsworth certainly does not drop away. In *The Spirit Level*, 'Tollund' brings to mind his earlier piece, 'The Tollund Man', which broods on ancient and contemporary atrocity, and seeks unavailingly a healing music or poetic formula when the poet asserts, 'I could risk blasphemy, | Consecrate the cauldron bog | Our holy ground'. As the long sentence unwinds of which these quoted words are the opening, we find ourselves taken back towards, rather than away from, the violence. Heaney is in Yeatsian territory, the world of 'Meditations in Time of Civil War' and 'Nineteen Hundred and Nineteen' (much of Heaney's own contact

eaney, *The Redress of Poetry* (London: Faber, 1995), p. 189.
ney is quoted from Stan Smith, 'Seamus Heaney: The Distance Between', in *Chosen* Corcoran, p. 45.

with Romanticism is fruitfully mediated through his response to Yeats). 'The Tollund Man' concludes thus: 'Out there in Jutland | In the old man-killing parishes | I will feel lost, | Unhappy and at home.' The fineness of this derives from the refusal to resolve the tensions out of which the poem is made.

In 'Tollund', Heaney writes a poem that implicitly answers his earlier piece. We are not exactly in the world of 'Tintern Abbey', since Heaney is not describing a return visit (a central feature of 'The Tollund Man' was that its mood was proleptic, anticipatory). Yet, like Wordsworth's poem, Heaney has found his way through to a new and uncomplacent serenity, and one might wish to apply to his poem his words about Kavanagh's 'Innishkeen Road': 'The poet's stance becomes Wordsworth's over Tintern Abbey, attached by present feelings but conscious that the real value of the moment lies in its potential flowering, its blooming, in the imagination' (Heaney, 'From Monaghan to the Grand Canal: The Poetry of Patrick Kavanagh', *P*, p. 117). He does so by revisiting less a place than a poetic career. Heaney's poem begins with a memory of standing 'a long time out in Tollund Moss' in a landscape at once 'Hallucinatory and familiar'. The adjectives yoke together heterogeneous perspectives, and bespeak the poet's need and ability to straddle two worlds and various opposites: Ireland and Jutland, imagination and memory, invention and reality. The Jutland world is one in which he is still 'at home', though he is no longer 'unhappy'. Rural Derry does not seem far away from the 'swept and gated farmyard'; yet Jutland is quickly regarded as providing the setting for a literary fiction in the third stanza: 'It could have been a still out of the bright | "Townland of Peace", that poem of dream farms | Outside all contention.' That notion sounds desirable, but possibly illusory, and the poem immediately turns away from any immersion in a pastoral that might, in Keats's terms, turn cold. The run-on lines assert a freedom from encasement in artistic dream, and the poem discovers—in a way that is a source of encouragement—that 'Things had moved on'.

This moving on shows, for Heaney, in the fact that the imagined landscape of one of his great lyric triumphs reveals traces of change. Not only has a 'standing stone' 'been resituated and landscaped', but also there are now 'tourist signs' 'In Danish and in English'. In the earlier poem the poet's linguistic alienation is stressed, as he says the names, 'Watching the pointing hands | Of country people, | Not knowing their tongue'. In the later work, 'we' (Heaney and his wife, one presumes) are 'at home beyond the tribe'. With chastened hopefulness, the poem likens them to 'ghosts who'd walked abroad | Unfazed by light, to make a new beginning'. In its self-conscious angling of earlier work, 'Tollund' reminds us that one bequest of Romanticism is the evolving and shaped literary career.

That Romantic poetry continues to sustain Heaney's imagination is apparent in his poem 'Wordsworth's Skates', included in his *District and Circle* (2006). The poem is a parable of the way the Romantic refuses to inhabit tamely only its own historical space. Heaney sees but rejects 'the bootless runners lying toppled | In dust in a display case, | Their bindings perished'. In place of this spiritless vision of the past as a material junk yard, his impulse is to return to the poem's original intimation of its immortality: 'Star in the window', the poem opens, offering an emblem of the way in which Romantic vision beacons to a later poet. The poem's lineation and rhythms manage both to stay in touch with a metrical ground, yet mimetically to imply movement 'from the clutch of earth'. Heaney closes with a rekindled vision of 'the reel of them on frozen Windermere | As he flashed from the clutch of earth along its curve | And left it scored'. The lines suggest that Wordsworth's imagination needed the earth's diurnal course, yet they allow him briefly to have 'flashed from the clutch of earth', temporarily to have eluded the gravitational 'clutch' which at the same time makes his skating possible. 'Flashed' recalls the 'strength of usurpation' celebrated by Wordsworth in the Crossing the Alps passage in *The Prelude*, Book VI, 'when the light of sense | Goes out in flashes that have shewn to us | The invisible world' (1805, 534–6). Heaney imagines, in his tribute to Wordsworth, that the Romantic poet used, but went beyond, the 'light of sense' to reveal, if not an 'invisible world', a world that is newly interpreted, as is implied by the poem's final pun. 'Scored' refers to both the marks left on the ice and the 'score' bequeathed by the Romantic poet writing about his experience: a score into which, in turn, Heaney breathes his own music.[38]

V

In his study of American Modernist poetry, as noted in the Introduction to the present book, Albert Gelpi argues for a 'subtler continuity between Romanticism and Modernism beneath the avowed discontinuity'. Continuity does not preclude difference: 'For the Romantics', Gelpi writes, 'absolute experience predicated aesthetic failure, but the Modernists could postulate the absolute only as an ultimate gauge of technical achievement.'[39] Gelpi's terms help to clarify the inheritance and choices available to poets who are, in turn, post-Romantic and writing after Modernism. Derek Mahon's awareness of the dilemmas facing, and opportunities open to, the poet results in a light-wristed, ˜avely witty stance; Mahon is a poet who likes his Romanticism at a remove,

Scuttle for Dorothy Wordsworth', the first of two poems in 'Home Fires' in the same vol-
˜ Heaney's attunement to more diminished but achingly human forms of Romantic

˜oherent Splendor, pp. 2, 4–5.

refracted through Symbolist or Decadent prisms, through the lyric purity of a Jaccottet, or through a mocking echo of Stevens's late-Romantic 'rage for order': 'Somewhere beyond the scorched gable end and the burnt-out buses | there is a poet indulging | his wretched rage for order— | or not as the case may be.' The poet's 'posture is grandiloquent and deprecating', and Mahon's own deprecating grandiloquence suggests his desperately ironic relationship to the Romantic tradition. The cold beauty and arrested perfection of Keats's 'Ode on a Grecian Urn' give way in Mahon's terminal vision to 'The Apotheosis of Tins'. Here, the tins speak for a condition of derelict, parodically aesthetic freedom 'from the historical nightmare', as the poem offers a mock-celebration of their 'saintly | devotion to the notion of permanence | in the flux of sensation | and crisis'.[40]

More recently, however, Mahon's allusions to Keats demonstrate that the Romantic poet has become one of his exemplary figures. The seventh stanza of 'Ode to a Nightingale' (starting, in Mahon's text, '*Thou was not born for death, immortal Bird!*') stands at the head of the epigraphs to *The Hudson Letter* (1995). In loose-knit sections, full of allusions, echoes, and literary revisitings, the poem describes Mahon's life in America and celebrates 'the resilience of our lyric appetite' (I).[41] The Keatsian epigraph stands in enigmatic and suggestive relationship to the sequence. Though the bird is not 'born for death', the poet of *The Hudson Letter* feels mortality pressing upon him. In the final section 'The Small Rain' (XVIII) Mahon writes in elegiac mode, 'the friends and contemporaries begin to go'. Part of the pathos of Keats's stanza is the gap, yet link, between art, figured as immortal bird-song, and human suffering, plangently embodied in the image of 'the sad heart of Ruth' (66). Mahon wears his own 'sad heart' very much on his sleeve—and 'at night to lie', as he puts it, 'empty of mind, heart hammering'; yet his poem's endless weaving in and out of other texts suggests a frail trust in poetry as able to embrace, if not offer to stay against, existential confusion. '*Now more than ever seems it rich to die*', he writes in xviii, borrowing Keats's line from stanza 6 of the 'Ode to a Nightingale', 'into an oceanic, a molecular sky'. 'Molecular' sets up a scientific friction with the consciousness-drowsing 'oceanic', and the poem is in no mood to find salvation in any naïve reprise of Romantic lyricism. Nevertheless, 'the secret voice of nightingale and dolphin' are included in the poem's final litany of what constitutes essential compass points of poetic perception—along with 'the homeless, no rm. at the inn', and typically of Mahon, 'the gaseous planets'.

---

[40] These two poems are quoted from Derek Mahon, *Poems, 1962–1978* (Oxford: Oxford University Press, 1979).

[41] Quotations are from Mahon, *The Hudson Letter* (Loughcrew: Gallery, 1995). Interestingly, Mahon's revision of the section for his *Collected Poems* (Loughcrew: Gallery, 1999), omits the allusions to Keats.

Nature may betray the heart that loved her, but the poem finishes with a plea, 'Take us in; take us in!', that one might think is covertly uttered by many contemporary Northern Irish poems in their cunning, heartfelt solicitations of Romantic poetry. Though it is quoted playfully at the head of 'Sappho in "Judith's Room"' (section XIII), Susan Sontag's recommendation that 'in place of a hermeneutics we need an erotics of art' comes close to a manifesto for Mahon in *The Hudson Letter*. The 'erotics of art' include, for the author of this work, a belated, melancholy, yet energized and energizing responsiveness to Romantic poetry.[42]

[42] For a recent example of Mahon's response to Romantic poetry, see his 'Biographia Literaria', a poem in the *Times Literary Supplement*, 5 May 2006, in which Mahon writes about Coleridge's literary life with a mixture of admiration and pathos (p. 15).

7

'Just Another Twist in the Plot': Paul Muldoon's 'Madoc: A Mystery'

I

'*Madoc* started with Byron. I did a little edition of selected poems of Byron,' Paul Muldoon remarked in a 1994 interview. Responding to his interviewer's praise for the rhyme of *Bucephalus / syphilis* (wittily included in the section whose sur-title is '[Nietzsche]'), he also said: 'I'm a great fan of Byron, and I really like these totally crazy rhymes.' The interview is a medium in which the contemporary poet is able to act as surreptitious (or ostentatious) critic or champion of his own work, and one needs, especially with so wily a writer as Muldoon, to be careful about accepting too gratefully all proffered leads: crumbs from his beguiling if sometimes indigestible poetic feast. And, as Tim Kendall has argued, 'the roots of Muldoon's poem go further back, beyond the Byron edition'.[1] But it is clear that in his reconfigurations of Romantic comedy, Muldoon, like Auden and Kavanagh, owes much to the example of Byron, even if he refuses merely to imitate and ends up producing a poker-faced poem that prizes the unpinnable-down more than the satirically deadly. 'A lot of the time', he comments after his praise for Byron, 'I just love to say, "Let's see what happens. Just how near the edge can you go without dissolving into outright doggerel?" '[2] If in 'Madoc: A Mystery' (hereafter 'Madoc') he is at his most post-Romantic and arguably his most post-colonial, he is so in ways that reward an openness to 'what happens' in the poem's language, and what that language makes happen.

This linguistic openness accompanies a complexly uncommitted ethics. Whereas Byron attacks, Muldoon insinuates, rarely allowing fewer than two interpretations of a viewpoint. Byron's digressions serve at the very least to acquaint us with a speaker who is our witty companion. Moreover, he can tell a story even while performing Shandyesque feats of self-consciousness: in *Beppo*, in which Muldoon finds 'Byron at its brilliant best', the narrator asserts:

---

[1] Tim Kendall, *Paul Muldoon* (Bridgend: Seren, 1996); hereafter Kendall, p. 157.
[2] Lynn Keller, 'An Interview with Paul Muldoon. Conducted by Lynn Keller', *Contemporary Literature*, 35/1 (1994), quotations in paragraph on pp. 15, 18.

'But to my tale of Laura,—for I find | Digression is a sin, that by degrees | Becomes exceeding tedious to my mind, | And, therefore, may the reader too displease' (393–6).[3] Digressing, he confides; teasing, he narrates. Muldoon's characteristic lyric in 'Madoc' works at a beguiling tangent to Byron's mode of address. Frequently there is an air of quotation, of free indirect discourse, of relished immersion in the demands and possibilities of diction, grammar, and syntax. Delighting in slow-moving, enjambed sentences that pause at the ends of lines, so much poetic water gathering towards a long fall into yet another pool of bathos, deflation, or poker-faced irony, the poetry has a characteristically droll but not self-pleased air of attending to its own unfurlings. Muldoon, too, can tell a story, but his story is as much meta-narrative as narrative, as much about the possibilities of decoding and finding the ubiquitous key as about the retelling of real or imaginary events. Yet, while irony may be pervasive, it is hard to know how much such irony is at the service of the moral positions or literary stances that half edge into view: disapproval of colonialism, whether carried out by Europeans in America or, in a covert subtext, by the English in Ireland, or glancing criticism of the poetry of Seamus Heaney, associated through a number of echoes with Southey, as when we are told that 'Southey will stay completely in the dark' '[Malebranche]'.

An earlier poem, 'I Remember Sir Alfred', concludes with a description of 'a hare', 'dislodged' by Sir Alfred McAlpine, patron saint of road building. The hare 'goes by leaps and bounds', Muldoon writes, 'Across the grazing, | Here and there, | This way and that, by singleminded swervings'. 'Singleminded swervings', mimicked by the 'this way and that' movement of the lines, is a phrase that serves as a description of the trajectories taken by Muldoon's poems. They are forever mocking the view (expressed in 'I Remember Sir Alfred') that 'The shortest distance between two points | Is a straight line'. The word 'swervings' recalls the first of Harold Bloom's six revisionary ratios in *The Anxiety of Influence*, the Lucretian term *clinamen*, glossed in the epigraph to the relevant chapter from A. R. Ammons's poem 'The City Limits' as 'the guiltiest | swervings of the weaving heart' and by Bloom himself as the 'swerve' and as 'necessarily the central working concept of the theory of Poetic Influence': a theory which for Bloom exists in large part to explain the predicament and perilous achievements of those poets writing in the wake of the 'vast visionary tragedy' of Romanticism. Muldoon's dealings with Romantic poetry have more than a smack of 'singleminded swervings' about them. They are responsive, with their own wry twist, to Bloom's sense that there is in all acts of critical or creative interpretation a ''Pataphysical sense of the arbitrary', an 'apocalyptic

---

[3] Paul Muldoon, 'Introduction,' in *The Essential Byron* (New York: Ecco, 1989), p. 5.

absurdity'.[4] It is not the case that Muldoon can be made to fulfil Jarryesque laws of lawlessness or abide by the codes of Blakean irony or Beckettian absurdity. Rather, his way with words often appears to issue in a materialist come-uppance so far as high-falutin ideas or ideals are concerned. That is, as this chapter will argue, by no means the whole story, and yet, like the Auden of *Letter to Lord Byron*, Muldoon explores the refusal of reality to conform to human will or desire.

As the phrase which gives this chapter its title shows, Muldoon sees this refusal as reflected in language's ability to undercut itself. South, the poem's subsequent narrator, seeks to escape Unitel, a monolithic, Big Brother state; but mouthing the opening lines of 'Kubla Khan' (now serving as a password involving voice and facial recognition) gets him only so far. Romantic fantasy has been co-opted by the Orwellian state, and he will end up, cut to ribbons by razor-wire, as 'just another twist in the plot', where 'twist' wincingly revives a dead metaphor. The only liberation possible, one might hazard, is that offered by doubleness of meanings, and entrapment in 'Madoc' coexists with an almost frightening liberty of interpretation. Fantasy collides with history, the imaginative with the actual, the mental with the physical. 'Madoc' holds parallels, opposites, and contradictions in suspension through a parodic style that thrives on the liaisons set going by verbal and thematic rhyme or off-rhyme. Muldoon's declared master here is Byron, of whom he writes: 'Byron's mature style is wonderfully discursive, ranging from Aristotle through hitting the sack to hitting the bottle of sack, while relishing the rhyme on "Aristotle" and "bottle" along the way; he reminds us again and again that poetry can be serious without being solemn, that it might even be *fun*.'[5] The poem's riddles, its teasingly rhymed and cross-referencing lyrics that play poker-faced, post-modern games with the reader, represent a challenging version of a poetry that might 'be serious without being solemn' and 'might even be *fun*'.

As with Kavanagh, all the 'fun' lies in how Muldoon says a thing, since the poem's premiss is darkly fantastical. It imagines what might have happened had Coleridge and Southey carried through their Pantisocratic scheme and visited America. Real and imagined history interweave, the whole poem running 'parallel to the parallel | realm to which it is itself the only clue', as '[Pascal]' puts it. The notion of 'parallel' realms—possibly belittled even as it is articulated—relates to Muldoon's emphasis in *To Ireland, I*, of the specifically Irish 'idea of a parallel universe, a grounded groundlessness', an idea which he sees as offering 'an escape clause, a kind of psychological trapdoor, to a people

---

[4] Bloom, *Anxiety of Influence*, pp. [18], 42, 10, 42, 43. In the interview with Lynn Keller, Muldoon remarks: 'We're touching a little bit on Harold Bloom's theory. I'm not an expert on "the anxiety of influence," but I can see the argument for that', before he goes on to add the pluralist rider: 'Basically, I'm a person who can see some value in a great many of the theories that come floating by' (p. 8).

[5] Muldoon, 'Introduction' to *Essential Byron*, pp. 5–6.

from under whose feet the rug is constantly being pulled, often quite literally so'.⁶ The comment, like the reference to 'the parallel | realm', intrigues through its reworking of a longing crucial to Romanticism, the desire for 'some world far from ours', as Shelley has it, 'Where music and moonlight and feeling | Are one' ("To Jane: "The keen stars were twinkling"', 22–4). In '[Pascal]' the writing opens itself with darkly comic inventiveness to the infinite silence of the eternal spaces between the actual and the virtual; Jefferson is 'beside himself with glee', where 'beside himself' plays on a conventional phrase meaning 'excited' to suggest that he is somehow his own double, rather as in *Alastor* 'A Spirit seemed | To stand beside' the Poet (479–80). That he 'finishes off a carafe | | of his best Médoc', where the wine name half rhymes with the poem's title intimates that in the chasm between parallel realms lies the 'clue' to the poem's 'mystery' (its subtitle). The comment quoted from *To Ireland, I* casts light, too, on the sub-textual and sometimes overt concern in 'Madoc' with 'a people from under whose feet the rug is constantly being pulled'; among the poem's parallels is entanglement with post-colonial concerns as Muldoon plays his own variations on a central Romantic legacy: the twin sense of the work of art as autonomous and as reconfiguring the real.

Muldoon sums up the bewildering narrative, as he imagines representing the work to 'a Hollywood producer', in the following terms:

this is a story of two youthful poets who set up a little colony in North America and, for various reasons, went their separate ways. One [Southey] turned into bit of a demagogue, or worse, a despot—as Frost says, 'I never dared be radical when young for fear of being conservative when old'—and the other [Coleridge] subsided into drug abuse. . . . [Coleridge] joins, briefly, the Lewis and Clark expedition, then finds himself in the western part of the United States moving from tribe to tribe, while the other, Robert Southey, embarks on this disastrous course of self-aggrandizement and increasing self-delusion.

This clarification ('When you put it like that, it's very, very simple') is poker-faced. Muldoon dispenses with the bantering first-person narrator of Byron's *Don Juan* and Auden's *Letter to Lord Byron*: his story is, as he tells us in the same interview, 'told within the framework of a descendant, we think, of Southey's. It's set a little bit in the future, and it's all retrieved from the back of his eye by some remarkable device, which will probably be available to us very shortly, and this guy [South] has a very strange vision of the world.'⁷ This 'strange vision' involves ditching the lyric self and seeing perception as unavoidably technologized; the Aeolian harp has become an iPod-like machine scrambling and rearranging. Muldoon or South houses the supposed cerebral functionings of the latter under appropriate or pseudo-appropriate philosophical

---

⁶ Muldoon, *To Ireland, I*, p. 7. ⁷ Keller, 'Interview', pp. 11, 12, 11.

sur-titles—as in '[Heraclitus]', which links the poem's narrative technique (images derived from the 'remarkable device' or 'retinagraph' attached to Southey's eyeball) to the philosophy of continual flux:

> So that, though it may seem somewhat improbable,
> all that follows
> flickers and flows
> from the back of his right eyeball.

This mode of perception mocks, yet sanctions, the subjective view of the Romantic. South's 'eyeball' may not be 'Transparent' in an Emersonian sense; but, as a means of connecting with the 'improbable', it serves as a guide to post-Romantic marvels.

Southey's own *Madoc* (1805) is an officially pro-colonialist work that tells the legendary story of how Madoc, a twelfth-century Welsh prince, sailed to America and, in the words of the poem's epigraph, 'overthrew | The bloody altars of idolatry, | And planted in its fanes triumphantly | The cross of Christ'.[8] I say 'officially' to take on board Christopher Smith's admittedly qualified suggestion that we read Southey's *Madoc* as 'a *cautionary* tale, which ... exposes the never-ending human and natural cost of inter-cultural struggles for territories and resources'. 'Was that', as Smith goes on to ask, 'what Southey intended?'[9] Muldoon plays fast and loose with intentions, but his version never overlooks the 'cost of inter-cultural struggles for territories and resources'. The story of Madoc enjoyed currency in the sixteenth century, supporting English claims to the New World. Prince Madoc was supposed to be, in Hugh Brogan's words, 'either the ancestor of the Indians or the begetter of their tongue', and, as Brogan notes in a remark relevant to 'Madoc', 'the quest for Welsh-speaking Indians was to last into the nineteenth century'.[10] In '[Dee]' Muldoon quotes from Southey's account of '*The historical facts on which this poem is founded*', 'facts' which include Madoc's response to the disputed succession of his father's kingdom ('*north Wales*'): '*Madoc . . . abandoned his barbarous country, and sailed away to the west in search of some better resting-place*'. Madoc, for Muldoon and, possibly, for Southey himself, is a forerunner of Pantisocratic ambitions. Indeed, in '*better resting-place*', Muldoon suggests the link between the longing for a Romantic 'elsewhere' at the heart even of a seemingly egalitarian enterprise such as Pantisocracy and proto-colonial exploration. At the same time, Muldoon's method allows him to depict without endorsing a 'singleminded' moral perspective. The only thing that is 'singleminded', in fact, about 'Madoc'

---

[8] Robert Southey, *Madoc*, ed. Lynda Pratt, vol. 2 of *Robert Southey: Poetical Works, 1793–1810*, gen. ed. Lynda Pratt, 5 vols. (London: Pickering & Chatto, 2004).

[9] Christopher J. Smith, *A Quest for Home: Reading Robert Southey* (Liverpool: Liverpool University Press, 1997), p. 327.

[10] Hugh Brogan, *The Penguin History of the USA*, 2nd edn (London: Penguin, 1999), p. 4.

is its opposition to single-mindedness. As already suggested, it would be too single-minded to ascribe such opposition solely to Byron's influence. Rather, Muldoon pursues a form of writing that identifies intertextuality with inspired acts of imaginative serendipity. That said, Byron's and Muldoon's common ground is that sketched by the Romantic poet in *Don Juan* (XIV. 3), where the reader is at once told and challenged: 'For me, I know nought; nothing I deny, | Admit, reject, contemn; and what know *you*?' (17–18): 'know nought', that is, as a metaphysical certainty. At the same time, Byronic forthrightness gives way in 'Madoc' to Muldoonian drollery.

The volume (*Madoc*) in which 'Madoc' appears includes a number of mischievous preludes to the long poem. In one of these pieces, 'The Briefcase', Muldoon writes a sonnet, or a slippery version of a sonnet (its fourteen lines are disposed in a repeated quatrain and tercet), in which the poet's 'eelskin' briefcase threatens a tricksy metamorphosis into a 'supple' creature capable of heading out of the poet's control towards the 'sea'. 'By which', the speaker adds, 'I mean the "open" sea.' That '"open" sea' might stand for a place of endlessly possible interpretation, a reflexive reading encouraged by the fact that the briefcase, which the poet dare not put down for fear of it 'slinking' off towards the sea, 'contained only the first | inkling of this poem'. 'This poem' might be 'The Briefcase', but it might also be the long poem 'Madoc'; and in 'The Briefcase' Muldoon re-stages a post-modern version of the vagaries and uncontrollability of inspiration offered by Coleridge in his Preface to the published text of 'Kubla Khan'.

II

'Madoc' may seem to subject Romantic dreams of transcendence to relentless derision; yet the derision is so relentless that the reader suspects a residue of attachment to those dreams. What for Auden is 'The Trap', an abstract, quasi-Marxist concept, manifests itself cruelly as a physical trap in '[Anaxagoras]', in which 'Daniel Boone | | comes on a beaver caught in two separate | traps', where the trap is triggered by the line-ending. The poem continues: 'It has gnawed both drubs | to the bone. | | This beaver, like the woodchuck, is an emissary | from the Great Spirit.' Off-rhyme is itself a trap that points up how 'separate' are the worlds of physical matter and longed-for 'Spirit'. Muldoon relies on techniques of mock-portentousness such as the use of 'This' in 'This beaver', the deixis seeming to claim for the beaver a special status, a status that is both confirmed and held up for sceptical inspection in the assertion that follows. The beaver's role as 'emissary | from the Great Spirit' is rendered problematic by the deadpan tone, the distracting off-rhyme of 'emissary' with the earlier 'Missouri', and the odd mix in the diction: if 'Great Spirit' conjures up the religious beliefs of the American Indian, the Latinate 'emissary' derives from a different culture. Daniel Boone is himself an ambiguous figure, at once pioneer of future settlement and having more than a little in common with the Native Indians whom he fought (he was, in fact, court-marshalled though acquitted for supposedly conspiring with the Indians and being a British agent).[11] Byron praises Boone in *Don Juan* (VIII. 61 and following), as an example of a figure who retreated from the corruptions of civilization; Muldoon repeats this praise, *Don Juan*, VIII. 61, composing the central section of '[Carnap]', but his praise seems ironical, given that '[Carnap]' is, in a highly Byronic way, debunking the creator of *Don Juan*. Byron 'himself is his own ball-and-chain', enslaved by his need to sublimate feelings of shame about his clubfoot. Entrapment connects the disparate sections; freedom, as so often in 'Madoc', is exposed as a fiction. Boone is seen by Byron as 'killing nothing but a bear or buck', but Muldoon implies that the American frontiersman thereby shares in the will to violence which pervades 'Madoc'.

If here the pendulum swings in the direction of undercutting a Romantic dream of freedom, however ironized that original dream may itself have been (it serves mainly as a means of attacking 'thy great joys Civilization!', *Don Juan*, VIII. 68. 538), elsewhere—especially when Coleridge features in the poem—it oscillates unsteadily to and fro. Here is the first of the three sections of '[Feuerbach]', the precursor text of '[Quine]', already discussed in Chapter 6:

> The tinkle
> of an Aeolian harp.
>
> Eels.
> Elvers.
>
> An inkle
> of black crêpe.

Engels wrote of Feuerbach:

Then came Feuerbach's *Essence of Christianity*. With one blow it pulverised the contradiction, in that without circumlocutions it placed materialism on the throne again. Nature exists independently of all philosophy. It is the foundation upon which we human beings, ourselves products of nature, have grown up. Nothing exists outside nature and man, and the higher beings our religious fantasies have created are only the fantastic reflection of our own essence.[12]

'Nature exists independently of all philosophy' might be one of Muldoon's themes in 'Madoc', yet Engels comes round at the end of this passage to confirming the intuition of many Romantic writers; Blake, a champion of the poetic imagination, traces in *The Marriage of Heaven and Hell* the process by which 'men forgot that All deities reside in the human breast' (p. 38). Muldoon's poem

---

[11] Ibid, 224–5.
[12] Frederick Engels, *Ludwig Feuerbach and the End of Classical German Philosophy* (Moscow: Progress, 1946), pp. 19–20.

cannily explores what in Engels is inadvertent ambivalence. '[Feuerbach]' starts, 'The tinkle | of an Aeolian harp'; the word 'tinkle' discrediting the visionary music of Coleridge's famous conversational poem 'The Eolian Harp'. Then two lines follow, each made of a single noun: 'Eels. | Elvers.' The lines possibly refer to Montale's 'L'anguilla' ('The Eel') in which the Italian poet fuses matter and spirit in a dizzying synthesis. 'The Eel' values, in its darting enjambments and love of the unpredictable, 'the spark announcing | that all sets forth when all that's set forth | is a charred thing, a buried stump', in Muldoon's own translation. The lines that might serve as an epigraph for a post-Romantic poetry that asserts a 'spark' of hope, however ambiguous, in the face of destruction.[13] The poem also provides what Francesco Zambon calls 'the most achieved refiguration Montale has offered of his own poetry', Zambon pointing to the very Muldoonian fact that 'L'ANGUILLA is an anagram of LA LINGUA'.[14] Closer to home, the short lines take us back to the eel-like 'The Briefcase' containing the first 'inkling' of itself. That poem is dedicated to Heaney, and the reference to 'Eels' forms part of the intertextual game played with Heaney's work in 'Madoc', alluding to Heaney's 'Vision', the seventh poem in his 'A Lough Neagh Sequence' (from *A Door into the Dark*).[15] In an ironic reworking of Romantic 'vision', Heaney turns the sight of eels moving 'through the grass like hatched fears | | Towards the water' into a nightmarish sense of 'the horrid cable' binding him, 'his world's live girdle'. Heaney, often thought of as a Wordsworthian celebrant of place, here, suggests a fear of being trapped. Muldoon's equivalent to Heaney's 'cable' is a teasingly weightless 'inkle | of black crêpe', where the rhyme between 'tinkle' and 'inkle' offers a comically post-Romantic parallel to rhymes such as 'things' and 'imaginings' in Shelley's 'Mont Blanc' (version A, 139, 143). Heaney's 'horrid cable' turns into a potential thread through a labyrinth in Muldoon in the second and third sections of '[Feuerbach]':

> His pirogue
> reels
>
> through a sulphurous
> brook

---

[13] Translation quoted from Jamie McKendrick (ed.), *The Faber Book of Twentieth-Century Italian Poems* (London: Faber, 2004); first published in Paul Muldoon, *Moy Sand and Gravel* (London: Faber, 2004).

[14] Francesco Zambon, *L'iride nel fango: L'anguilla di Eugenio Montale* (Palma: Nuova Pratiche Editrice, 1994); quoted in Eugenio Montale, *Collected Poems, 1920–1954*, trans. and annotated Jonathan Galassi (New York: Farrar, Straus and Giroux, 1999), p. 595.

[15] Tim Kendall detects a 'sly allusion' to the second poem in the sequence, 'Beyond Sargasso' (Kendall, p. 153).

> What if Coleridge were to plait
> a geyser's
>
> cobalt-
> azure
>
> into a less than ideal
> rope whereby
>
> to wheedle-
> warp
>
> himself into the well, well, well
> of his own fontanelle.

Muldoon privileges the autonomous life of his words, which, over and above their contribution to 'meaning', seem to enjoy prior existence as sonic and verbal units, experienced in a delicious, baffling series of moments. His lines come close to parodying the idea of the poetic line; sometimes they exaggerate the enjambing function of the line-break as words hang before us; sometimes they invite a degree of scrutiny that seemingly leaves the reader very little the wiser, as when the neologistic 'wheedle-| warp' is broken across a line: little the wiser, that is, except for a heightened relish of possible double meanings. Here, for example, after 'wheedle', with its suggestions of 'insidious coaxing', 'warp' brings into play the notion of a subsequent making 'crooked or perverted' (*OED*); at the same time, it calls to mind the idea of a 'rope used in ... warping' (the process of stretching threads 'lengthwise in a loom to be crossed by the weft' (*OED*)). The twin meanings correspond to the poem's fascination with the ways in which the physical and the metaphysical or metaphorical criss-cross and entwine. Coleridge is imagined lowering himself into his own 'fontanelle', an imagining which involves gibe and admiration. The gibe is there in the word 'fontanelle', which has regressive associations, since it means the 'membranous space in an infant's skull at angles of parietal bones' (*OED*). That the 'fontanelle' rhymes with 'the well, well, well' sparks further suggestions. This 'well' may well be the 'deep well of unconscious cerebration' in the phrase of Henry James which John Livingston Lowes applies to the workings of Coleridgean creativity.[16] But such an allusion coexists with the tut-tutting implied by 'well, well, well', an idiom expressing a cluck of mild disapproval—here, one presumes, of the poet's re-entry into his own skull: an idiom which finds a precedent in Coleridge's own openings to 'This Lime-Tree Bower My Prison' and 'Dejection: An Ode'.

If Coleridge is going somewhere in his drunken boat of inspiration, his 'pirogue' (or 'piragua', that is, a 'long narrow canoe made from a single tree-trunk') may be guiding him, rather as the boat voyage of Shelley's *Alastor*

---

[16] John Livingston Lowes, *The Road to Xanadu: A Study in the Ways of the Imagination* (1927; London: Pan, 1978), p. 52.

guides the Poet, only towards his doom, here a distinctly unwelcoming 'sulphurous | brook'. Yet, if the rope, in section three, is less than 'ideal', there is a Rimbaudian alchemy involved in plaiting 'a geyser's | | cobalt- | azure'. Muldoon does not end the section with a question mark, despite opening with the Coleridgean enquiry, 'What if', and the absence of the question mark means that we dwell on the process rather than the outcome of the events described. Coleridge opens up 'The Eolian Harp' to new vistas when he enquires, 'And what if all of animated nature | Be but organic Harps diversely fram'd . . .?' (44–5). Muldoon leaves the door ajar; Coleridge's efforts may 'less than ideal' in the double sense of being necessarily bound up with the material and not as impressive as they might be.

But they hold out, in however minimal a form, the possibility of renewal. The ironies and deflations of 'Madoc' are evident. Yet Coleridge is associated with a shaking-up of the factual kaleidoscope that gives him much in common with Muldoon. Although Bucephalus, the talking stallion taken on board when the Pantisocrats stop off in Ireland, is made to sound absurd when he opines 'that *Madoc* means the "greatest, greatest good"' ('[Mill]'), or when he asserts posthumously, in a later poem, '[Heidegger]', the most vaunting of his attempts to claim a Celtic bedrock for American culture, that 'Madoc himself is, above all, emblematic | | of our desire to go beyond ourselves', Coleridge goes beyond himself in ways that complicate the poetry's irony. Indeed, for Kendall, 'Coleridge unlocks the mystery of Madoc by discovering that to locate what Muldoon has called the true "home" or "inheritance" requires not fidelity to a tribe or fixed identity, but escape from them'.[17] If the comment is suggestive, Coleridge's 'escape' involves regression as well as a desirable fluidity of identity, as is shown by his sense that the Spokane chief's wife ('lent' by the chief in exchange for a Sheffield knife and some kinnikinnick) is a version of his boyhood love, Mary Evans.

Surreal, nightmarish, and hallucinatory, the career of the Coleridge figure suggests Muldoon's latent sympathy. Coleridge talks with a Westernized Indian chief, Joseph Brant, now 'nominally "King of the Mohawks"' ('[Occam]'), after undergoing a journey akin to that envisaged in his own 'Kubla Khan'; he is bullied 'into | the formal gardens and unfathomable fountains | | of this, the summer palace | of the Old Man of the Mountains' ('[Maimonides]'). The passage thematizes the poem's fascination with Romantic Orientalism; those 'formal gardens and unfathomable fountains' represent an imaginative fantasy to which Muldoon is knowingly responsive. Elsewhere, Coleridge is represented by Muldoon in ways that cut for and against his role as representative of the metamorphosizing poetic imagination. In the second part of '[Whitehead]',

[17] Kendall, p. 170.

Muldoon quotes from a 1797 letter sent by Coleridge to Cottle: '*I am fearful that Southey will begin to rely too much on* story & event *in his poems to the neglect of those* lofty imaginings *that are peculiar to, & definitive of, the* POET.' Muldoon would have enjoyed the fact that the conventions of print when dealing with an italicized quotation mean that the phrases italicized (or underlined) by Coleridge appear in roman typeface, so that 'lofty imaginings' pit themselves against 'story & event' as though the successful outcome for the former of that battle were, indeed, constitutive of the nature of a 'POET'. But Coleridge's 'lofty imaginings' look as bumptious in 'Madoc' as in the original, where they precede an account by him of the '20 years' of labours necessary for the successful undertaking of 'an Epic Poem'.[18] The status of 'lofty imaginings' is perilous in 'Madoc', since its 'imaginings' often deflate or debunk the notion of 'loftiness'.

At the same time, Coleridge seems a Muldoonian surrogate, albeit a somewhat hapless one, when he undergoes experiences that bear in hallucinatory ways on his own writing. In '[Gramsci]', for instance, Muldoon goes on a fishing expedition, turning up echoes of the Romantic poet's work, as 'Coleridge casts a paternoster into the murky stream'. A 'paternoster' is 'weighted fishing tackle with hooks at intervals' (*OED*); it also brings the Lord's Prayer to mind in a poem about forgetting, a source of cultural authority lost in the wilderness where Coleridge 'has himself only a remote || idea of his whereabouts'. 'Himself' earns its place as an echo of Bucephalus's account, in the previous poem, 'of our desire to go beyond ourselves'. Coleridge is lost in the here-and-now, a confusion that mocks his lack of clarity yet indicates his inability sturdily to claim a stable identity, an inability which counts in his favour. He reprises Southey's earlier blankness about the burning down of the Pantisocratic encampment by the Ulster Protestant scout Cinnamond; there, Southey takes a while before he has 'even the faintest idea | of what's happened'. But the two poets' responses to dislocation differ drastically. Southey's reaction is to build Southeyopolis, a none-too-subtle giving of form to the siege mentality of Protestant Ulster. In Coleridge's case, the 'remote || idea' is both colloquial idiom and challenging to be heard as a ghostly intimation of the Romantic poet's intermittent flirtation with Platonic Ideas; indeed, chapter 10 of *Biographia Literaria* contains an abstruse footnote by Coleridge on the true meaning of 'idea' which, *pace* Hume, meant for Plato in the plural 'mysterious powers, living, seminal, formative, and exempt from time' (i. 97).

Muldoon sets this intertextual filament quivering, even as his phrasing secures itself from any privileging of the Platonic. The centre of the poem might be said to demonstrate a self-reflexive sense of coming to a pause, of

---

[18] Samuel Taylor Coleridge, *Selected Letters*, ed. H. J. Jackson (Oxford: Oxford University Press, 1987), p. 58.

'the mind's self-experience' in Coleridge's phrase.[19] Muldoon proffers allusions to the presiding image of 'The Eolian Harp' and the end of 'Frost at Midnight' when he has Coleridge unable to remember why he cut up wind-chimes 'and strung them like icicles | | in the thatch'. In 'Frost at Midnight' Coleridge imagines as one of the possibilities through which divinely sponsored harmony between humans and nature shows itself the very scene that surrounds him, one in which 'the secret ministry of frost' turns the 'eave-drops' into 'silent icicles, | Quietly shining to the quiet Moon' (72, 70, 73–4). Muldoon allows these associations a brief phantasmal life; they crowd on to the poem's touchlines, before a bleaker, post-modern wind blows: 'Still no take | on the line'. The line is the fishing line, but also the poetic line and the line that leads from Coleridge to Muldoon. Amusingly, Coleridge turns from his paternoster to some kind of drug, 'his so-called Paddy Nostrum' in search of inspiration.

'Madoc' may evidently set Coleridge against Southey, druggy assimilator into Native American culture against despotic colonialist; but, more covertly, it invites us to weigh the claims of Coleridge as poetic avatar with those of Byron. Strikingly, '[Gramsci]' gives way to '[Carnap]' and ['Benjamin]' in which Byron cuts less of a dash than might be expected. Even his sexual encounter with 'The Contessa' turns quickly into textual byplay as we learn that 'a little dribble down her chin | is the only sign of their earlier antics | when she winkled the "semen" out of "semantics"' ('[Carnap]'). The result is of subtraction from Byronic self-idealization; a story he might have told Murray and his friends about 'tooling' in a swashbucklingly man-of-the-world letter is, when recounted by Muldoon, aloofly comic. The effect is to laugh at Byron rather than with him. Coleridge's escape into drugs seems, by contrast, generous in its trust in new possibilities. So, in '[Huxley]' the doors of perception open, and their opening is not only ironic in its impact, as the word 'himself' is used again, this time with a favourable import: 'Coleridge is himself the blossom in the bud | of peyote'. Muldoon's inflections rarely escape an ironic leash, but this hallucinatory miniaturization reads like a post-modern reversal of Coleridge's own dilations, as when in 'Religious Musings' he asserts: ' 'Tis the sublime of man, | Our noontide Majesty, to know ourselves | Parts and proportions of one wondrous soul' (126–8). Subsequent sections seesaw between Byron and Coleridge; '[Bakhtin]' may even offer, through its sur-title, a suggestion of hybrid modes of discourse, yet the poem appears to prefer Coleridge's minute observation of 'the glair- | | glim | of mica and feldspar | | on the collar | of Southey's closely-knit byrnie' to the fact that 'the flossofer | declaims | | from Byron'. Muldoon himself is about to quote stanzas from Byron, so the 'flossofer' is on uncomfortably intimate terms with the philosopher, or cod-philosopher, organizing 'Madoc'.

---

[19] Coleridge, *Biographia Literaria*, i. 124.

Coleridge and Byron do precariously unite in this phase of the poem as adversaries of Southey. At times Muldoon appears to take up the satiric rapier and cudgels of *Don Juan* and *The Vision of Judgment*, quoting, as indicated, whole stanzas from Byron, as in '[Marcuse]', which consists of the stanza beginning 'He had written praises of a regicide' from *The Vision of Judgment*, or '[Gadamer]', made up of the stanza from the same poem opening 'He had sung against all battles, and again'. By this stage, Southey has turned from Pantisocratic idealist into a Kurtz-like colonial despot, 'couchant on a tavelin | Of vairs and minivers' ('[Bergson]'), where the mincing sounds mime a corrupt self-indulgence. Southey is still able to experience anguished doubt about the idea that there are Welsh-speaking descendants of Madoc in America, when, in '[Whitehead]', entitled solely, one presumes, because of the subject of the last line, he 'wakes in a cold sweat; | penguins don't have white heads', thus discrediting the false etymology propounded by Bucephalus, talking horse and fanatical believer in the Celtic origins of America. But if there is a sly amusement that Southey, the would-be Pantisocrat, developed authoritarian leanings and into a full-blown despot, there is also a sense that Byron's hatred for him emerges from hurt and insecurity. Southey is the villain of Muldoon's piece, but not in a straightforward way. The constant quotation from his and Coleridge's 'The Devil's Walk' may cut against Southey's subsequent repression of his radical past, but it links the adversaries in a common diabolism. The hobbling Byron's humiliating sprawl over a cobble in a Pisan street ('As he sprawls there, a group of boys | begins to jeer, "*Diavolo*"') leads him to write to Southey 'to propose | he either retract the "Satanic" canard | or give him satisfaction. (This missive's intercepted by Kinnaird)' '[Benjamin]'. The episode, as imagined by Muldoon, suggests that Byron's challenge to Southey is fuelled by the need to compensate for his shaming sprawl in a Pisan street.

Malcom Kelsall has written shrewdly on Byron's need in his poetry 'to reconstitute his own heroic status', and that this 'heroic status' had to have about it an oppositional quality. 'The liberationist ethic requires the hegemonic tendency to justify its opposition,' writes Kelsall (with Jefferson in mind).[20] Byron, one might speculate, hated Southey because in Southey he saw his ambivalent other. Certainly, at points in 'Madoc' it is as though Muldoon has tapped into that understanding of Byron's complex dealings with Southey shown by Jerome McGann: McGann comments that 'in drawing the portrait of the "sad trimmer" poet (*Don Juan*, III. 82) in the likeness of Robert Southey, Byron's poem creates an unusual palimpsest in which the faces of Southey and Byron, those arch-antagonists, are superimposed on each other. The two men

---

[20] Malcom Kelsall, 'Byron's Politics', in *The Cambridge Companion to Byron*, ed. Drummond Bone (Cambridge: Cambridge University Press, 2004), pp. 51, 54.

are, in the full meaning of that paradoxical phrase, "Twin opposites".[21] Muldoon's poem is uncannily alive to the twinnings that occur between apparent opposites, and it ends up close to 'the flaunting of its own contradictions' which McGann sees as constituting the integrity-salvaging nature of 'romantic irony' in *Don Juan*. Muldoon's post-modernist ironies, however, have forfeited the longing apparent in Byron's text 'to transcend its own contradictions'.[22] In 'Madoc' virtually all is quotation and intertextual play; the author affects to abdicate his role as ethical arbiter, ghosting the poem's wraith-like voices. When in '[Lacan]', 'The wraith pokes its tongue in Southey's ear— | "Rhythm in all thought, and joyance everywhere"— | before leaving only a singe on the air', Coleridge's great affirmation in 'The Eolian Harp' reduces to a mocking reminder of once-held ideals. That Coleridge added the lines in an errata slip to *Sibylline Leaves* (1817) only emphasizes the gaps and lacks of which the section speaks: the main gap is that between word and reality; the principal lack is of any capacity to incarnate Romantic ideals. We are left only with quotation, the hallmark of the post-modern text, in which former imaginative fires leave 'only a singe on the air'.

III

Yet that elegiac undercurrent implies that Muldoon is not simply or complacently happy to retreat into textuality. The knowingly derided 'desire to go beyond ourselves' is both the core of this decentred poem and the aura that haunts it. This desire has something in common with Romantic dreams of transcendence; it speaks, less flatteringly, of the will to extend territorial ownership or to plunder the land of others, a strong motif throughout the poem; and it expresses, metapoetically, the poet's longing to escape particular perspectives. The use of Thomas Moore's work is a case in point. '[Bentham]' quotes from Thomas Moore in a way that allies Romantic 'fancy' with slavery. The first stanza consists, with variations, of four lines printed in Moore's 'Epistle VII, To Thomas Hume Esq., M. D., from the City of Washington':

> *In fancy now, beneath the twilight gloom,*
> *come, let me lead thee o'er this 'second Rome',*
> *this embryo capital, where fancy sees*
> *squares in morasses, obelisks in trees.*

---

[21] Jerome J. McGann, 'Lord Byron's Twin Opposites of Truth [*Don Juan*]', in *Byron*, ed. Jane Stabler, Longman Critical Readers (London and New York: Longman, 1998), p. 42.

[22] Ibid. For an excellent and relevant discussion, see Stabler, 'Byron, Postmodernism and Intertextuality', in *Cambridge Companion to Byron*, pp. 265–84.

Moore's tone, as befits a satirist of American Utopian hopes, is sardonic: the '*obelisks*' serve as one of Muldoon's motifs suggesting aestheticizing dreams of grandeur, and appear in a quotation from Southey's *Thalaba* ('The fluted cypresses | rear'd up their living obelisks'), used on three occasions, including the closing poem. Muldoon allows Moore's satirical rhetoric its own space and voice, and between the one Irish poet's and the other's view of America there is some affinity. Moore writes in the Preface to *Epistles, Odes, and Other Poems* (1806) that he 'went to America with prepossessions by no means unfavourable, and, indeed, rather indulged in many of those illusive ideas with respect to the purity of the government, and the primitive happiness of the people, which I had early imbibed in my native country'. But, he asserts, 'I was completely disappointed in every flattering expectation which I had formed.'[23] Muldoon pokes fun at Moore as well as drawing fully on his forebear's satirical accents, depicting him as a literary pole-climber, largely through struttingly empty duels that result in strategically valuable friendships, and one assumes that he will have noted that Moore's disillusionment extends to 'the American Indian', treated, in his view, in too 'flattering' a light by Jefferson. Later on, in the poem from which Muldoon quotes, Moore writes:

> Oh! was a world so bright but born to grace
> Its own half-organized, half-minded race
> Of weak barbarians swarming o'er its breast,
> Like vermin gendered on the lion's crest?
> Were none but brutes to call that soil their home,
> Where none but demi-gods should dare to roam?
> Or, worse, thou mighty world! oh! doubly worse,
> Did Heaven design thy lordly land to nurse
> The motley dregs of every distant clime,
> Each blast of anarchy and taint of crime
> Which Europe shakes from her perturbèd sphere,
> In full malignity to rankle here?

Muldoon does not spare us the details of the savage acts perpetrated by the American Indians, yet 'Madoc' treats the American Indians with sympathy and can be regarded as an elegy for them.[24] Moore's Whiggish scorn for the 'half-organized, half-minded race' of the Indians looks fatuous when set against

---

[23] Thomas Moore, *The Poetical Works of Thomas Moore, Reprinted from the Early Editions, with Explanatory Notes, Etc.* The 'Albion' Edition (London and New York: Frederick Warne Co., n.d.), p. 97. This edition is used for the present author's quotations from Moore's poems. Muldoon's quotations from Moore differ in details.

[24] For this view, see Clair Wills, *Reading Paul Muldoon* (Newcastle upon Tyne: Bloodaxe, 1998), p. 156. Wills adds the crucial point that 'it is impossible to ignore the new energies which are released by the clash of cultures, languages and verbal styles which occurs throughout the poem'; ibid.

'[Spinoza]', which consists of a letter from Red Jacket, an Indian chief whose ironies work at the expense of the white settler: he sends his thanks to the white men for '*their good wishes towards us in attempting to teach us your religion. Perhaps your religion may be peculiarly adapted to your condition. You say that you destroyed the Son of the Great Spirit. Perhaps this is the merited cause of all your troubles and misfortunes.*'

Muldoon's 'Madoc' is post-Romantic, in that it questions whether the imagination is able to resist or is in cahoots with fantasies of colonial ownership and cultural origins. It allows Pantisocratic fantasies to play themselves out, sometimes entwining themselves with the serendipitous rhymes of history. Three historical Welsh-Americans—Meriwether Lewis, John Evans, and Thomas Jefferson—all feature in the poem, Evans appearing as a would-be rediscoverer of 'Welsh Indians' and as a figure parallel both to the talking horse Bucephalus, an extreme nationalist (in Northern Irish terms), and Alexander Cinnamond, 'the Scots- | Irish scout', who leads the party to 'Ulster' and 'fondles a tobacco- | pouch made from [a] scrotal sac': Cinnamond is one of those for whom human sovereignty is a key belief. Or, as he puts it at the end of '[Protagoras]': 'Mon is the mezjur of all thungs.' The pleasure taken there in mimicking Cinnamond's Ian Paisley-like accent is characteristic of the poem's delight in the 'thunginess' of language, caught also in the record of Whitehouse, one of the members of the Lewis and Clark expedition in '[Schelling]': '*These Savages has the Strangest language of any we have ever Seen. They appear to us to have an Empediment in their Speech or bur on their tongue. We take these Savages to be the Welch Indians if their be any Such.*' Such a collage technique captures the unadorned authenticity of fantasy, as a motive working behind exploration and settlement. Yet, if it supplies a groundedness for fantasy, it suggests, too, its groundlessness, leaving us with only the material signifier, illiteracies and all. The unbearable groundlessness of language is another motif of the poem, one that quietly ghosts its celebration of different discourses, manifesting itself in the Chebutykinesque refrain 'de dum de dum', present in '[Schiller]' and in poems such as '[Copernicus]', where 'De dum', with its mockery of an iambic beat alternates with the exalted 'Te Deum' associated with Pantisocratic hopes. All human hopes reduce to 'de dum', a meaningless ou-boum of a sound, as meaningless as the compulsion to fight wars, each particular, all resolving into a seeming inevitability; so, in '[Anaxagoras]', Muldoon writes, 'In the light of the X Y Z affair | America and France are limbering up for war.'

Elsewhere, language mimes a quicksilver vanishing act, its questions, as in '[Aenesidemus]', 'What are we to make of . . . ?', implying that causes and consequences are so multifarious they defy decoding. This poem begins 'We doubt even that we doubt', alluding to the scepticism about scepticism that one finds in Byron's 'So little do we know what we're about in | This world, I doubt if doubt itself be doubting' (*Don Juan*, IX. 135–6). Yet in Muldoon's words the reader can hear what Bakhtin calls 'intonational quotation marks',[25] as the poem studiously asks about Sara Coleridge's capture or voluntary flight and the trail followed by Bucephalus. The final stanza strikes a typical note: 'In any case, both | trails are already cold, | both almost certainly false.' In the poem, ghostly miniature narratives spark into life and gutter: for example, Sara's feelings for her children and her motives for leaving (if she 'did go willingly'). So, too, do philosophical themes: are people capable of agency (later when Coleridge meets the King of the Mohicans the same issue of free will is raised, but raised parodically)? The question of free will is, in fact, among the poem's major themes, one that bears on its relationship with its Romantic roots. In 'The Key', one of the volume's preliminary pieces before 'Madoc', the speaker comments: 'These past six months I've sometimes run a little ahead of myself, but mostly I lag behind, my footfalls already pre-empted by their echoes.' The opening of 'Burnt Norton' comes to mind in this Bloomian moment of *apophrades*—if echoes pre-empt footfalls, the author is somehow displaced from any role as originator of meaning. At the same time, one may also read the lines as asserting the primacy of Muldoonian echoes. There may, too, be a chime with Homi Bhabha's idea of the 'time-lag', created by what Bhabha calls 'the return of the subject' and involving 'an agency that seeks revision and reinscription'. Indeed, the interruptions of narrative and re-imaginings of event and history in 'Madoc' speak of an impulse towards 'liminal interrogation', in Bhabha's phrase, though Muldoon might be not wholly comfortable with Bhabha's outlawing of 'the liberal ironist' for whom, in Bhabha's view, 'an empowering strategy' is never available.[26]

Muldoon's ironies may not uncomplicatedly offer an 'empowering strategy' for post-colonial liberation. But he breathes new, if post-modernist, life into the Romantic quest poem, even if linguistically the poem performs the impossibility of escaping its own enigmatic codes. So, the linsey woolsey from which the teeny-weeny key is hung that might open the valise containing the code finally deciphered as 'CROTONA' means both 'a dress material of coarse wool' and 'a strange medley in talk or action or nonsense' (*OED*), the latter approximating a description of Sara's Coleridge's quasi-Joycean babble. Just as Byron's sole positive in *Don Juan* seems to be the poetry itself, 'A versified Aurora Borealis, | Which flashes o'er a waste and icy clime' (VII. 2. 11–12), so Muldoon's poem is, in Clair Wills's words, 'an epic of language, a story told not just

---

[25] Mikhail Bakhtin, 'From the Prehistory of Novelistic Discourse', in *Modern Criticism and Theory*, 2nd edn., ed. David Lodge, rev. and expanded by Nigel Wood (Harlow: Longman, 2000), p. 125.
[26] Homi K. Bhabha, *The Location of Culture* (1994; London and New York: Routledge, 2004), pp. 274, 275.

through, but about language'.²⁷ Kendall makes the good point that Muldoon, aware of language as a 'weapon of colonisation', tries to redress the balance, packing the poem with Native American diction.²⁸ But pleasure in language is rarely complacent; even when an implicitly self-reflexive epigraph for 'Madoc' and its relationship with Romantic poetry emerges, Bucephalus's '"*Eadem,* de dum, *sed aliter*"', the idea that the poem is 'the same but other' is interrupted by the travestying 'de dum' and mocked by the fact that the speaker 'strains for effect' ('[Scaliger]'); later, Southey's nib is 'stiff with grume, de dum', having been stuck into Cinnamond's eyes, and language more generally is rarely able to uncouple itself from violence and power.

With a seemingly urbane humour, much of the language swithers between the shelter of words and the horror of physical violence. The section ('[Burnet]') devoted to the fate of one of the Pantisocratic band, Burnett, gagged by his own penis after Cinnamond's raid, is a graphic example: the grotesquely imagined execution comes across through mincing off-rhymes that are themselves linguistically poised 'on the brink | of speech' even as they describe the inability to speak.²⁹ Romantic rhetoric—here a Wordsworthian song of 'the inherent worth | of the earth'—is always, Muldoon implies, merely that: a rhetoric, ready to be undermined by the physical savagery of which people are capable. In his excursus on the attractions and dangers of thought, especially Pyrrhonist scepticism, Byron asserts his belief in one idea: that of '*Lykanthropy*,' since 'Men become wolves on any slight occasion' (*Don Juan*, IX. 20. 158, 160). Tellingly, in his edition's selective choice of material from *Don Juan*, Muldoon includes central stanzas from canto VIII about the siege of Ismail in which Byron makes us conscious of 'All that the mind would shrink from of excesses' (977). 'Madoc' teems with brutality, wolfish behaviour, often carried out by the colonialists, sometimes by the Native American tribes. In his 'remake', to use the word employed in 'The Key', of Southey's poem and his response to Byron's great *ottava rima* poems, Muldoon leaves us in no doubt of the human capacity for cruelty: 'The woodchuck has had occasion | to turn into a moccasin' is the entirety of '[Empedocles]', the phrase 'has had occasion' a pseudo-polite euphemism for the process by which the woodchuck has undergone change in one of Muldoon's most chilling metamorphoses; 'Cinnamonds' trews are so very becoming' because 'they're made from the epiderms, de dum, | of at least four, maybe five, hapless Gros Ventre women' ('[Croce]'). 'Becoming', a conventional term of appreciation for the fit between clothes and person, turns into a shockingly

---

[27] Wills, *Reading Paul Muldoon*, p. 154.

[28] Kendall, p. 161. Kendall speaks of Muldoon's use of 'native American words' as 'tacitly celebrating and commemorating a culture on the verge of being wiped out'.

[29] Kendall (p. 171) compares the fate of an IRA man in Muldoon's play *Six Honest Serving Men*.

apposite term; the monotonous 'de dum' comes out of 'epiderms', mocking a collapse into brutalism.

Here language exposes its own falsities. In other places, language defeats the would-be idealist by insisting on its nominalism, as in '[Hobbes]', where Coleridge cannot 'argue from this faded blue | turtle's splay | above the longhouse door to a universal | idea of "blue" or "turtle"'. The rhyme of 'universal' and '"turtle"' reduces philosophical argument to absurdity. Or language serves only to imagine the same dull round as in '[Vico]', or it lists items that merely 'go smattering into the void' ('[Democritus]'). Yet in both instances something is retrieved from 'the void', if only in '[Democritus]' the pleasure of imagining with such precision, enumerating with such care, 'the astonishing clutter necessary had Pantisocracy "actually" got underway', as Nicholas Roe puts it.[30] The poem is, as Roe observes, 'appropriately associated with the materialist philosopher Democritus' and, as the same critic notices, includes a reference to '*the* cast-iron skillet' (emphasis added), doubtless containing the hot milk which scalded Coleridge's foot and led to the composition of 'This Lime-Tree Bower My Prison'.[31] Still, as the poem unfolds, its rhymes and off-rhymes convert its list of things into a litany of words, and the allusion to the genesis of 'This Lime-Tree Bower' reminds us that even as poems can be referred back to biographical origins, those origins can give rise to imaginative creations. If all goes to the void, the void might also be regarded as that from which all imagination comes. Muldoon's dealings with things, then, remind us of the material, 'the struggling sphere in which ideas are buffeted', in Roe's fine phrase; but they demonstrate, too, the ability of the imagination to turn words into quasi-magical counters.[32] A similar duplicity is at work in '[Vico]', which mimics and seems to deride the effect of a 'rondo' achieved by Coleridge in his most famous conversation poem, 'Frost at Midnight'.[33] The poem depicts a 'hand-wringing, small grey squirrel' on a treadmill made up of innumerable mechanical parts, all listed before, at the close, we return, though without any epiphanic illumination, to the 'hand-wringing, small grey squirrel'. The poem parodies William Carlos Williams's post- and, indeed, anti-Romantic notion that 'A poem is a small (or large) machine made of words'; here it is a mechanical contraption devoid of spirit, making fun of Vico's notion of cyclical cultural movements.[34] Yet the bravura of the performance, best appreciated

---

[30] Nicholas Roe, 'Pantisocracy and the Myth of the Poet', in *Romanticism and Millenarianism*, ed. Tim Fulford (Basingstoke: Palgrave, 2002), p. 91.

[31] Ibid.   [32] Ibid.

[33] Coleridge wrote thus of his motives for revising 'Frost at Midnight': 'The six last lines I omit because they destroy the rondo, and return upon itself of the Poem'; quoted in Nicholas Halmi et al. (eds), *Coleridge's Poetry and Prose* (New York: Norton, 2004), p. 123 n. 1.

[34] 'Author's Introduction to *The Wedge*', in *Selected Essays of William Carlos Williams* (New York: New Directions, 1969), p. 256.

when the poem is read aloud, its series of 'and's accumulating force, again asserts the power of the poet's imagination.

The 'mystery' of 'Madoc' lies in its clear-sighted, post-Romantic demonstration that words are irreducible to things, that poetry, inextricable as it may be from history, is not quite the same thing as history. Yet so much of the poem's language shows that words are contaminated even as they are recycled or rediscovered. Or it reveals that words fight a near-Beckettian battle against wordlessness. So, in the expanding—or should it be contracting?—universe of the last poem, '[Hawking]', *The Brief History of Time* casts its darkness visible over the sudden evaporation of words: 'It will all be over, de dum, | in next to no time— | | long before "The fluted cypresses | rear'd up their living obelisks" | | has sent a shiver, de dum, de dum, | through Unitel, its iridescent Dome.' 'De dum' off-rhymes with 'time', as though the iambic measure were merely a way of whiling away the hours. The collocation of 'fluted cypresses' and 'iridescent Dome' sets sardonically side by side, and finds equally wanting, the earthly paradises of Southey's *Thalaba*, Book 6, in which 'fluted cypresses rear'd up | Their living obelisks', and Coleridge's 'dome' in 'Kubla Khan' (or Shelley's 'dome of many-coloured glass' in *Adonais*). Yet those 'fluted cypresses', quoted earlier by South as he was attached to the retinagraph (in '[Anaximenes]'), are the mantra of rebellion. Southey, who in 'Madoc' is a tyrannical figure, bequeaths a verbal legacy that can be turned against tyranny; Coleridge, who in the poem is a more benevolent character, finds the 'dome' of his 'Kubla Khan' encompassing the dystopian world of Unitel. The 'shiver' may suggest the *frisson* of running up against the limits of poetry, even if that *frisson* is a verbal event made possible by a poem; but it also hints at the complex and unreliable nature of poetic legacy. Yet Muldoon's post-Romantic irony in 'Madoc' is generously accommodating; it includes in its range of effects the satirical and the elegiac, and its scepticism about language is inseparable from its relish for the proliferations of meaning.

8

'Deep Shocks of Recognition' and 'Gutted' Romanticism: Geoffrey Hill and Roy Fisher

I

This chapter will explore the work of two very different poets to demonstrate, in part, the variety and tenacity of Romantic legacies and renewals in contemporary British poetry. It would be absurd to suggest that Romantic poetry is the sole literature with which Geoffrey Hill engages, any more than it is the only literature to beguile Roy Fisher, to whom this chapter's second section will be devoted. As Andrew Michael Roberts notes, 'Hill's influences are eclectic and his explorations adventurous', even as Roberts observes that amongst these influences 'Romantic and Modernist poets figure prominently'.[1] More than this, Hill's poetry involves a prolonged meditation on, and wrestle with, the English language itself. In 'Poetry and Value', the second and last of the Tanner Lectures on Human Values delivered in 2000 at Brasenose College, Oxford, he concludes: 'A poem issues from reflection, particularly but not exclusively from the common bonding of reflection and language; it is not in itself the passing of reflective sentiment through the medium of language.'[2] Yet it is germane to my argument that an acknowledged influence on Hill's view here (for all his lecture's dislike of the 'Romantic-confrontational')[3] is the Coleridge of *Aids to Reflection*, especially the Coleridge who describes 'incomparably well' a 'disinterested force in the nature of language itself' 'in the sudden blaze of a sentence at the beginning of *Aids to Reflection*': 'For if words are not THINGS, they are LIVING POWERS, by which the things of most importance to mankind are actuated, combined, and humanized.'[4] This Coleridgean sentence restores to words a living power which in turn confers life on things and detects throughout the history of the language a vital process. In 'Englands of the Mind', Seamus Heaney speaks of Hill as 'sustained by the Anglo-Saxon base',

---

[1] Andrew Michael Roberts, 'Geoffrey Hill', in *Literary Encyclopedia*, online. First published 1 Oct. 2004; rev. 11 Jan. 2006.
[2] Geoffrey Hill, *Rhetorics of Value*, The Tanner Lectures on Human Values, delivered at Brasenose College, Oxford, 6 and 7 March 2000, online, p. 283.
[3] Ibid. 272.   [4] Ibid. 282.

indeed as possessing a vision of England that might be described 'as Anglo-Romanesque, touched by the polysyllabic light of Christianity but possessed by darker energies which might be acknowledged as barbaric'.[5] Hill's post-Romantic relish for the Janus-faced nature of language shows in his critical prose and in his poetry, as in his demonstration in *Style and Faith* of Hooker's ability to be 'magisterially persuasive in ranging across the senses of the word "common"'.[6]

Hill's concern with Romantic poetry is evident across his poetry and prose. An example is his brooding admiration for Wordsworth in his essay 'Redeeming the Time':

In Wordsworth's 'Ode: Intimations of Immortality . . .', published in 1807, the line

> Heavy as frost, and deep almost as life!

is a weighed acknowledgement of custom's pressure; stanza eight is allowed to settle onto this line. However, the poet immediately breaks continuity, thrusts against the arrangement, the settlement, with a fresh time-signature

> O joy! that in our embers
> Is something that doth live . . .

It has been pointed out that in this poem 'the prevailing rhythm is merely iambic' and the Ode has been further described as 'broken-backed'. Saintsbury may be technically correct; but Wordsworth's strategy of combining a pause with a change of time-signature within the 'merely iambic' prevailing rhythm overrides both the propriety and the pressure. It could be suggested, in response to C. C. Clarke's criticism, that the Ode is indeed broken but that the break, far from being an injury sustained, is a resistance proclaimed. If language is more than a vehicle for the transmission of axioms and concepts, rhythm is correspondingly more than a physiological motor. It is capable of registering, mimetically, deep shocks of recognition.[7]

Hill both pinpoints the nature and source of one of the most affecting transitions in Romantic poetry, and suggests a legacy of Wordsworth's practice, the recognition that language is 'capable of registering, mimetically, deep shocks of recognition'. The recognition frees poetry from being merely the conveyor of 'axioms and concepts', and here Hill's affinity with the Romantic sense of poetic language is at its deepest. He goes to cite and draw support from Gerard Manley Hopkins's view that 'when [Wordsworth] wrote that ode human nature got another of those shocks' which Hopkins sees as occurring throughout history.[8] For Hill, the 'shock' reverberates; indeed, he picks up Hopkins's phrase '*seen something*' to assert, 'If Wordsworth has indeed "seen something" he has seen, or foreseen, the developing life-crisis of the nineteenth century.'[9]

---

[5] Heaney, *Finders Keepers*, p. 78.
[6] Geoffrey Hill, *Style and Faith* (New York: Counterpoint, 2003), p. 52.
[7] Hill, 'Redeeming the Time', in *The Lords of Limit: Essays on Literature and Ideas* (London: André Deutsch, 1984), p. 87.
[8] Ibid.   [9] Ibid. 88.

This is a large claim, and constructs a link between rhythm and vision that has its origins in Romantic poetics: one thinks of Shelley's comment in *A Defence of Poetry* that 'All the authors of revolutions in opinion' are poets to the degree that their 'periods are harmonious and rhythmical' (p. 679). Hill's prose itself conveys one of the 'deep shocks of recognition' of which he speaks, consciously turning the almost despairing 'deep' of Wordsworth's 'deep almost as life' into a depth associated with a 'resistance proclaimed'. As Eric Griffiths has shown, Hopkins and Hill, in using the words 'shock' and 'shocks', are alert to their importance in Wordsworth himself: 'one of Wordsworth's own words', as Griffiths puts it, 'for the experience of vision and recoil upon the self', as in, to take just one of Griffiths's examples, the poem 'There was a boy', which ended up in Book v of *The Prelude* (and which is also central to Seamus Heaney's understanding of poetry).[10] In that passage Wordsworth tells how, while the boy 'hung | listening, a gentle *shock* of mild surprize | Has carried far into his heart the voice | Of mountain torrents' (1805, v. 406–9, emphasis added); there the switch of tense 'Has carried' moves from the past into something more indeterminate, while the effect of 'far', as De Quincey remarked, makes of the heart an interior and sublimely echoic space.[11] For Heaney, tuned to Wordsworth's sense of discovery, the lines illustrate how the boy-poet 'becomes imprinted with all the melodies and hieroglyphs of the world; the workings of the active universe, to use another phrase from *The Prelude*, are echoed far inside him'.[12] For Hill, however, one suspects that 'deep shocks of recognition' bear witness less to a sense of uncanny power than to a troubled awareness of responsibility. Recognition here means the act of acknowledging the validity or genuineness or character or claim of—as well as the act of identifying as known before. Wordsworth, that is, acknowledges that 'life' can inflict a condition of near-powerless passivity on us, unless we find in ourselves the capacity to identify as known before a prior and alternative condition: that of 'joy'. Enacted in the transition, then, in Hill's words, is a 'resistance proclaimed', but the proclamation is not made, or elsewhere made in Hill, with a decisive conviction of poetry's power to transcend, or to enable transcendence. Though the possibility of that power is rarely rejected wholly, Hill, like Keats, is alive to 'the menace of the high claims of poetry itself'.[13] The 'deep shocks of recognition' incurred in the process of writing poetry involve a conviction that poetry is answerable speech.

---

[10] Eric Griffiths, 'Hill's Criticism: A Life of Form', in *Geoffrey Hill: Essays on his Work*, ed. Peter Robinson (Milton Keynes: Open University Press, 1986), p. 180.

[11] 'This very expression, "far", by which space and its infinities are attributed to the human heart, and to its capacities of re-echoing the sublimities of nature, has always struck me as with a flash of sublime revelation', quoted from Wu (ed.), *Romanticism*, p. 474 n.

[12] Seamus Heaney, 'The Indefatigable Hoof-Taps: Sylvia Plath', in *Government of the Tongue*, p. 163.

[13] Hill's words in 'Poetry as "Menace" and "Atonment"', in *Lords of Limit*, p. 5.

Moreover, the 'shocks' are those experienced within language and cadence. Peter McDonald wonders whether 'it was not until some of *Canaan* that Hill began to find the creative ways of registering the "deep shock of recognition" that Hopkins's sense of rhythm represents', and he writes sensitively about 'the stepped lineation' of a poem such as 'Of Coming into Being and Passing Away', which concludes by enlisting the support of

> visions of truth or dreams
> as they arise—
>   to terms of grace
> where grace has surprised us—
> the unsustaining
>   wondrously sustained[14]

Hill's own poem comes into being and passes away before our eyes, wonder co-existing with doubtful scepticism in a movement which McDonald describes well. One would want to supplement his account by pointing out how the syntax mimes surprise and the wondrous sustaining of what seems unsustaining, and by drawing attention to the ineluctably Romantic idiom deployed by Hill: 'visions of truth or dreams' compounds memories of the close of 'Ode to the Nightingale', where the perplexed Keats asks, 'Was it a vision, or a waking dream?' (79), and of the end of 'Ode on a Grecian Urn', where the Urn stubbornly asserts, '"Beauty is truth"' (49). The idiom, moreover, is ineluctably Romantic, not simply because affirmations of quasi-transcendental meaning are being made, but also because, in Keats as in Hill, such affirmations are also—in context—put to the test. Hill ends by opening a dialogue with the Shelley who in *Adonais* hymns

>   that sustaining Love
> Which through the web of being blindly wove
> By man and beast and earth and air and sea,
> Burns bright or dim, as each are mirrors of
> The fire for which all thirst. (481–5).

Shelley's 'sustaining Love' sustains the 'web of being', but in itself is a belief founded on the poet's need to affirm; Hill's sense of humans as 'unsustaining', yet 'wondrously sustained', challenges Shelley's readiness to shape implicitly fictive absolutes from his immersion in the Dantescan and Platonic tradition. In so doing, his sense of surprising grace may owe as much to Wordsworth's 'peculiar grace, | A leading from above, a something given' ('Resolution and Independence', 50–1) as to any Bunyanite tradition.

---

[14] Peter McDonald, *Serious Poetry: Form and Authority from Yeats to Hill* (Oxford: Clarendon Press, 2002), pp. 198, 192. 'Of Coming into Being and Passing Away' is quoted from *Canaan* (London: Penguin, 1996).

It is, moreover, the case that 'deep shocks of recognition', of moments when Hill's syntax and rhythms enact a rethinking in and of his poems in ways that recall Wordsworth's example in the 'Ode: Intimations of Immortality', pervade his writing, pre- and post-*Canaan*. 'The Death of Shelley', the third section of 'Of Commerce and Society', is itself split into two parts. The poem opens with Romantic quest as undergoing a shocking change, scarcely recognizable in the modern age, to which it appears merely to have bequeathed 'Slime; the residues of refined tears', an effect that cuts against Shelleyan refinement and against contemporary 'slime'. At the end of the first part, Hill's rhythms enact the pointlessness of Percy Bysshe Shelley as Perseus, 'clogged sword, clear, aimless mirror— | With nothing to strike at or blind | in the frothed shallows'. Romantic quest does not lead to the fire for which all thirst, but peters out among the 'frothed shadows'. In the second section, though, the poem 'thrusts against the arrangement', even as it seems to consolidate it:

> Rivers bring down. The sea
> Brings away;
> Voids, sucks back, its pearls and auguries.
> Eagles or vultures churn the fresh-made skies.

These lines suggest that cultures 'repeat the same dull round over again', in Blake's words from the 'Conclusion' to 'There Is No Natural Religion [b]' (*c.*1788). But Blake's rider—'If it were not for the Poetic or Prophetic character'—is also relevant to lines which guardedly reassert the 'Poetic . . . character' (p. 3). The 'fresh-made skies' which may be churned by eagles rather than vultures grace the lines with a flickering and momentary post-Romantic hope, since the belief in the 'fresh-made' is central to any sense of Romanticism's continuity.

Again, in the following poem in 'Of Commerce and Society', 'Statesmen have known visions', where Auschwitz is depicted as impossible to come to terms with, a 'fable | Unbelievable in fatted marble', it is, as Henry Hart points out, to Shelley's 'notion that poets should be the world's unacknowledged legislators' that Hill, with immense caution, turns his attention.[15] If 'Artistic men prod dead men from their stone', 'prod' sounds callous as well as awakening. But, as the memory of concentration camps undergoes degenerating indifference in those consciously echoing, self-engrossed sounds—'a fable | Unbelievable in fatted marble'—Hill registers a 'resistance proclaimed': the effect is to shock us and himself out of 'decent' indifference. In recoil from the shock of those lines is the final stanza, building towards the loaded restraint of 'At times it seems not common to explain'. The word 'common' is charged with meaning, as it was for Wordsworth, swinging between delight in ordinariness, 'all

---

[15] Henry Hart, *The Poetry of Geoffrey Hill* (Carbondale: Southern Illinois University Press, 1986), p. 75.

the sweetness of a common dawn' (*The Prelude*, 1805, V. 337), and fear of time's erosions that enthrall us to 'the light of common day' ('Ode: Intimations of Immortality', 76). For Hill, in this context, the word rejects the sub-Movement notion of poetry as a rather intelligent bloke chatting to some other rather intelligent blokes, and brings out the 'uncommonness' of poetry if it is remind us of our civic and historical, our 'common' experience. Here the change of time signature is achieved by a break with rhythmic breaks, by the last stanza's return to regular pentameters, especially in the concluding line. Ghosting 'seems' is the poet's disciplined humility about the prophetic mantle that he is reluctantly assuming, and there is a Wordsworthian or a Shelleyan admission of subjectivity in the word.

But what gives Hill the right to assume such a mantle? His detractors dislike Hill's supposed self-importance. Sometimes one may feel that such critics miss Hill's self-mockery. In recent work, there is a quasi-Byronic delight in getting in his self-descriptions first; so *Scenes from Comus* (2005), if not a 'versified Aurora Borealis' (*Don Juan*, VII. 2. 11), participates in 'a grand and crabby music' (I. 19), while a surly delight in self-caricature shows itself throughout *The Triumph of Love* (1998), as when the poet imagines a detractor saying of him, 'Rancorous, narcissistic old sod—what | makes him go on?' (XXXIX). The line-ending, there, blunts the edge of criticism, since it briefly turns loathing into repressed wonder, but Hill's self-condemnations give the lie to the notion that he is guilty of complacent self-importance. So, in *The Triumph of Love* CIII, he speaks of 'the presiding | judge of our art, self-pleased *Ironia*' and provides a sardonic self-condemnation that cuts to the heart of what Hills has always felt to be most questionable about poetry: the solace it finds not only in artifice but also in guilty self-examination which can easily turn into 'self-pleased *Ironia*'. One is inclined to ask: if he is found guilty, who will scape whipping? For Hill recognizes, more than just about any other contemporary writer, that he writes, to quote from 'Poetry as "Menace" and "Atonement" ', 'in the context of that obsessive self-critical Romantic monologue in which eloquence and guilt are interwined, and for which the appropriate epigraph would be one abrupt entry in Coleridge's 1796 Notebook: "Poetry—excites us to artificial feelings—makes us callous to real ones."[16] In *The Enemy's Country*, Hill draws on Davenant for the 'conceit of "the vast field of Leaning, where the Learned ... lye ... maliciously in Ambush" and where one must "travail ..." as "through the Enemy's country" '. Yet his revision of 'vast field of Leaning', via Hugh MacDiarmid's quoted wish for 'a learned poetry wholly free | Of the brutal love of ignorance', into 'vast apparatus of Opinion', aligns him—perhaps despite himself—with

---

[16] *Lords of Limit*, pp. 3–4.

those Romantic-period writers, notably Godwin and Shelley, who were sworn foes to 'Opinion'.[17] In canto 8 of *Laon and Cythna* Shelley (or Cythna) asserts: 'opinion is more frail | Than yon dim cloud now fading on the moon | Even while we gaze, though it awhile avail | To hide the orb of truth' (9. 3271–4). Romantic writing finds as much substance in its enmities as in utopian hopes. Wordsworth, for one, writes with scorn for those who 'fall off . . . | To selfishness, disguised in gentle names | Of peace and quiet and domestic love, | Yet mingled not unwillingly with sneers | On visionary minds' (*The Prelude*, 1805, II. 452–6). Yet the Shelleyan image begs the question: how do we differentiate between the frail cloud of opinion and the orb of truth? Hill's view is less that he can lay bare 'truth' than that he can commend and enact in the bloody fray of his poems 'actuated self-knowledge, a daily acknowledgement | of what is owed the dead' (*The Triumph of Love*, CXIX). 'Actuated' recalls his quotation from Coleridge about words being 'LIVING POWERS, by which the things of most importance to mankind are actuated, combined, and humanized'. Even in his echo of this Coleridgean passage, his alliteration mimes a self-chastizing movement from agency to attention (from 'actuated' to 'acknowledgement').

Turning on his critics, whom he aligns with Croker, the 'noteless blot on a remembered name' (327) dispatched by Shelley in *Adonais*, a work which rolls its sleeves up and gets stuck into some fairly vigorous literary infighting as well as offering the most majestic vision of poetry's power in the language, Hill writes in the antepenultimate poem (CXLVIII) of *The Triumph of Love*:

> So—Croker, MacSikker, O'Shem—I ask you:
> what are poems for? They are to console us
> with their own gift, which is like perfect pitch.
> Let us commit that to our dust. What
> ought a poem to be? Answer, *a sad*
> *and angry consolation*. What is
> the poem? What figures? Say,
> *a sad and angry consolation*. That's
> beautiful. Once more? *A sad and angry*
> *consolation*.

Hill mocks his own exaltation of poetry: 'That's | beautiful', exhaled across the line-ending, mimics a falling back on the stereotypical, but he will not jettison the 'consolation' offered by poetry's 'gift'. This gift is said to be 'like perfect pitch'. Hill contrasts 'pitch' with 'tone' to the latter's detriment when he argues that in the posthumously published *The Varieties of Metaphysical Poetry* 'Eliot

---

[17] Hill, *The Enemy's Country: Words, Contexture, and Other Circumstances of Language* (Stanford, Calif.: Stanford University Press, 1991), pp. xi, xii.

aims at pitch but, for the most part, succeeds only in tone', and his work baffles that comfortable relationship with the reader achieved by 'tone'.[18] Whether the opposition does justice to Eliot is questionable; the very blurring of pronouns in *Four Quartets* of which Hill appears to complain lies behind the success of the encounter with the familiar compound ghost, even though Hill claims that his 'objection . . . has nothing to do with deliberated indeterminacy of pitch'.[19] But 'pitch', implying, in Peter McDonald's helpful gloss, 'a quality of deliberated alertness in the use of a word or phrase, in which even the intended meaning has taken stock of the misconstructions to which it is liable', is a forceful presence in the passage.[20] The translated phrase from Leopardi ('a sad and angry consolation') is repeated four times in the section, each time with a different lineation as if to point up the possibility of re-emphasis and even 'deliberated indeterminacy'. As '*a sad | and angry consolation*', poetry leaves behind 'sadness', recovering the nerve of its anger; as '*A sad and angry | consolation*', poetry, or 'the poem', seems to use up its mixed emotional energies in the attempt to offer 'consolation'. 'Perfect pitch' is itself a phrase where 'pitch' goes awry, one senses consciously so, since the phrase seems to forget the struggle in which the poem is engaged. The phrase, confessing its inadequacy through 'like', might be said to 'bear witness, | Despite [itself], to what is beyond us', to adapt lines from the final sonnet of Hill's earlier sequence, 'Funeral Music'. In so doing, it recovers authenticity, bearing the sweat of struggle, gazing towards a 'distant sphere of harmony', while being part of a poem that has no easy retort to 'What figures?', a question that leads to no Shelleyan avalanche of 'figures', but only to a self-discrediting yet clung-to formulation. 'Once more?' may mock Hill's adversaries, as though he were teaching them the ABC of primary poetics, but it concedes, too, that he is enmeshed in a struggle for poetry's heart and soul which cannot be won merely by rhetorical display. To this degree, Hill stands bareheaded in the unsheltered glare of a post-Romantic mindscape. Yet his defence of poetry is in accord with the intransigent insistence in Shelley's *A Defence of Poetry* that poetry is itself and not another thing. Shelley, acutely conscious of poetry's duty to connect with 'moral improvement', asserts that poetry differs from 'Ethical science', that it 'awakens and enlarges the mind itself by rendering it the receptacle of a thousand unapprehended combinations of thought' (p. 681).

Indeed, Hill's post-Romantic engagement with defences of poetry in *The Triumph of Love* is apparent in poem LXX in the sequence. First of all, one notes Hill's effort to include in the poem what in his essay 'Redeeming the Time' he

---

[18] Hill, *Style and Faith*, p. 156.   [19] Ibid. 157.

[20] McDonald, *Serious Poetry*, p. 205. For a discriminating discussion of Hill and Eliot, see Thomas Day, 'Sensuous Intelligence: T. S. Eliot and Geoffrey Hill', *Cambridge Quarterly*, 35/3 (2006), pp. 255–80.

criticizes George Eliot for excluding from *Advice to Working Men by Felix Holt*: that is, 'the antiphonal voice of the heckler', though the heckler seems within Hill himself; the poem's words exemplify what Coleridge, praising 'Parentheses', calls, in a letter of 1810 quoted by Hill, 'the *drama* of Reason—& present the thought growing, instead of a mere Hortus siccus'.[21] Thought is shown less as growing than as chopping itself down in the questions, 'But where is it? | Where has it got us?' The poem ricochets between its italicized phrases: between the possibly Yeatsian 'Active virtue' of the opening—a phrase which may be drawn from *Per Amica Silentia Lunae*, but is here applied to poetry's struggle to find 'a noble vernacular' that will connect poetic 'passion' to 'the public weal'—and the '*Intrinsic value*' of the second half. For all the rueful self-doubt, both halves rise to affirmations that are recognizably indebted to Romantic *exempla*. The first half ends: 'Still, I'm convinced that shaping, | voicing, are types of civic action' and proposes Wordsworth's 'two | Prefaces' (those to *Lyrical Ballads*, 1800, and to *Poems*, 1815), along with 'his great | tract on the Convention of Cintra', as embodiments of 'witnessing', here of 'witnessing | to the praesidium in the sacred name | of things betrayed' . '[W]itnessing | to the praesidium' suggests bearing witness to a body of power-makers unsympathetic to poetry, and doing so 'in the sacred name | of things betrayed'. Below the surface of Hill's poem there may be a memory of a passage in which enjambments enact losses of footing and stealthy betrayals, Wordsworth's nightmarish experience of 'long orations which in dreams I pleaded | Before unjust Tribunals, with a voice | Labouring, a brain confounded, and a sense | Of treachery and desertion in the place | The holiest that I knew of, my own soul' (*The Prelude*, 1805, X. 376–80).

Certainly 'things betrayed' seems Wordsworthian in its sense of something beyond poetry to which poetry owes allegiance. Turning to '*Intrinsic value*', the title of the first of his two Tanner Lectures of 2000, Hill owns his unease, but he identifies poetry's value with the capacity to house both 'fact and recognition'. Recognition of the fact of intrinsic value entails, according to Hill's lecture, 'stubborn attentiveness over a broad and varied range of a given world' until 'reflective language itself becomes a redemptive agent of the author's self-deceptions, willed and unconscious evasions, ethical sentimentality and political shape-shifting'.[22] It seems part of Hill's post-Romantic predicament that he can write about the need for such 'stubborn attentiveness' with more force than he can attend to any 'given world', save that of linguistic structures which commend 'attentiveness'. Hill does not chant any 'spousal verse | Of this great consummation' (1003–4 of *Home at Grasmere*, where the lines appear in Gill's edition) as he seeks to bind word to world, but he does envisage 'imponderables

---

[21] Hill, *Lords of Limit*, p. 90.   [22] Hill, *Rhetorics of Value*, p. 264.

brought home | to the brute mass and detail of the world; | there, by some, to be pondered'.

In the same passage, Wordsworth also speaks of 'how exquisitely . . . | The external world is fitted to the mind' (1009, 1011). Blake annotates this with sardonic fury: 'You shall not bring me down to believe such fitting & fitted I know better & Please your Lordship' (p. 667). But Hill, for all his debt to Blake, apparent in his early 'Genesis', continually stages a contest in his poetry between 'the mind' and the 'external world', self and history, language as vision and language as clog and encumbrance, 'inertial drag'.[23] So, at the close of the first sequence in *Scenes from Comus* he writes: 'That weight of the world, weight of the word, is. | Not wholly irreconcilable'. The Wordsworthian weight of the word 'is', followed by a full stop, braces itself against the 'weight of the world'. Hill inserts that full stop to enact the intransigent counterpoint of weights. When we cross the line-ending, we get a fine echo and reworking of the Narrator's lament in Shelley's *The Triumph of Life* that God has 'made irreconcilable | Good and the means of good' (230–1). *The Triumph of Life* seems central to Hill's recent work; it cannot have escaped him as being close to the title of *The Triumph of Love*. Jeffrey Wainwright remarks on the affinity between 'The baleful cast of Hill's poem' and Shelley's fragmentary masterpiece, whose 'chariot . . . like that of Hegel's History, rides over the bodies of the slain, and is checked only by the image of Dante "returned to tell | | . . . the wondrous story | How all things are transfigured except love". There is', he goes on to comment, 'no such "wondrous story" available in *The Triumph of Love.*'[24] Wainwright misses the ambivalent irony of Shelley's tribute: no absolute escapes an unblest 'transfiguration' in *The Triumph of Life*, unless it is placed outside human figuration. There is little sense that Hill's poem is more toughly 'baleful' than Shelley's, as the critic implies. Hill is assuredly not offering 'moral uplift', so pleasingly and disconcertingly absent from *Measure for Measure*, as he notes in poem CXX. But *The Triumph of Love* has its authority figures, however ironized as points of light. Poem CXXX lists some of them, including 'Milton—the political pamphlets. Blake | in old age reaffirming the hierarchies. | Péguy *passim*, virtually'. 'Virtually' may dampen this mood of praise, and the allusion to Blake, 'reaffirming the hierarchies', is oblique; Hill may possibly be referring to the Romantic poet's asserted preference for Christianity over Greek and Roman culture. The section concludes with what feels like an equivalent to a desolate song of despair, Hill finishing the poem as he does its predecessor and the next three with the refrain '*ta-Rah ta-Rah ta-rarara Rah*'. Yet even if the poem's nearest approach to a 'wondrous story' is its

---

[23] Hill, *Lords of Limit*, p. 87.
[24] Jeffrey Wainwright, *Acceptable Words: Essays on the Poetry of Geoffrey Hill* (Manchester; Manchester University Press, 2005), p. 72.

glimpse of 'sad and angry consolation', it is no less driven to pursue, to quest, to keep 'still | writing' (CXLIX).

Moreover, Hill has been brooding on two texts which preoccupied Shelley in his final years: Milton's *Comus*, with its motifs of enchantment and goodness, and Calderón's *La vida es sueño*, whose influence can be heard in Rousseau's question to the 'shape all light' (352) in *The Triumph of Life*: 'If, as it doth seem, | Thou comest from the realm without a name | | Into this valley of perpetual dream, | Show whence I came, and where I am, and why— | Pass not away upon the passing stream' (395–9). There the rhyming and off-rhyming on 'dream' suggests an experience that is endlessly unsatisfying but sick with hope for certainty. With due allowance for Hill's sturdy commitment to the 'weight of the world', something comparable infuses *The Orchards of Syon* (2002), a sequence in which the 'realm without a name' blends with Hopkins's 'Goldengrove' (from 'Spring and Fall'). A Calderónesque sense of life as a dream, alleviated only by the 'sufficient act' of poetry, colours the sequence. So, in section XV, Hill stages a last-minute stumbling upon a partial source of recompense:

> Presentable
> tribute to the passing down of kings,
> *Poiesis* a sufficient act, I almost
> forgot to say this. Otherwise
> the transient ever-repeated dream,
> the all-forgetful. *La vida es sueño*
> or something other. Other, that is, than death.

Poiesis, making, briefly redeems us from 'the transient, ever-repeated dream', where the adjectives have a Shelleyan conviction of time as always transient.

In the poem quoted above from *Scenes from Comus* Hill writes about the need to believe in poetry's power allied with the need to accept its possible limits. For all the sequence's allusions to Milton, the theme is resonantly post-Romantic. So the 'almosts' in lines 2 and 3 inch towards a minimal affirmation: 'Almost. | Almost we cannot pull free; almost we escape | | the leadenness of things.' Hill is likely to recall the work performed by Wordsworth's use of the same word in the line from 'Ode: Intimations of Immortality' discussed in 'Redeeming the Time': 'Heavy as frost, and deep almost as life'. Then the fourth and fifth lines half-mock the poet's ambition: 'Almost I have walked | the first step upon water': the poet sees himself sardonically as a near-miracle-worker and half implies that he is a fraud to nourish ambitions of 'escape'. The next phrases continue the tug of war between limits and transcendence. 'Nothing beyond' seems to dispose of transcendence, though, for once, there may be a Larkinesque note in Hill (one thinks of the end of 'High Windows'): perhaps there is a 'Nothing beyond'. This negative form of assertion may suggest the tenacious if crabbily ironic nature of Hill's approach to 'the sublime, a mode wholly archaic yet always available to us again, provided a survivor of the old line comes to us'.[25] The poem moves on to assert that 'The inconceivable is a basic service', presumably a service performed by poetry which seeks to reconceive the 'base' from which we understand reality. *Pace* Christopher Ricks who has written brilliantly on the 'Two-faced, or two-edged' work undertaken by hyphens in Hill's poetry, this punctuation device is, the poet tells us, 'not-necessary for things I say', and yet 'not-necessary' employs a hyphen.[26] Conceptually, the poem has been hyphenated throughout: 'things I say' captures in a seemingly straightforward way Hill's conviction that the poet needs to 'say things', to utter the world through his words. What is necessary—and here the poem repeats virtually its first line, but this time with a new sense of discovery—is 'weight of the world, weight of the word'.

As Wallace Stevens says in 'The Course of a Particular', 'there is a resistance involved'. Poetry needs to deal with, without surrendering to, 'the brute mass and detail of the world'. It must acknowledge, but not submit to, 'the inertial drag of speech', the 'gravitational pull' of everyday language.[27] The programme of Wordsworth's Preface to *Lyrical Ballads* may seem to be under attack here. But Wordsworth got it right in that Preface, according to *The Triumph of Love*, LIV, in objecting to the 'undeniable powers of this world', powers whom Hill identifies with the abuse of thought and words: 'For the essentials of the cadre, Wordsworth's | "savage torpor" can hardly be bettered | or his prescience refuted.' His voice allowed by the lineation to alight with biting fury on ' "savage torpor" ', Hill alludes to the Preface to *Lyrical Ballads* where Wordsworth draws out the significance of the fact that in the poems 'the feeling therein developed gives importance to the action and situation, and not the action and situation to the feeling'. Wordsworth stresses the 'general importance' of 'this mark of distinction' and its contemporary relevance: 'For a multitude of causes, unknown to former times, are now acting with a combined force to blunt the discriminating powers of the mind, and unfitting it for all voluntary exertion to reduce it to a state of almost savage torpor'; the Preface lays the blame on 'the great national events which are daily taking place, and the encreasing accumulation of men in cities' (p. 599). Hill stops short of the prophetic role he seems to wish to assume: 'A

---

[25] Harold Bloom, 'The Survival of Strong Poetry', Introduction to Geoffrey Hill, *Somewhere is Such a Kingdom: Poems, 1952–1971* (Boston: Houghton Mifflin, 1975), p. xvi. See also Andrew Michael Roberts's discussion of the 'relationship of Romantic irony to the postmodern sublime' in his 'Romantic Irony and the Postmodern Sublime: Geoffrey Hill and "Sebastian Arrurruz" ', in *Romanticism and Postmodernism*, ed. Edward Larrissy (Cambridge: Cambridge University Press, 1999), pp. 141–56; quoted phrase, p. 156. Roberts argues that 'Hill employs Romantic irony in relation to postmodernist elements in his work, and employs postmodernist irony in relation to Romanticism' (p. 156).

[26] Christopher Ricks, 'Geoffrey Hill 2: At-One-Ment', in *The Force of Poetry* (1984; Oxford: Oxford University Press, 1987), p. 327.

[27] Hill, *Lords of Limit*, p. 87.

simple text would strike them | dumb, and is awaited': a latter-day version of *Lyrical Ballads*, perhaps. But he ends the previous section with an illustration of, and an appeal to, the mind's 'discriminating powers', one which is impossible to imagine without the example of Wordsworth's poetry. Hill celebrates 'that all-gathering general English light, | in which each separate bead | of drizzle at its own thorn-tip stands | as revelation' (LIII). The line-endings beautifully enhance the movement from the eye's greeting of particulars to the mind's and imagination's construction of 'revelation': the 'separate bead' is allowed a 'separate' line while its position 'at its own thorn-tip' also 'stands' free for observation. Hill affirms, though 'all-gathering general English light' may conceal a latent reference to imperialist nostalgia, while 'stands | as revelation' can be read as stopping short of affirming revelation's full presence. But Hill's '*moral landscape*', indebted to reflection on Wordsworth, is one 'in which particular grace, | individual love, decency, endurance, | are traceable across the faults' (*The Triumph of Love*, LI).

Wordsworth's 'faults' are, in part, the subject of 'Elegiac Stanzas, On a Visit to Dove Cottage', a poem in Hill's first volume, *For the Unfallen*. The title is typically allusive, here calling to mind one of Wordsworth's finest poems, 'Elegiac Stanzas, Suggested by a Picture of Peele Castle' (as Haughton notes[28]). In that poem, written after the death by shipwreck of the poet's brother John, Wordsworth asserts: 'A power is gone, which nothing can restore; | A deep distress hath humanized my Soul' (35–6). Hill's poem, in turn, senses in Wordsworth's 'Greatly-aloof, alert, rare | Spirit' 'a power' which 'nothing can restore'. For Hill, Wordsworth's rhetoric is, in the end, 'clear-obscure'. The oxymoron balances on an ambivalent high wire. His 'tongue broody in the jaw', Wordsworth may brood to good purpose, as his stockdove broods over its own sweet voice in 'Resolution and Independence' (line 5), but he is also 'moody', a poet who can be egotistical as well as sublime. If he gropes beyond 'custom towards love', 'love' reverts, both in the poet and in his admirers, to 'the custom to approve'. All is entropically turned in on itself in this parable of poetic reception. But though his poem raises only two cheers for a poet apostrophized as 'near-human spouse and poet', and as at once 'conditioned' and 'authentic', Hill also sustains a strain of elegy that carries conviction; there is lament as well as irony in the fact that Wordsworth has bequeathed a legacy which leaves 'Sentiment upon the rocks', at once securely located in the 'mountains' surrounding Grasmere and also, more colloquially, broken down, in danger of going under, 'on the rocks'.[29]

---

[28] Hugh Haughton, ' "How Fit a Title . . .": Title and Authority in the Work of Geoffrey Hill', in *Geoffrey Hill: Essays on his Work*, ed. Robinson, p. 134.

[29] Henry Hart writes of the poem's close: 'But while Hill resurrects the romantic spirit and places it on firm foundation, he simultaneously exclaims that romantic "sentiment," like the Christian spirit from which it partly derives, is "on the rocks," irrevocably shattered' (*Poetry of Geoffrey Hill*, pp. 38–9).

Doubleness governs Hill's view of Romantic poetry. For one thing, he approaches the word 'Romantic' with great wariness, asserting in his essay 'The Conscious Mind's Intelligible Structure—A Debate' that 'no such simple entity as the Romantic tradition can be discovered', yet stating in the same piece that 'one might suggest that Romanticism had (and has) both false and true masks'; the false marks 'gleams amid the fecundity of money', in Hill's phrase, offering a Gatsby-like debasement of transcendence; the true mask he is gnomic about, but he sees the second of two ways of shaping it as deriving from responsible and creative uses of 'syntax'.[30] If for Hill etymology is history, then syntax for him is poetry. So, in his 'Elegiac Stanzas' all is suspended in a poem without a main verb, both Wordsworth's magnificent, ambivalent example and our later, queasily ambiguous response. There is no 'such simple entity as the Romantic tradition', for Hill, because the Romantics themselves are alive to fissures, decreations, recoils of the self upon the self. This tendency is described in favourable terms in his essay 'Poetry as "Menace" and "Atonement"':

> Readers of the *Biographia Literaria* may note that Coleridge's concern is not so much with thought as with 'the mind's self-experience in the act of thinking' and that this 'self-experience' is most clearly realized by the process of 'win[ning one's] way up against the stream' ... For Matthew Arnold, in his essay 'The Function of Criticism at the Present Time', the crucial vindication of Burke's integrity is his capacity to 'return ... upon himself' ... It is, of course, a frequently observed fact that the first word of the final stanza of Keats's 'Ode to a Nightingale' ('Forlorn! the very word is like a bell') echoes the last word of the preceding stanza ('Of perilous seas, in faery lands forlorn'). The echo is not so much a recollection as a revocation; and what is revoked is an attitude towards art and within art. The menace that is flinched from is certainly mortality ... but it is also the menace of the high claims of poetry itself. ... We perhaps too readily assume that the characteristic Romantic mode is an expansive gesture ('Hail to thee, blithe Spirit! Bird thou never wert'). That which MacKinnon has described, in speaking of Kant, as a 'tortuous and strenuous argument whose structure torments the reader' is equally a paradigm of Romantic-Modernist method:
>
>> Not, I'll not, carrion comfort, Despair, not feast on thee;
>> Nor untwist—slack they may be—these last strands of man
>> In me or, most weary, cry *I can no more*. I can;
>> Can something, hope, wish day come, not choose not to be.[31]

Gathered here is an anthology of Romantic turns and returns, the very substance of so many poems by Hill: Coleridge's 'self-experience in the act of thinking'; Burke's 'capacity', noted so brilliantly by Arnold, 'to return upon himself', to concede the significance of the French Revolution, despite his dislike of it; Keats's repeated use of 'forlorn' at the start of the last stanza of the Nightingale

---

[30] Hill, 'The Conscious Mind's Intelligible Structure—A Debate', *Agenda* 4/1 (1971–2), pp. 15, 15–16.

[31] Hill, *Lords of Limit*, p. 5.

Ode, 'less a recollection than a revocation'; and finally lines from Hopkins, suggestively presented as a 'paradigm of Romantic-Modernist method'. Long before critics had presented the divorce between Romanticism and Modernism as deeply questionable, a Modernist fabrication, Hill, almost in a hyphenated aside, brings Keats and Hopkins together as fellow practitioners. Indeed, the lines from Hopkins anticipate that mimetic use of stress and rhythm central to Hill's own poetic efforts to convey 'the mind's self-experience in the act of thinking'.

Poems are experiences for Hill, not simply verbal constructions about experience. And the experience is lodged in the words. Arguing against Austin in 'Our Word is Our Bond', and in support of Ransom's claim that 'the density or connotativeness of poetic language reflects the world's density', Hill turns for support to Wordsworth to show how recalcitrance and possibility not only coexist but also generate one another: 'The word "blind" upon which Wordsworth homes in so often is itself a compounding of blankness and intuition: at one time [and here he quotes from 'Resolution and Independence'] 'Dim sadness, and blind thoughts I knew not nor could name', at another [and here he quotes from 'Michael'] 'A pleasurable feeling of blind love'. Words such as 'perplexity' and 'gleam' in Wordsworth, he continues, thrive on 'the sense that without the perplexity there would be no gleam and that the "blindness" embodies them both'.[32] Wordsworth is said by Hill in an interview to illustrate how in the greatest poets (Donne, Herbert, Vaughan, Milton, and Dante are also mentioned), 'the language seems able to hover above itself in a kind of brooding, contemplative, self-rectifying way'.[33] This 'double quality' of which Hill speak in connection with Wordsworth is there in his own best poems where language hovers above itself by being intimately aware of itself. 'Too near the ancient troughs of blood | Innocence is no earthly weapon,' says the speaker of 'Ovid in the Third Reich', 'weapon' rhyming haplessly, it would seem, with the toneless dullness of 'Things happen'. But if Ovid here ends up celebrating 'the love-choir', this is partly because 'Innocence' recovers its Blakean nerve at some level of its being; and does so as Hill remodels the expected phrase 'no earthly use' in a way that brings out that there must be, has to be, some way of combating 'earthly weapons'. Innocence is not sentimentalized, but its value is recovered, even as in the earlier 'Holy Thursday' Hill comes close to that condition which critics of Blake used to call 'Organized Innocence'.[34] 'Lo, she lies gentle and innocent of desire | Who

[32] Ibid. 151.
[33] Carl Phillips, Interview: 'Geoffrey Hill, The Art of Poetry LXXX', *Paris Review*, 154 (Spring 2000), p. 283.
[34] For a recent allusion to the idea, see Geoffrey H. Hartman's observation, one relevant to Hill's poetic concerns and procedures, that 'Blake's phrase "organized innocence" ... suggests that ... the creative must undergo a process of intellectual mediation and emerge as a powerful second immediacy' ('A Life of Learning', Charles Homer Haskins Lecture for 2000, online). Blake, in fact, wrote in the margin of the manuscript of *The Four Zoas*: 'Unorganizd Innocence, An Impossibility | Innocence dwells with Wisdom but never with Ignorance' (p. 838).

was my constant myth and terror', the speaker concludes, with how much overconfidence it is hard to say.

'Mighty figures straining to free themselves from the imprisoning marble': in 'Poetry as "Menace" and "Atonement"', Hill quotes Michael Meyer's 'commonplace image, founded upon the unfinished statues of Michelangelo', but he says that the image suits words more than sculpture.[35] Certainly he is all too aware of the fact that, as Coleridge puts it, in a passage in *Biographia Literaria* which Hill uses, 'our chains rattle, even while we are complaining of them'.[36] But there are moments when Romantic models help Hill to free his 'mighty figures' from the 'imprisoning marble' of language, when he moves beyond the kind of ironized stand-off in his relations with Romantic poetry apparent in 'The Death of Shelley'. In 'Funeral Music', Hill suggests that the Romantic mode may seem to lead to a dead end, yet that it opens up new possibilities: 'Some parch for what they were', ends sonnet 6, a post-Romantic meditation on the 'pristine fields' of childhood; 'others are made | Blind to all but one vision, their necessity | To be reconciled'. Henry Hart sees 'Some' as a synonym for Wordsworth and 'others' as recalling 'Blake'; reconciliation seems as Coleridgean as Blakean, but the mapping is helpful in the way in which it shows Hill's tactic of measuring himself against the Romantics.[37] 'I believe', the poem concludes, 'in my | Abandonment, since it is what I have'. Dispossession is the condition that the great poets in the post-Romantic tradition are often conscious of themselves as possessing; that off-rhyme between 'have' and 'believe' confirms the minimal, sad assertion being made here.

A finely creative yet critical dialogue with Romantic poetry informs the sonnet sequence 'An Apology for the Revival of Christian Architecture in England', in which Hill inwardly comprehends, but obliquely distances himself from, nostalgia for what in an epigraph he quotes Coleridge describing as 'the spiritual, Platonic old England'. In some of his most flawlessly lyrical and harmonious writing, Hill evokes and critiques the 'Platonic': so, in 'Loss and Gain', 'Platonic England grasps its tenantry', where the verb's two meanings ('hold tightly' and 'exploit' as in a 'grasping' landlord) disconcert the concept, and where the ending is charged with suggestions:

> Vulnerable to each other the twin forms
>
> of sleep and waking touch the man who wakes
> to sudden light, who thinks that this becalms
> even the phantoms of untold mistakes.

The writing conjures up a Romantic state of being visited by 'twin forms | | of sleep and waking': the 'Ode to a Nightingale', or 'La Belle Dame Sans Merci', or

---

[35] Hill, *Lords of Limit*, p. 2.   [36] Ibid. 142.
[37] Hart, *Poetry of Geoffrey Hill*, p. 138.

'the two worlds of life and death' (1. 195) in *Prometheus Unbound*, or Rousseau in *The Triumph of Life* come to mind as multiply complex precursors. Do the 'forms', in context, have a 'Platonic' colouring? If so, is this colouring stained by the aspersions that have just been cast on 'Platonic England', possibly guilty of exploiting 'its tenantry'? There is a waking 'to sudden light', as in a Romantic epiphany, but such awakenings are themselves often ambivalent: 'the light of common day' in Wordsworth's 'Ode: Intimations of Immortality' is, for example, an apparent enemy of 'the visionary gleam'. Light may not seize the man's 'brain | With frantic pain' (23–4), as in Blake's 'Mad Song', but it may lure him to think that 'phantoms of untold mistakes' may be laid to rest. 'Phantoms' harks back to Romantic diction, recalling Shelley's 'phantoms of a thousand hours' recalled in 'Hymn to Intellectual Beauty' (64); it implies both a haunting by 'untold mistakes', where the mistakes are countless and repressed in that they have never have been 'told', and a sense of the necessary subjectivity and unreliability of the man's thoughts. Hill uses the Romantic legacy to make possible the poem's balance between ruthless critique and sympathy.

In the sequence, Keats is a pervasive presence, the model for Hill's luscious evocations and a point of departure for the later poet's ironies. So the third poem, entitled 'Who Are These Coming to the Sacrifice?', singles out a line from 'Ode on a Grecian Urn', in which Keats changes his poem's time signature; but it does so, as Hart observes, 'to set off an avalanche of contrasts'.[38] Yet, though the poem's 'you' survives, 'though still not quite yourself', the poem's air of a period piece, depicting an 'elopement', is as ekphrastically aware of art's limitations as is Keats's poem—which can do nothing to rescue the little town's streets from 'desolateness'. The 'young | ferns' renewing themselves among the 'vitrified tears' might describe a model in which later poetry revives earlier work, and in which 'the bric-a-brac of loss and gain' in played out 'in each room' or, metapoetically, each stanza. The modern poet, though, ends up caught between a past of 'long-laid dust' and a future which will make new demands; he sees his wary, ensnaring double in the final image: 'Guarding its pane | the spider looms against another storm.' Further storms await the poet.

In more recent work, Hill sustains a heightened, if still double, view of Romanticism's bequest. His use of Blake in *Canaan* is a case in point: a reference point for righteous anger and for the apparent uselessness of that anger. 'Churchill's Funeral' takes for its fifth section's epigraph lines from Blake's *Jerusalem* that constitute a cultural elegy: '. . . every minute particular, the jewels of Albion, running down | The kennels of the streets & lanes as if they were abhorr'd'. The poem also alludes to Blake's 'London' when it refers to 'the harlot | of many tears', recalling how 'the youthful Harlots curse | Blasts the new-born

---

[38] Ibid. 232.

Infants tear | And blights with plagues the Marriage hearse' (14–16). But its mood is consciously at odds with, even as it is sustained by, Blake's visionary righteousness. The poem is written in quatrains as is Blake's lyric, but for Blake's rhyme it substitutes unrhymed, embittered, and mainly two- or three-stress lines. 'The brazed city | reorders its own | destruction', it opens, where 'brazed' meaning 'soldered with alloy' also suggests 'razed' and 'brazen'. But quasi-apocalyptic warnings issue through tight lips. '[R]eorders its own | destruction' shrugs its shoulders at modern folly that would 'reorder', as in order again from a catalogue or give instructions for, 'its own | destruction', where the noun falls with a weary rather than a portentous sound. '[T]he harlot | of many tears' is now an all too familiar figure, almost an image for a corruption that can never be expunged, yet also—and here the urgency of Blake's poem breaks through—an image of potential ruined: that 'harlot | of many tears' might be a sainted figure, too. 'Whose Jerusalem— | at usance for its bones' | redemption and last | salvo of poppies' is the poem's end, its 'last | salvo'. 'Usance', 'the time allowed by commercial usage for payment of foreign bills of exchange', implies that the city is in financial and moral debt; but whether the dead bones of the city's finest hours can live again, whether they can be 're-deemed', both saved and bought back, is an open question, as is the nearly analogous question whether Blakean vision might ultimately be realized, or at least, whether its force might be recognized.

Such doubt and anxiety fitfully burn away in other recent poems in which Hill's imagination is energized by the Romantic inheritance, even as it is aware of its participation in moments of transient affirmation. 'To John Constable: In Absentia' from *Canaan* alludes to the Romantic painter's work after the death of his wife. True to its Latin epigraph (which translates as 'Alas! from what a slender thread hangs that which makes life more radiant'), the poem employs an elegant blank verse broken by short lines and stress shifts to communicate a double sense of the twinning of sadness and joy. Hill calls up the Wordsworth of the 'Ode: Intimations of Immortality', who elegizes the human condition by affirming 'the human heart by which we live' (203), when he asserts, 'We suffer commonly, where we are quite alone'. The line does justice to that peculiarly powerful conjunction in Wordsworth whereby 'We suffer commonly' yet, in doing so, 'are quite alone'. In Hill, 'suffer' turns into a transitive verb across the line-ending when we find its object, 'not the real but the actual natures of things', once again entering that post-Romantic labyrinth in which the 'real' and the 'actual' jostle, yet demand that they be distinguished. More assuredly, Hill praises the Romantic artist's fight 'to engineer' (a verb itself not untroubled) 'a perceptible radiance—arched and spectral— | the abrupt rainbow's errant visitation'. Any number of Romantic texts cry out to be identified as precursors, but Shelley's 'dome of many-coloured glass' (*Adonais*, 462) comes to mind, for its praise of the 'many-coloured', even as the poem is lured by the

'the white radiance of Eternity' (463). 'Spectral', too plays its part, reworking the Poet's question in *Alastor* whether 'the bright arch of rainbow clouds' (213) may 'Lead only to a black and watery depth' (215). But the 'errant visitation' is finally affirmative, 'errant' suggesting the unbiddability of the 'visitation' rather more than its capacity for error, and harking back to the those 'evanescent visitations' praised by Shelley in *A Defence of Poetry* (p. 697).

Finally, it is to something very like the Romantic imagination, albeit one under fierce pressure, that Hill turns in *Without Title* (2006). In 'In Ipsley Church Lane 2' he asks whether 'the appearances, the astonishments' 'are annulled through the changed measures of light' and answers, 'Imagination, freakish, dashing every way, | defers annulment'. 'Freakish' may speak of and to Hopkins's love of the individual as well as a sense of the oddness of the imagination in modern contexts; and Hill may sound momentarily and strangely Derridean in 'defers annulment'. But the lines, like much of Hill's work, suggest the importance to him of the Romantic tradition in seeking both to proclaim an ethical resistance and to value authentic beauty in his own 'changed measures', until, as Pound has it, in a line which serves as an epigraph to the English poet's *Collected Poems*, 'In the gloom, the gold gathers the light against it'.

II

By contrast with Hill's complexly anguished yet positive response to Romantic poetry, Roy Fisher shows in his poetry an altogether warier and quieter engagement. Reviewing himself, Fisher writes with characteristic wryness: 'I think he's a Romantic, gutted and kippered by two centuries' hard knocks.'[39] It is Fisher's representation of this Romantic or post-Romantic 'self', albeit one that is 'gutted and kippered', on which the present section will focus. If Auden represents the words of the Romantics, among others as 'modified | In the guts of the living', Fisher's image of himself as a 'gutted' Romantic is even more visceral in impact. Yet, however 'gutted' his Romanticism, the poetry it produces is undeniably 'living'. A sign of Fisher's importance is that he turns out to be a poet hard to enlist in poetic camps. His 'Staffordshire Red', dedicated to Geoffrey Hill, reads, in part, as a good-humoured riposte to Hill's way with landscape and history. For Hill's tensed formalism, struggling to intimate ironic conflict between ideas and realities, transcendence and the sublunary, Fisher substitutes a conversational, short-lined free verse. Yet Fisher also shows that his style is capable of rhetorical daring as it stretches itself to suggest journeys between different realms: 'clefts cut in the earth | to receive us

---

[39] 'Roy Fisher Reviews Roy Fisher', *The Rialto*, 35 (1996), p. 31.

living' may, the poem half-speculates, be the more authentically there for being casually ambushed by the sidling imagination: 'I had not been looking for the passage, | only for the way.'⁴⁰ The Eliot of *Four Quartets* is audible behind those last-quoted lines, and in the ensuing movement away from discovery into the post-Shelley condition of 'vacancy'; the poem closes with a deadpan refusal to commit itself to meaning—'It was as it had been'—that is a signature of Fisher. Where Fisher differs from others writing in an empiricist manner is his awareness of that style's potential limitations; his poetry, for all its dislike of pretention and afflatus, is discontent with easy irony. What is admirable about his long poem *A Furnace* is the poem's recognition of what is at stake in the deployment of types of language. Fisher's Preface alerts us to the fact that, with altering degrees of intensity, the poem will address and incorporate opposites, tensions, and superimpositions: an industrialized version of Coleridge's Secondary Imagination, the poem 'is an engine devised, like a cauldron, or a still, or a blast furnace, to invoke and assist natural processes of change; to persuade obstinate substances to alter their condition'.⁴¹

Marjorie Perloff takes Pound and Stevens as contrasting types of modern poet: the latter (honoured by Harold Bloom and Helen Vendler) deriving his beliefs and stance from Romanticism, and offering 'a vision of Reality'; the former seeing Modernism as a break with Romanticism and concerned to make 'its processes imitate the processes of the external world as we have come to know it'.⁴² One problem with Perloff's antithesis is that it slices too cleanly. Poets in the so-called Stevens tradition often mirror through their verbal 'processes' 'the processes of the external world'; poets in the so-called Pound tradition do not entirely shun the prospect of 'a vision of Reality'. Another problem is that her 'we' in 'as we have come to know it' presumes the existence of common knowledge. This presumption underplays the efforts of a poet like Fisher to communicate his sense that knowledge of shared reality is likely to be individual and private. At the heart of his work is the unignorable fact of his own subjectivity.

Fisher, no less than any other contemporary poet, whether neo-Modernist or post-Movement in manner, is vexed by '*self*, that burr that will stick to one', in Shelley's phrase.⁴³ Fisher has a variety of strategies to represent the self. One is to work by analogy: to praise, say, Joe Sullivan (in 'The Thing about Joe

---

⁴⁰ Quoted from Roy Fisher, *Poems, 1955–1987* (Oxford: Oxford University Press, 1988).

⁴¹ Fisher, *A Furnace* (Oxford: Oxford University Press, 1986), p. vii. See my ' "Exhibiting Unpreparedness": Self, World, and Poetry', in *The Thing about Roy Fisher*, ed. John Kerrigan and Peter Robinson (Manchester: Manchester University Press, 2000), pp. 210–14, for further discussion of *A Furnace*. See also William Wootten, 'Romanticism and Animism in Roy Fisher's *A Furnace*', *Cercles*, 12 (2005), pp. 79–93.

⁴² Marjorie Perloff, *The Dance of the Intellect: Studies in the Poetry of the Pound Tradition* (Evanston, Ill.: Northwestern University Press, 1996), p. 22.

⁴³ Shelley, *Letters*, ii. 109.

Sullivan') in terms that are so resolutely other-centred that they grow reflexive. Fisher's couplets mime the pianist's 'mannerism of intensity' with such mimetic verve, 'such | quickness of intellect', that among the 'shapes' that 'flaw and fuse' are those of the poem's subject and its authorizing consciousness. Sullivan, the poem tells us, will 'strut', 'amble, and stride over | gulfs of his own leaving, perilously | | toppling octaves down to where | the chords grow fat again', and the performance is captured with a gusto which indicates that Fisher has desired at least one man's art and scope. Elsewhere, Fisher sets going a *dédoublement* that allows him to create and watch himself create. In 'The Memorial Fountain' he at once stages 'the scene' and gives himself a walk-on part at the close:

> And the scene?
> a thirty-five-year-old man,
> poet,
>   by temper, realist,
> watching a fountain
>
> and the figures round it
> in garish twilight,
>   working
> to distinguish an event
> from an opinion;
>   this man,
> intent and comfortable —
>
> Romantic notion.

'The Memorial Fountain' suggests the difficulty of escaping the 'self' (scarcely more unitary in Larkin than it is in Fisher: one thinks of the elongating perspectives that open up in poems such as 'Dockery and Son', threatening the self's sense of meaning and stability). Fisher's poem is a beautifully controlled illustration of the impossibility of distinguishing 'event' from 'opinion', if one sees those loaded terms as corresponding (roughly) to such binaries as 'objectivity' and 'subjectivity', 'description' and 'interpretation', 'fact' and 'metaphor'. The semi-humorous phrase, 'by temper, realist', implies that 'realism' is a 'construction' (to borrow Fisher's own proleptic word from the poem's opening). Yet to say one is 'by temper' a 'realist' may concede that 'realism' involves subjective preference, but it does not free one from the dilemma that poetic knowledge will negotiate between 'event' and 'opinion'. The poem can expose, but not escape, its dependence on the need for such negotiations. Language will not permit the self to be banished; words will only allow the self to be seen in an estranged way. There is a flicker of projected self-criticism in 'intent and *comfortable*' (emphasis added). The adjectives reveal Fisher's awareness that his poem's nimble self-monitoring is hardly putting the author under much duress. 'Romantic notion' attaches itself with calculated imprecision to the preceding passage to which it is connected by the suspended dash after 'comfortable': calculated, because, throughout the passage, Fisher is alert to the contribution made by his 'temper' to the construction of the 'scene', and he wishes to leave open the possibility not only that 'Objectivity is a Romantic notion because events tend to blur together', but also that awareness of such a possibility is itself 'Romantic'.[44] The poem displays an eloquent guardedness about the rewards of the self-scrutiny to which it is impelled; Fisher concedes and asserts, with the mimicked awkwardness of someone passing a not altogether favourable or unfavourable judgement on himself, the 'Romantic' nature of his poem's activity

Among Fisher's strategies for representing the self is to treat it as strands of tobacco to be rolled up in the Rizla paper of poetic self-reflexivity. Whether the ensuing smoke satisfies varies from poem to poem—and reader to reader. In such poems the 'I' may be the creation of the poem's winks and nods. The pronoun may try to unburden itself of foresuffering and endurance through time, refusing to commit itself to stable identity. Yet it is as sovereign an ego as any to be found in contemporary poetry. Discovering post-modernist 'anxieties about the reality of the observing "author" ' in the poetry, Bert Almon takes the view that Fisher is to be praised, in terms borrowed from Andrew Crozier, for not taking for granted 'an empirical self', and selects as an illustrative text 'Of the Empirical Self and for Me'. One may find the dedication ('for M. E.') less 'witty' than smart-alecky. But Almon also points out that 'the self is the source of Fisher's poem and must work to render perceptions accurately'.[45] Given that the poem knows this, it starts into contradictory life. Its opening expects to be contested:

> In my poems there's seldom
> any *I* or *you* —
>
> you know me, Mary;
> you wouldn't expect it of me —

Self-absorption sounds through the opening phrase—'In my poems'—and mocks itself in the hackneyed appeal, 'you know me, Mary'. Fisher asks to be taken seriously, but cannot be read straight. So, 'you' may be an invented 'alter ego'.[46] The very word is like a bell to toll us back to a sense that the sole self that counts is the subject as writer. But the poem is caught between affirming and denying the reality of what it calls in its title 'the Empirical Self'. After all, it goes on to spin a mini-plot of misconception and perceptual error. A passer-by mistakes for '*a cup | of coffee*' the 'glasses of white milk' that the poem's 'I'

---

[44] Bert Almon, '"If I Didn't Dislike Mentioning Works of Art": Roy Fisher's Poems on Poetics', *Ariel*, 22/3 (1991), p. 12.

[45] Ibid. 8, 12, 16. [46] Ibid. 13.

and 'you' are drinking. The passer-by is said to be 'A tall man', walking 'what looks like a black dog': as Almon points out, 'The dog may be a black dog, if it is a dog at all', and even the detail of the man being 'tall' is subtly disquieting. The two sitting on the seemingly substantial 'bench under the window' are 'invisible ghosts'. No sooner does the man cease speaking than he 'vanishes' across an expressive line-ending. Yet the notion of error brings into play the possibility of truth; the poem both 'dramatizes perceptual uncertainty' and depends for doing so on the notion of perceptual certainty.[47] If the man is wrong about the milk being coffee, that is because the speaker is right about the coffee being milk. The poem finds itself needing to believe in, even as it questions, the self and the world. However ironically, the idea of an absolute self shows in the title's distinction between 'the Empirical Self' and 'Me', where 'Me' may briefly put one in mind of 'the Me myself' in that central monument to American Romantic Transcendentalism, Whitman's *Song of Myself*, section 4. There is an intriguing affinity, too, between Fisher's phrasing and the Whitman who in 'As I Ebb'd with the Ocean of Life' asserts that 'before all my arrogant poems the real Me stands yet untouch'd, untold, altogether unreach'd, | Withdrawn far, mocking me with mock-congratulatory signs and bows, | With peals of distant ironical laughter at every word I have written'.[48]

Fisher's turns on the self are as low-key as Whitman's are operatic, and in the suspended 'So —' that follows, the poem hits a pause. The moment gathers to itself the to-and-fro implications of what has gone before. 'So' may imply that the self and the world are unreliable, given to vanishing. It may imply the need to stand back from that conclusion, even to contest it—or at least, to allow the possibility of a different mode of interpreting. In the ensuing question, 'What kind of a world?', Fisher confirms yet resists the poem's push towards indeterminacy. The question suggests that the world cannot be defined and that the poet does, and yet does not, wish to define it. Elliptically Fisher asserts, 'Even | love's not often a poem': the reader of his poetry learns to expect this kind of effect where the diction is simple but the impact is obscure. To the degree that they demand the reader's involvement, such effects energize the process of response. But at times they risk mannerism. Here Fisher means, one presumes, that there is a gap between feeling and art, that even if the 'you' were a real other loved by the poet, there would be no assurance that a 'poem' would ensue. The following assertion is also suspended across a line-break, though this time less precariously: 'The night | has to move quickly.' 'The night' emerges as a distinct if ephemeral fact; in having 'to move quickly' it is subject to the same imperative as the poem in pursuit of its meaning and the reader in the wake of the poem. 'Sudden rain' followed by

---

[47] Ibid.
[48] Walt Whitman, *The Complete Poems*, ed. Francis Murphy (Harmondsworth: Penguin, 1975).

'Thunder bursts across the mountain' recalls the symbolic plot of 'What the Thunder said' in *The Waste Land*. Yet, like Eliot, Fisher proposes a symbolic meaning without committing himself to it. Still, the less agitated lineation is the strongest clue to a new trust in language:

> Thunder bursts across the mountain;
> the village goes dark with blown fuses,
> and lightning-strokes repeatedly
> bang out their own reality-prints
> of the same white houses
> staring an instant out of the dark.

As the 'lightning-strokes repeatedly | bang out their own reality-prints', they serve as images of Fisher's own verbal activity, his words 'banging out' (on a typewriter, perhaps) 'their own reality-prints'. In fact, so snug is the fit between word and referent that the passage verges on a traditional metaphoric identification, and plays with the capacity of language to persuade one of such an identification. As in Williams's work, the poem's denial of metaphor is not, in practice, complete. The 'houses | staring an instant out of the dark' suggest reality's impingement, through language, on consciousness. Yet 'reality-prints' may imply, too, in the best empirical manner, that the world is known only through possibly unreliable sense-impressions. But this is only one of several implications, and when Ian Gregson writes of these lines that 'the transformation of reality into "prints" suggests the distortions of representation' he is too quick to allow 'transformation' to slide into 'distortions'.[49] There is a further self-reflexive twist in the use of 'prints': the word draws attention to the representation of 'reality' on the printed page looking up at the reader, challenging him or her to decide whether 'transformation' is 'distortion'.

For all its resolute indeterminacy, then, the poem displays a fascination with the very things—self and reality—that it seeks to present as elusive. In 'If I Didn't', indeterminacy and scepticism prove to be riven with paradox. If one has decided in advance that reality is indeterminate, one has made a determinate interpretation; if one is committed to scepticism, scepticism turns into a kind of faith in the rightness of scepticism. At their best, Fisher's poems string along and outmanoeuvre these self-cancellings, as 'If I Didn't' shows. The poem begins with a characteristic assertion of diffidence, Fisher shaping a tangled scenario in which he is forward about his backwardness in being forward: 'If I didn't dislike | mentioning works of art'. These opening two lines separate themselves from the main clause by means of an emphatic gap. The effect, as often in Fisher, is of uneasy parody. Part of the opening registers

---

[49] Ian Gregson, 'Music of the Generous Eye: The Poetry of Roy Fisher', in *Contemporary Poetry and Postmodernism: Dialogue and Estrangement* (Basingstoke: Macmillan, 1996), p. 190.

a genuine 'dislike' of artistic chat; part recognizes that the poet, by writing about writing, is forever 'mentioning works of art'. Here this contradiction gives impetus to the self-reflexive journey on which, almost with a guilty rush, the poem embarks:

> I could say
> the poem has always
> already started, the parapet
> snaking away, its grey line guarding
> the football field and the sea . . .

'I could say' places the lines after it in a conditional mood. But the line also suggests—especially after 'always'—that were the poet to 'say' what, in fact, he goes on to say, he would only be saying what a poem always, in some sense, does say. Ian Gregson points out that 'the words "poem" and "parapet" are connected to each other through an ambiguity achieved by parataxis—a parataxis characteristic of later Fisher in the way it deliberately questions boundaries'.[50] Gregson's own prose seems inadvertently to join in the self-reflexive dance. It is hard not to feel that 'parataxis' has been provoked by alliteration and echo; the boundary between poem and critical discourse is blurred with worrying ease, and 'parataxis' emerges too conveniently as a label to justify Fisher's elliptical transitions. What saves the poem is its 'snaking' away from the banal observation that the poem is a poem and has been written 'already'.

In the following lines 'always already' repeats itself— '—the parapet | has always already started | snaking away'—but this time the phrase has no need for the surprise-inducing line-break. It may be that the repeated phrase conveys, in Almon's words, 'a sense of the continuous present both in the poem . . . and the world'.[51] But to communicate this is to make 'the world' a place of continual, inexhaustible activity. The poem enlarges its scope through this hardly intended hint of celebration; 'under whatever progression', as it goes on to say, it 'takes things forward'.

The couplet from which these phrases are quoted is isolated, as though the poet were rescuing from the surrounding flux the poem's principle of being, a commitment to taking 'things forward'. Fisher is self-aware, yet freed from self-reflexive paralysis, because word and world have begun to mesh in his lines. As is often the case when his poems work, the poem's 'movements' from now on are sure and surprising; commitment to forward movement gives way (as the poem moves forward) to a sense of 'looking down | between the moving frames', a looking down that takes the poet back into the past, or at least into a dimension 'close to recall'. Here the poem does not play games merely; it opens up new territory as it develops. The poet leads himself, and yet is led,

---

[50] Ibid. 182–3.   [51] Almon, ' "If I Didn't Dislike" ', p. 16.

with a bemused tentativeness, into the domain of memory; of 'those other movements' Fisher writes, reluctantly owning up to ownership, 'All of them must be mine, | the way I move on', and then moves on into the past:

> and there I am,
> half my lifetime back,
> on Goodrington sands
> one winter Saturday,
>
> troubled in mind: troubled
> only by Goodrington beach
> under the gloom, the look of it
> against its hinterland
>
> and to be walking
> acres of sandy wrack
> sodden and unstable
> from one end to the other.

Again, one is struck by the way concern with subjectivity comes to the fore. Fisher makes strange his presence ('and there I am') by placing himself in a 'there' that turns out (after the line-ending) to be 'half my lifetime back'. He plays up and plays down a 'troubled' element; he was, we assume in the past ('one winter Saturday') 'troubled in mind', but this confessional gesture is immediately cancelled by the next, seemingly appositional phrase, 'troubled | only by Goodrington beach . . .'. Yet that second instance of being 'troubled' will not stay attached wholly to the first and might refer less to the past time than to a present feeling of being 'troubled' by a past memory. Lending support to this reading is the untethered syntax of 'and to be walking', as though the 'walking' were less remembered than current. It is as if the past memory has turned, by virtue of being conjured up in the poem, into a present image for the poet's 'movement' into the past. In Neil Corcoran's words (describing a general condition of Fisher's work), 'landscape' undergoes 'displacement into mindscape'.[52] Hauntingly, the self discovers itself 'walking | acres of sandy wrack', momentarily recalling the Wordsworth who sees in his mind's eye the Leech-gatherer wandering continually. The terrain of poem and self may be 'sodden and unstable', but the poem traces it 'from one end to the other'.

This terrain seems post-Romantic rather than post-modernist. With its emphasis on 'movement', 'If I Didn't' brings to mind Perloff's description of the Poundian 'rule . . . that anything goes as long as the poet knows, in Charles Olson's words, how to "keep it moving" '.[53] But Fisher's design is far less restlessly open than Olson's dictum suggests, and comes to a provisional

---

[52] Neil Corcoran, *English Poetry since 1940* (London: Longman, 1993), p. 172.
[53] Perloff, *Dance of the Intellect*, p. 22.

pause, as is often the case in the work of the poets discussed in this book, as it articulates a keenly plangent sense of experiential and poetic self-discovery. Fisher serves, in this respect, as an appropriate poet with whom to finish a critical tale of work that is still ongoing. In their capacity to exceed paraphrase and explication, the post-Romantic writers studied in this volume recall, to return to the first chapter's presiding trope, those figures who, in Fisher's poem 'Barnadine's Reply', 'ride out of the air and vanish, | and never once stop to say what they mean'. Yet, if they 'vanish', they do so into the minds of their readers, thus ensuring the emergence of voices still to be accomplished.

Bibliography

ABRAMS, M. H., *The Correspondent Breeze: Essays on English Romanticism*. New York: Norton, 1984.

—— *Natural Supernaturalism: Tradition and Revolution in Romantic Literature*. New York: Norton, 1971.

—— 'Structure and Style in the Greater Romantic Lyric' (1965). In vol. 1 of *Romanticism: Critical Concepts in Literary and Cultural Studies*, ed. Michael O'Neill and Mark Sandy, 4 vols. London: Routledge, 2006.

ADAMS, S. L., and HARPER, G. MILLS (eds.), 'The Manuscript of Leo Africanus'. In *Yeats Annual No. 1* (1982).

ALMON, BERT, ' "If I Didn't Dislike Mentioning Works of Art": Roy Fisher's Poems on Poetics'. *Ariel* 22/3 (1991).

AUDEN, W. H., *Collected Poems*, ed. Edward Mendelson. London: Faber, 1991.

—— *The Dyer's Hand and Other Essays*. London: Faber, 1963.

—— *The Enchafèd Flood; or, The Romantic Iconography of the Sea*. 1951; London: Boston, 1985.

—— *The English Auden: Poems, Essays and Dramatic Writings, 1927–1938*, ed. Edward Mendelson. London: Faber, 1977.

—— *Juvenilia: Poems, 1922–1928*, ed. Katherine Bucknell. London: Faber, 1994.

—— *Prose and Travel Books in Prose and Verse*, i: *1926–1938*, ed. Edward Mendelson. London: Faber, 1996.

—— and MACNEICE, LOUIS, *Letters from Iceland*. London: Faber, 1937.

BAKER, CARLOS, *The Echoing Green: Romanticism, Modernism, and the Phenomena of Transference in Poetry*. Princeton: Princeton University Press, 1984.

BAKHTIN, MIKHAIL, 'From the Prehistory of Novelistic Discourse'. In *Modern Criticism and Theory*, 2nd edn., ed. David Lodge, rev. and expanded by Nigel Wood. Harlow: Longman, 2000.

BATE, JONATHAN, *The Song of the Earth*. London: Picador, 2000.

BATE, WALTER JACKSON, *The Burden of the Past and the English Poet*. Cambridge, Mass.: Harvard University Press, 1970.

BAYLEY, JOHN, *The Romantic Survival*. 1957; London: Chatto & Windus, 1969.

BECKETT, LUCY, *Wallace Stevens*. Cambridge: Cambridge University Press, 1968.

BEER, JOHN, *Post-Romantic Consciousness: Dickens to Plath*. Basingstoke: Palgrave, 2003.

BISHOP, ELIZABETH, *The Complete Poems, 1927–1979*. London: Hogarth Press, 1984.

BHABHA, HOMI K., *The Location of Culture*. 1994; London and New York: Routledge, 2004.

BLAKE, WILLIAM, *Blake: Complete Writings*, ed. Geoffrey Keynes. Oxford: Oxford University Press, 1966.

—— *The Complete Poetry and Prose of William Blake*, newly rev. edn., ed. David V. Erdman, commentary by Harold Bloom. New York: Anchor–Doubleday, 1988.

—— *Milton: A Poem*, ed. with intro. and notes by Robert N. Essick and Joseph Viscomi. London: William Blake Trust/Tate Gallery, 1993.

BLAMIRES, HARRY, *Word Unheard: A Guide through Eliot's 'Four Quartets'*. London: Methuen, 1969.
BLOOM, HAROLD, *The Anxiety of Influence: A Theory of Poetry*. 1973; London: Oxford University Press, 1975.
—— *Poetry and Repression: Revisionism from Blake to Stevens*. New Haven: Yale University Press, 1975.
—— 'The Survival of Strong Poetry'. Introduction to Geoffrey Hill, *Somewhere is Such a Kingdom: Poems, 1952–1971*. Boston: Houghton Mifflin, 1975.
—— *Wallace Stevens: The Poems of Our Climate*. Ithaca, NY: Cornell University Press, 1977.
—— *Yeats*. New York: Oxford University Press, 1970.
BORNSTEIN, GEORGE, *Transformations of Romanticism in Yeats, Eliot, and Stevens*. Chicago: University of Chicago Press, 1976.
—— 'Yeats and Romanticism'. In *The Cambridge Companion to W. B. Yeats*, ed. Marjorie Howes and John Kelly. Cambridge: Cambridge University Press, 2006.
—— *Yeats and Shelley*. Ithaca, NY: Cornell University Press, 1970.
BOZORTH, RICHARD R., ' "But Who Would Get It?": Auden and the Codes of Poetry and Desire'. *ELH* 62/3 (1995).
BRITZOLAKIS, CHRISTINA, *Sylvia Plath and the Theatre of Mourning*. Oxford: Clarendon Press, 1999.
BROGAN, HUGH, *The Penguin History of the USA,* 2nd edn. London: Penguin, 1999.
BROMWICH, DAVID, 'Elizabeth Bishop's Dream Houses'. *Raritan* 4/1 (1984).
BUNTING, BASIL, *Collected Poems*. Oxford: Oxford University Press, 1978.
BURKE, EDMUND, *Reflections on the Revolution in France,* ed. with intro. by Conor Cruise O'Brien. Harmondsworth: Penguin, 1968.
BYRON, GEORGE GORDON, LORD, *Byron*, ed. Jerome J. McGann. Oxford Authors. Oxford: Oxford University Press, 1996.
CARSON, CIARAN, *The Irish for No.* 1987; Newcastle upon Tyne: Bloodaxe, 1988.
CHASE, RICHARD, 'from *Walt Whitman Remembered*' (1955). In *Walt Whitman: A Critical Anthology,* ed. Francis Murphy. Harmondsworth: Penguin, 1969.
COLERIDGE, SAMUEL TAYLOR, *Biographia Literaria, or, Biographical Sketches of my Literary Life and Opinions,* ed. James Engell and W. Jackson Bate, 2 vols. London: Routledge, 1983. Vols. 7.1 and 7.2 of *The Collected Works of Samuel Taylor Coleridge,* gen. ed. Kathleen Coburn, 16 vols. Princeton: Princeton University Press, 1969–2002.
—— *Coleridge: Poetical Works,* ed. Ernest Hartley Coleridge. 1912; London: Oxford University Press, 1967.
—— *Opus Maximum,* ed. Thomas McFarland with Nicholas Halmi. Vol. 15 of *The Collected Works of Samuel Taylor Coleridge*. Princeton: Princeton University Press, 2002.
—— *Coleridge: Poetical Works,* ed. Ernest Hartley Coleridge. 1912; London: Oxford University Press, 1967.
—— *Samuel Taylor Coleridge: Selected Letters,* ed. H. J. Jackson. Oxford: Oxford University Press, 1987.
COOK, ELEANOR, *Poetry, Word-Play, and the Word-War in Wallace Stevens*. Princeton: Princeton University Press, 1988.

CORCORAN, NEIL, *English Poetry since 1940*. London: Longman, 1993.
—— 'One Step Forward, Two Steps Back: Ciaran Carson's *The Irish for No*'. In *The Chosen Ground: Essays on the Contemporary Poetry of Northern Ireland*, ed. Neil Corcoran. Dufour: Seren, 1992.
—— *Seamus Heaney*. London: Faber, 1986.
COSTELLO, BONNIE, *Elizabeth Bishop: Questions of Mastery*. Cambridge, Mass.: Harvard University Press, 1991.
CRANE, HART, *The Complete Poems and Selected Letters and Prose of Hart Crane*, ed. Brom Weber. New York: Liveright, 1966.
CRONIN, RICHARD, *Shelley's Poetic Thoughts*. London: Macmillan, 1981.
CURRAN, STUART, 'Figuration in Shelley and Dante'. In *Dante's Modern Afterlife: Reception and Response from Blake to Heaney*, ed. Nick Havely. Basingstoke: Macmillan, 1998.
DAVIE, DONALD, *Collected Poems*. Manchester: Carcanet, 1990.
DAVIES, DAMIAN WALFORD, and TURLEY, RICHARD MARGGRAF (eds.), *The Monstrous Debt: Modalities of Romantic Influence in Twentieth-Century Literature*. Detroit: Wayne State University Press, 2006.
DAY, AIDAN, *Romanticism*. London: Routledge, 1996.
DAY, THOMAS, 'Sensuous Intelligence: T. S. Eliot and Geoffrey Hill'. *Cambridge Quarterly*, 35/3 (2006).
DE MAN, PAUL, 'Image and Emblem in Yeats'. In *The Rhetoric of Romanticism*. New York: Columbia University Press, 1984.
DENTITH, SIMON, 'Heaney and Walcott: Two Poems'. *Critical Survey*, 11/3 (1999).
ELIOT, T. S., *The Annotated 'Waste Land' with Eliot's Contemporary Prose*, ed. Lawrence Rainey. New Haven: Yale University Press, 2005.
—— *The Complete Poems and Plays*. London: Faber, 1969.
—— *Inventions of the March Hare: Poems, 1909–1917*, ed. Christopher Ricks. 1996; San Diego: Harcourt, 1998.
—— 'Observations'. *Egoist*, 5 (May 1918).
—— *On Poetry and Poets*. London: Faber, 1957.
—— *The Sacred Wood*. London: Methuen, 1920.
—— *Selected Essays*, 3rd edn. London: Faber, 1951.
—— *To Criticize the Critic*. London: Faber, 1965.
—— *The Use of Poetry and the Use of Criticism*. London: Faber, 1933.
ELLMANN, RICHARD, *The Identity of Yeats*. London: Macmillan, 1954.
EMERSON, RALPH WALDO, 'Quotation and Originality'. In *Emerson's Prose and Poetry: Authoritative Texts, Contexts, Criticism*, ed. Joel Porte and Saundra Morris. New York: Norton, 2001.
EMPSON, WILLIAM, *Collected Poems*. London: Hogarth Press, 1984.
ENGELS, FREDERICK, *Ludwig Feuerbach and the End of Classical German Philosophy*. Moscow: Progress, 1946.
FISHER, A. S. T., 'Auden's Juvenilia'. *Notes and Queries*, 21 (1974).
FISHER, ROY, *A Furnace*. Oxford: Oxford University Press, 1986.
—— *Poems, 1955–1980*. Oxford: Oxford University Press, 1988.
—— 'Roy Fisher Reviews Roy Fisher'. *The Rialto*, 35 (1996).
FITZGERALD-HOYT, MARY, 'Grounding Keats's Nightingale: Ciaran Carson's *The Irish for No*'. *Canadian Journal of Irish Studies*, 19/2 (1993).

FORBES, DEBORAH, *Self-Consciousness in Mid-Twentieth-Century American Poetry.* Cambridge, Mass.: Harvard University Press, 2004.

FOSTER, ROY, *W. B. Yeats,* ii: *The Arch-Poet, 1915–1939.* Oxford: Oxford University Press, 2003.

FRANKLIN, GEORGE, 'Instances of Meeting: Shelley and Eliot: A Study in Affinity'. *ELH* 61 (1994).

FROST, ROBERT, *Collected Poems.* London: Cape, 1943.

FRYE, NORTHROP, *Anatomy of Criticism: Four Essays.* Princeton: Princeton University Press, 1957.

GARBER, FREDERICK, *Wordsworth and the Poetry of Encounter.* Urbana: University of Illinois Press, 1971.

GARRATT, ROBERT F., *Modern Irish Poetry: Tradition and Continuity from Yeats to Heaney.* Berkeley: University of California, 1988.

GELPI, ALBERT, *A Coherent Splendor: The American Poetic Renaissance, 1910–1950.* 1987; Cambridge: Cambridge University Press, 1990.

GERRARD, NICCI, 'The Face of Human Evil', *Observer,* 17 Nov. 2002.

GORDON, LYNDALL, *Eliot's Early Years.* 1977; Oxford: Oxford University Press, 1978.

GREGSON, IAN, 'Music of the Generous Eye: The Poetry of Roy Fisher'. In *Contemporary Poetry and Postmodernism: Dialogue and Estrangement.* Basingstoke: Macmillan, 1996.

GRIFFITHS, ERIC, 'The Divine Comedy Collides with the Modern "Vision Thing"'. *The Guardian Review,* 8 Jan. 1998. *Guardian Unlimited.* Online.

—— 'Hill's Criticism: A Life of Form'. In *Geoffrey Hill: Essays on his Work,* ed. Peter Robinson. Milton Keynes: Open University Press, 1986.

HALMI, NICHOLAS, et al. (eds.), *Coleridge's Poetry and Prose.* New York: Norton, 2004.

HART, HENRY, *The Poetry of Geoffrey Hill.* Carbondale: Southern Illinois University Press, 1986.

HARTMAN, GEOFFREY H., 'A Life of Learning'. Charles Homer Hashins Lecture for 2000, online.

HAUGHTON, HUGH, ' "How Fit a Title . . .": Title and Authority in the Work of Geoffrey Hill'. In *Geoffrey Hill: Essays on his Work,* ed. Peter Robinson. Milton Keynes: Open University Press, 1986.

—— 'Power and Hiding Places: Wordsworth and Seamus Heaney'. In *The Monstrous Debt,* ed. Damian Walford Davies and Richard Marggraf Turley. Detroit: Wayne State University Press, 2006.

HEANEY, SEAMUS, *District and Circle.* London: Faber, 2006.

—— 'The Drag of the Golden Chain'. *Times Literary Supplement,* 12 Nov. 1999.

—— *The Essential Wordsworth.* New York: Ecco, 1988.

—— *Finders Keepers: Selected Prose, 1971–2001.* London: Faber, 2002.

—— *The Government of the Tongue.* 1988; London: Faber, 1989.

—— *North.* London: Faber, 1975.

—— *Opened Ground: Poems, 1966–1996.* London: Faber, 1998.

—— *Preoccupations: Selected Prose, 1968–1978.* London: Faber, 1980.

—— *The Redress of Poetry.* London: Faber, 1995.

HECHT, ANTHONY, *The Hidden Law: The Poetry of W. H. Auden.* Cambridge, Mass.: Harvard University Press, 1993.

HEMANS, FELICIA, *Selected Poems, Letters, Reception Materials*, ed. Susan J. Wolfson. Princeton: Princeton University Press, 2000.
HERD, DAVID, 'Pleasure at Home: How Twentieth-Century American Poets Read the British'. In *A Concise Companion to Twentieth-Century American Poetry*, ed. Stephen Fredman. Oxford: Blackwell, 2005.
HILL, GEOFFREY, *Canaan*. London: Penguin, 1996.
—— *Collected Poems*. Harmondsworth: Penguin, 1985.
—— 'The Conscious Mind's Intelligible Structure—A Debate'. *Agenda*, 4/1 (1971–2).
—— *The Enemy's Country: Words, Contexture, and Other Circumstances of Language*. Stanford, Calif.: Stanford University Press, 1991.
—— *The Lords of Limit: Essays on Literature and Ideas*. London: André Deutsch, 1984.
—— *The Orchards of Syon*. London: Penguin, 2002.
—— *Rhetorics of Value*. The Tanner Lectures on Human Values. Delivered at Brasenose College, Oxford, 6 and 7 March 2000, online.
—— *Scenes from Comus*. London: Penguin, 2005.
—— *Speech! Speech!* New York: Counterpoint, 2000.
—— *Style and Faith*. New York: Counterpoint, 2003.
—— *The Triumph of Love*. London: Penguin, 1998.
—— *Without Title*. London: Penguin, 2006.
HOGLE, JERROLD E., *Shelley's Process: Radical Transference and the Development of his Major Works*. New York: Oxford University Press, 1988.
HORTON, PATRICIA, 'Romantic Intersections: Romanticism and Contemporary Northern Irish Poetry'. Ph.D. dissertation, Queen's University of Belfast, 1996.
HUGHES, TED, *Collected Poems*, ed. Paul Keegan. London: Faber, 2003.
—— Introduction to *A Choice of Coleridge's Verse*. London: Faber, 1996.
HUNT, LEIGH, *The Autobiography of Leigh Hunt*, 3 vols. London: Smith, Elder & Co., 1850.
JACCOTTET, PHILIPPE, *Selected Poems: Philippe Jaccottet*, trans. and intro. by Derek Mahon. Harmondsworth: Penguin, 1988.
JEFFARES, A. NORMAN, *W. B. Yeats: A New Biography*. London: Continuum, 2001.
JOYCE, JAMES, *Ulysses*, ed. Jeri Johnson. Oxford: Oxford University Press, 1993.
KAVANAGH, PATRICK, *Collected Poems*, ed. Antoinette Quinn. London: Allen Lane, 2004.
—— *A Poet's Country: Selected Prose*, ed. Antoinette Quinn. Dublin: Lilliput, 2003.
KEATS, JOHN, *John Keats*, ed. Elizabeth Cook. Oxford Authors. Oxford: Oxford University Press, 1990.
—— *The Poems of John Keats*, ed. Jack Stillinger. London: Heinemann, 1978.
KELLER, LYNN, 'An Interview with Paul Muldoon. Conducted by Lynn Keller'. *Contemporary Literature*, 35/1 (1994).
KELSALL, MALCOLM, 'Byron's Politics'. In *The Cambridge Companion to Byron*, ed. Drummond Bone. Cambridge: Cambridge University Press, 2004.
KENDALL, TIM, *Paul Muldoon*. Bridgend: Seren, 1996.
KERMODE, FRANK, *Romantic Image*. London: Routledge, 1957.
KEYES, SIDNEY, *The Collected Poems*, ed. with a memoir and notes by Michael Meyer. London: Routledge, 1988.
LARKIN, PHILIP, *Collected Poems*, ed. with intro. by Anthony Thwaite. London: The Marvell Press and Faber, 1988.
LARRISSY, EDWARD, *Blake and Modern Literature*. Basingstoke: Palgrave, 2006.

—— (ed.). *Romanticism and Post-Modernism*. Cambridge: Cambridge University Press, 1999.

LONGENBACH, JAMES, *Wallace Stevens: The Plain Sense of Things*. New York: Oxford University Press, 1991.

LOVEJOY, ARTHUR O., 'On the Discrimination of Romanticisms', *PLMA* 39 (1924); repr. in vol. 1 of *Romanticism: Critical Concepts in Literary and Cultural Studies*, ed. Michael O'Neill and Mark Sandy, 4 vols. London: Routledge, 2006.

LOWE, PETER, *Christian Romanticism: T.S. Eliot's Response to Percy Shelley*. Youngstown, NY: Cambria, 2006.

LOWELL, ROBERT, *Collected Poems*, ed. Frank Bidart and David Gewanter, with the editorial assistance of DeSales Harrison. London: Faber, 2003.

LOWES, JOHN LIVINGSTON, *The Road to Xanadu: A Study in the Ways of the Imagination*. 1927; London: Pan, repr. 1978.

MCDONALD, PETER, *Serious Poetry: Form and Authority from Yeats to Hill*. Oxford: Clarendon Press, 2002.

——'Yeats and Remorse'. *Proceedings of the British Academy*, 94 (1998).

MCGANN, JEROME J., *Fiery Dust: Byron's Poetic Development*. Chicago: University of Chicago Press, 1968.

—— 'Lord Byron's Twin Opposites of Truth [*Don Juan*]'. In *Byron*, ed. Jane Stabler. Longman Critical Readers. London and New York: Longman, 1998.

—— 'Romanticism and its Ideologies'. *Studies in Romanticism*, 21 (1982). Repr. in *Romanticism: Critical Concepts in Literary and Cultural Studies*, ed. Michael O'Neill and Mark Sandy, ii.

MCKENDRICK, JAMIE, 'Bishop's Birds'. In *Elizabeth Bishop: Poet of the Periphery*, ed. Linda Anderson and Jo Shapcott. Newcastle upon Tyne: Bloodaxe, 2002.

—— (ed.), *The Faber Book of Twentieth-Century Italian Poems*. London: Faber, 2004.

MACNEICE, LOUIS, *Selected Literary Criticism*, ed. Alan Heuser. Oxford: Clarendon Press, 1987.

MAHON, DEREK, 'Biographia Literaria'. *Times Literary Supplement*, 5 May 2006.

—— *Collected Poems*. Loughcrew: Gallery, 1999.

—— *The Hudson Letter*. Loughcrew: Gallery, 1995.

—— Introduction. In *Selected Poems: Philippe Jaccottet*. Harmondsworth: Penguin, 1988.

—— *Poems 1962–1978*. Oxford: Oxford University Press, 1979.

—— *Selected Poems*. 1990; London: Penguin in association with Oxford University Press, 1993.

MALLARMÉ, STEPHANE, *Collected Poems*, trans. Henry Weinfield. Berkeley: University of California Press, 1994.

MASON, EMMA, ' "Love's the Burning Boy": Hemans's Critical Legacy'. *The Monstrous Debt*, ed. Damian Walford Davies and Richard Marggraf Turley. Detroit: Wayne State University Press, 2006.

MILTON, JOHN, *Poetical Works*, ed. Douglas Bush. London: Oxford University Press, 1969.

MOLINO, MICHAEL R., 'Heaney's "Singing School": A Portrait of the Artist'. *Journal of Irish Literature*, 16/3 (1987).

MONTAGUE, JOHN, *Collected Poems*. Loughcrew: Gallery Press, 1995.

MONTALE, EUGENIO, *Collected Poems, 1920–1954*, trans. and annoted by Jonathan Galassi. New York: Farrar, Straus and Giroux, 1999.

MOODY, A. DAVID, *Thomas Stearns Eliot, Poet*, 2nd edn. Cambridge: Cambridge University Press, 1994.
MOORE, THOMAS, *The Poetical Works of Thomas Moore, Reprinted from the Early Editions, with Explanatory Notes, Etc.* The 'Albion' Edition. London and New York: Frederick Warne and Co., n.d.
MOYLE, J., '"A New Byronism": T. S. Eliot's "Bored But Courteous" Poetry', *Byron Journal*, 26 (1998).
MULDOON, PAUL (ed.), *The Faber Book of Contemporary Irish Poetry*. London: Faber, 1986.
—— Introduction. In *The Essential Byron*. New York: Ecco, 1989.
—— *Moy Sand and Gravel*. London: Faber, 2004.
—— *Poems, 1968–1998*. London: Faber, 2001.
—— *To Ireland, I*. Oxford: Oxford University Press, 2000.
The Norton Anthology of Poetry, 4th edn., ed. Margaret Ferguson, Mary Jo Salter, and Jon Stallworthy. New York and London: Norton, 1996.
O'BRIEN, CONOR CRUISE, 'Passion and Cunning: An Essay on the Politics of W. B. Yeats'. In *In Excited Reverie: A Centenary Tribute to William Butler Yeats, 1865–1939*, ed. A. N. Jeffares and K. G. W. Cross. London: Macmillan, 1965.
O'NEILL, MICHAEL, 'Cathestant or Protholic? Shelley's Italian Imaginings'. *Journal of Anglo-Italian Studies*, 6 (2001).
—— ' "Exhibiting Unpreparedness": Self, World, and Poetry'. In *The Thing about Roy Fisher*, ed. John Kerrigan and Peter Robinson. Manchester: Manchester University Press, 2000.
—— 'Poetry as Literary Criticism'. In *The Arts and Sciences of Criticism*, ed. David Fuller and Patricia Waugh. Oxford: Oxford University Press, 1999.
—— 'Poetry of the Romantic Period: Coleridge and Keats'. In *A Companion to Romance from Classical to Contemporary*, ed. Corinne Saunders. Oxford: Blackwell, 2004.
—— ' "Wholly Incommunicable by Words": Romantic Expressions of the Inexpressible', *The Wordsworth Circle*, 31 (2000).
—— and REEVES, GARETH, *Auden, MacNeice, Spender: The Thirties Poetry*. Basingstoke: Macmillan, 1992.
OWEN, WILFRED, *The Poems*, ed. and intro. by Jon Stallworthy. London: Hogarth Press, 1985.
PALEY, MORTON D., *Apocalypse and Millennium in English Romantic Poetry*. Oxford: Clarendon Press, 1999.
PARKER, MICHAEL, *Seamus Heaney: The Makings of the Poet*. Basingstoke: Macmillan, 1993.
PAULIN, TOM, *The Day-Star of Liberty: William Hazlitt's Radical Style*. London: Faber, 1998.
—— (ed), *The Faber Book of Political Verse*. London: Faber, 1986.
PERLOFF, MARJORIE, *The Dance of the Intellect: Studies in the Poetry of the Pound Tradition*. Evanston, Ill.: Northwestern University Press, 1996.
PERRY, SEAMUS, *Coleridge and the Uses of Division*. Oxford: Clarendon Press, 1999.
PETERFREUND, STUART, *Shelley among Others: The Play of the Intertext and the Idea of Language*. Baltimore: Johns Hopkins University Press, 2002.
PHILLIPS, CARL, Interview: 'Geoffrey Hill, The Art of Poetry LXXX'. *Paris Review*, 154 (Spring 2000).
PINSKY, ROBERT, 'The Idiom of a Self: Elizabeth Bishop and Wordsworth'. *American Poetry Review*, Jan.–Feb. 1980.

PLATH, SYLVIA, *Ariel.* 1965; London: Faber, 1968.
POUND, EZRA, *The Cantos.* London: Faber, 1968.
—— *Collected Shorter Poems.* London: Faber, 1984.
QUINN, ANTOINETTE, *Patrick Kavanagh: Born-Again Romantic.* Dublin: Gill & Macmillan, 1991.
QUINNEY, LAURA, *The Poetics of Disappointment: Wordsworth to Ashbery.* Charlottesville: University Press of Virginia, 1999.
RADER, MELVIN M., 'Shelley's Theory of Evil'. In *Shelley: A Collection of Critical Essays,* ed. George M. Ridenour. Englewood Cliffs, NJ: Prentice-Hall, 1965.
READ, HERBERT, *Adelphi,* 5 (Feb. 1933).
REEVES, GARETH, *T. S. Eliot's 'The Waste Land'.* New York: Harvester Wheatsheaf, 1994.
RICH, ADRIENNE, *Midnight Salvage: Poems 1995–1998.* New York: Norton, 1999.
RICKS, CHRISTOPHER, *Allusion to the Poets.* Oxford: Clarendon Press, 2002.
—— 'Geoffrey Hill 2: At-One-Ment'. In *The Force of Poetry.* 1984; Oxford: Oxford University Press, 1987.
—— *T. S. Eliot and Prejudice.* 1988; London: Faber, 1994.
ROBERTS, ANDREW MICHAEL, 'Geoffrey Hill'. In *Literary Encyclopedia,* online. First Published 1 Oct. 2004; rev. 11 Jan. 2005.
—— 'Romantic Irony and the Postmodern Sublime: Geoffrey Hill and "Sebastian Arrurruz"'. In *Romanticism and Postmodernism,* ed. Edward Larrissy. Cambridge: Cambridge University Press, 1999.
ROBINSON, PETER (ed.), *Geoffrey Hill: Essays on his Work.* Milton Keynes: Open University Press, 1986.
ROE, NICHOLAS, 'Pantisocracy and the Myth of the Poet'. In *Romanticism and Millenarianism,* ed. Tim Fulford. Basingstoke: Palgrave, 2002.
RUOFF, GENE W. (ed.), *The Romantics and Us: Essays on Literature and Culture.* New Brunswick, NJ: Rutgers University Press, 1990.
RZEPKA, CHARLES, 'Elizabeth Bishop and the Wordsworth of *Lyrical Ballads:* Sentimentalism, Straw Men, and Misprison'. In 'The "Honourable Characteristic of Poetry": Two Hundred Years of *Lyrical Ballads*', ed. Marcy L. Tanter, an online volume in the Romantic Circles Praxis Series, series ed. Orrin Wang, Nov. 1999.
SAID, EDWARD, *Culture and Imperialism.* London: Chatto, 1993.
SCHLEGEL, FRIEDRICH, 'Athenaum Fragments'. In *The Origins of Modern Critical Thought: German Aesthetic and Literary Criticism from Lessing to Hegel,* ed. David Simpson. Cambridge: Cambridge University Press, 1988.
SHACKLETON, SIR ERNEST, *South: The Story of Shackleton's Last Expedition, 1914–1917.* London: Heinemann, 1919.
SHAKESPEARE, WILLIAM, *The Norton Shakespeare,* gen. ed. Stephen Greenblatt. New York: Norton, 1997.
SHELLEY, PERCY BYSSHE, *The Letters of Percy Bysshe Shelley,* ed. Frederick L. Jones, 2 vols. Oxford: Clarendon Press, 1964.
—— *Percy Bysshe Shelley: The Major Works,* ed. Zachary Leader and Michael O'Neill. Oxford: Oxford University Press, 2003.
—— *The Poems of Shelley, ii: 1817–1819,* ed. Kelvin Everest and Geoffrey Matthews. Harlow: Longman, 2000.

SHELLEY, PERCY BYSSHE, *Shelley: Poetical Works*, ed. Thomas Hutchinson, rev. G. M. Matthews. London: Oxford University Press, 1970.

SMITH, CHRISTOPHER J., *A Quest for Home: Reading Robert Southey*. Liverpool: Liverpool University Press, 1997.

SMITH, GROVER, *T. S. Eliot's Poetry and Plays: A Study in Sources and Meaning*. Chicago: University of Chicago Press, 1956.

SMITH, STAN, 'Seamus Heaney: The Distance Between'. In *The Chosen Ground: Essays on the Contemporary Poetry of Northern Ireland*, ed. Neil Corcoran. Dufour: Seren, 1992.

SOUTHEY, ROBERT, *Madoc*, ed. Linda Pratt, vol. 2 of *Robert Southey: Poetical Works*, 5 vols. London: Pickering & Chatto, 2004.

SPENDER, STEPHEN (ed.), *A Choice of Shelley's Verse*. London: Faber, 1971.

—— *Eliot*. 1975; London: Fontana, 1986.

—— *New Collected Poems*, ed. Michael Brett. London: Faber, 2004.

—— *The Thirties and After: Poetry, Politics, People, 1933–75*. London: Fontana/Collins, 1978.

—— *World Within World*. 1951; London: Faber, 1977.

—— and LEHMANN, JOHN (eds.), *Poems for Spain*. London: Hogarth Press, 1939.

SPIEGELMAN, WILLARD, 'Landscape and Knowledge: The Poetry of Elizabeth Bishop'. *Modern Poetry Studies*, 6 (1975).

STABLER, JANE, 'Byron, Postmodernism and Intertextuality'. In *The Cambridge Companion to Byron*, ed. Drummond Bone. Cambridge: Cambridge University Press, 2004.

STAFFORD, FIONA, *Starting Lines in Scottish, Irish, and English Poetry: From Burns to Heaney*. Oxford: Oxford University Press, 2000.

STEAD, C. K., *The New Poetic: Yeats to Eliot*. 1964; Harmondsworth: Penguin, 1967.

STEINER, GEORGE, *Real Presences: Is There Anything in What We Say?* 1989; London: Faber, 1991.

—— (ed.), *The Penguin Book of Modern Verse Translation*. Harmondsworth: Penguin, 1966.

STEINMAN, LISA M., Introduction to *Romanticism and Contemporary Poetry and Poetics*, ed. Lisa M. Steinman for the Romantic Circles Praxis Series, series ed. Orrin Wang, July 2003, online.

STEVENS, WALLACE, *Collected Poems*. London: Faber, 1955.

—— *Collected Poetry and Prose*, ed. Frank Kermode and Joan Richardson. New York: The Library of America, 1997.

—— *Letters of Wallace Stevens*, ed. Holly Stevens. New York: Knopf, 1966.

—— *The Necessary Angel: Essays on Reality and the Imagination*. London: Faber, 1984.

—— *Opus Posthumous by Wallace Stevens*, ed. Samuel French Morse. New York: Vintage, 1982.

—— *The Palm at the End of the Mind: Selected Poems and a Play by Wallace Stevens*, ed. Holly Stevens. New York: Vintage, 1990.

TAYLOR, CHARLES, *Sources of the Self: The Making of the Modern Identity*. Cambridge: Cambridge University Press, 1989.

TENNYSON, ALFRED, LORD, *The Poems of Tennyson*, ed. Christopher Ricks. London: Longmans, 1969.

VASSALLO, PETER, 'From Petrarch to Dante: The Discourse of Disenchantment in Shelley's *The Triumph of Life*'. *Journal of Anglo-Italian Studies*, 1 (1991).

—— 'T. S. Eliot, W. B. Yeats and the Dantean "Familiar Compound Ghost" in *Little Gidding*'. *Journal of Anglo-Italian Studies*, 6 (2001).

VENDLER, HELEN, 'Ghostlier Demarcations, Keener Sounds'. In *Adrienne Rich: Poetry and Prose: Poems, Prose, Reviews and Criticism*, ed. Barbara Charlesworth Gelpi and Albert Gelpi. New York: Norton, 1993.

—— *On Extended Wings: Wallace Stevens' Longer Poems*. Cambridge, Mass.: Harvard University Press, 1969.

—— *Part of Nature, Part of Us*. Cambridge, Mass.: Harvard University Press, 1980.

—— *Seamus Heaney*. London: Faber, 1998.

WAINWRIGHT, JEFFREY, *Acceptable Words: Essays on the Poetry of Geoffrey Hill*. Manchester: Manchester University Press, 2005.

WASSERMAN, EARL R., *Shelley: A Critical Reading*. Baltimore: Johns Hopkins University Press, 1971.

WHITMAN, WALT, *The Complete Poems*, ed. Francis Murphy. Harmondsworth: Penguin, 1975.

—— *Leaves of Grass*. Intro. by Gay Wilson Allen. New York: The New American Library, 1958.

WILLIAMS, WILLIAM CARLOS, *Selected Essays*. New York: New Directions, 1969.

——*Selected Poems*, ed. with intro. by Charles Tomlinson. Harmondsworth: Penguin, 1976.

WILLS, CLAIR, *Reading Paul Muldoon*. Newcastle upon Tyne: Bloodaxe, 1998.

WOLFSON, SUSAN J., *The Questioning Presence: Wordsworth, Keats, and the Interrogative Mode in Romantic Poetry*. Ithaca, NY: Cornell University Press, 1986.

WOOTTEN, WILLIAM, 'Romanticism and Animism in Roy Fisher's *A Furnace*'. *Cercles*, 12 (2005).

WORDSWORTH, JONATHAN, *The Music of Humanity*. London: Nelson, 1969.

WORDSWORTH, WILLIAM, *The Prelude: The Four Texts (1798, 1799, 1805, 1850)*, ed. Jonathan Wordsworth. London: Penguin, 1995.

—— *William Wordsworth*, ed. Stephen Gill. Oxford Authors. Oxford: Oxford University Press, 1984.

WU, DUNCAN (ed.), *Romanticism: An Anthology*, 3rd edn. Oxford: Blackwell, 2006.

YEATS, W. B., 'Four Lectures by W. B. Yeats, 1902–4', ed. Richard Londraville. In *Yeats Annual No. 8*, ed. Warwick Gould. Basingstoke: Macmillan, 1991.

—— *Essays and Introductions*. London: Macmillan, 1961.

—— *Later Essays*, ed. W. H. O'Donnell, with assistance from E. Bergmann Loizeaux. New York: Charles Scribner's Sons, 1994.

—— *Letters*, ed. Allan Wade. London: Rupert Hart-Davis, 1954.

—— *Memoirs*, transcribed and ed. Denis Donoghue. New York: Macmillan, 1972.

—— *The Poems*, ed. Daniel Albright. London: Dent, 1990.

YEATS, W. B., ' "The Poet and the Actress": An Unpublished Dialogue by W. B. Yeats', ed. David R. Clark. In *Yeats Annual No. 8*, ed. Warwick Gould. Basingstoke: Macmillan, 1991.

—— *Selected Criticism and Prose*, ed. A. Norman Jeffares. London: Pan in association with Macmillan, 1980.

—— *Unpublished Prose*, ed. J. P. Frayne. New York: Macmillan, 1970.

—— *A Vision*. London: Macmillan, 1962.

—— *'The Wild Swans at Coole': Manuscript Materials*, ed. Stephen Parrish. Ithaca, NY: Cornell University Press, 1994.

ZAMBON, FRANCESCO, *L'iride nel fango: L'anguilla di Eugenio Montale*. Palma: Nuova Pratiche Editrice, 1994.

Index

Abrams, M. H. 12, 85, 107, 115
Albright, Daniel 42n, 55
Aligheri, Dante 13, 35–6, 39–42, 44–6, 78, 113–14, 179
   Commedia 44–6
   Paradiso 26
   Vita Nuova 46
Almon, Bert 186, 187, 189
Ammons, A. R.:
   'City Limits, The' 146
Arnold, Matthew 114, 115
Auden, W. H. 6, 10, 83–96, 97, 122, 125, 145, 183
   'Consider this and in our time' 87–9
   'Dame Kind' 85–9
   'Don Juan' 94–5
   The Enchafèd Flood 92
   'In Memory of W. B. Yeats' 5, 89–90
   'In Praise of Limestone' 84
   'In Time of War' 128
   Letters from Iceland 95
   Letter to Lord Byron 10, 13, 93–6, 147, 148
   'Light Verse' 93
   New Year Letter 92
   The Orators 93
   The Poet's Tongue 89
   'Richard Jefferies' 83
   'The Road's Your Place' 83–4
   'September 1, 1939' 91–2
   'Who stands, the crux left of the watershed' 84–7

Babbitt, Irving 114
Baker, Carlos 12n, 76n, 89, 90
Bakhtin, Mikhail 161
Bate, Jonathan 33
Baudelaire 13, 74
   'Le Voyage' 66
Bayley, John 87
Beckett, Lucy 106
Beddoes, Thomas Lovell 82
Beer, John 4
Bhabha, Homi 161
Bishop, Elizabeth 5, 10, 13
   'Casabianca' 28
   'Crusoe in England' 26
   'In the Waiting Room' 27–8
   'The Monument' 29–30
   'Sandpiper' 24–5
   'The Unbeliever' 27
Blake, William 1, 33, 34, 35, 45, 54, 92, 114, 174, 180
   'Auguries of Innocence' 24
   'The Ecchoing Green' 49
   'The [First] Book of Urizen' 27
   The Four Zoas 72
   'Introduction', *Songs of Experience* 91
   Jerusalem 47, 103, 181
   'London' 98, 181–2
   'Mad Song' 181
   The Marriage of Heaven and Hell 24, 47, 151
   'The Mental Traveller' 56, 87–8
   Milton 47, 105
   'Sick Rose, The' 132
   Songs of Innocence and of Experience 64, 98
   'There is No Natural Religion' 56, 169
   'The Tyger' 90
Blamires, Harry 78, 79
Bloom, Harold 11, 22, 35, 38n, 39, 43, 45n, 46, 51n, 52, 54, 56, 58n, 84, 118, 146, 176, 184
Bornstein, George 12n, 22, 32n, 34, 35, 38n, 40, 56, 58n, 70n, 75–6, 77, 80, 81
Bozorth, Richard R. 85
Britzolakis, Christina 29
Brogan, Hugh 149, 151
Bromwich, David 26n
Bucknell, Katherine 84n
Bunting, Basil 122
Burke, Edmund:
   Reflections on the Revolution in France 52
Byron, George Gordon, Lord 5, 10, 74–6, 145, 156
   Beppo 69–70, 145–6
   Childe Harold's Pilgrimage 53, 65, 75, 88, 116, 117–18
   Don Juan 70, 94–6, 119, 125, 128, 148, 150, 151, 157, 158, 161, 162
   'Ode to the Framers of the Frame Bill, An' 96
   'Stanzas to [Augusta]' 89
   The Vision of Judgment 157

Calderón de la Barca, Pedro:
   La vida es sueno 175

Carson, Ciaran 14, 121, 133–4
  'The Irish for No' 133
Chase, Richard 108
Clark, David R. 42
Coleridge, Samuel Taylor 18, 24, 25, 61, 80, 119, 133, 147, 151, 155, 156, 178, 180, 184
  Aids to Reflection 165
  Biographia Literaria 26, 32, 33, 53, 64, 101, 155, 180
  'Dejection: An Ode' 6, 7, 27, 31, 49, 62, 85, 86, 108, 153
  'The Devil's Walk' 157
  'The Eolian Harp' 33, 114, 133, 152, 154, 156, 158
  'Frost at Midnight' 156
  'Kubla Khan' 29–30, 40, 58, 64, 71–2, 147, 150, 164
  'Religious Musings' 72, 156
  'The Rime of the Ancient Mariner' 4, 58, 76, 115, 117
  'This Lime-Tree Bower My Prison' 115, 153, 163
Cook, Eleanor 105, 118, 119
Corcoran, Neil 132n, 133–4, 137, 190
Costello, Bonnie 26, 27, 30n
Crane, Hart 10, 13, 97
  'The Broken Tower' 15–16
Cronin, Richard 113n
Crozier, Andrew 186
Cullingford, Elizabeth 52
Curran, Stuart 44n

Davie, Donald:
  'Rejoinder to a Critic' 7
Davies, Damian Walford 12n
Day, Aidan 121
Day, Thomas 172n
De Man, Paul 50n
de Nerval, Gerard 68
De Quincey, Thomas 9
Denith, Simon 132n
Donne, John 179

Eliot, George:
  Advice to Working Men by Felix Holt 173
Eliot, T. S. 2, 10, 13, 60–82, 83, 97, 114
  Ash-Wednesday 123
  'Baudelaire' 74
  The Cocktail Party 65–6
  The Family Reunion 75
  Four Quartets 2, 60, 76–82, 97, 161, 172, 184
  'The Frontiers of Criticism' 82
  'Imperfect Critics' 63

'The Love Song of J. Alfred Prufrock' 61, 70, 97
  'Oh little voices of the throats of men' 61, 63–5
  'Rolled Over on Europe' 97
  'Varieties of Metaphysical Poetry' 171
  The Waste Land 13, 63, 67–73, 79, 86, 97, 188
  'What Dante Means to Me' 77
Ellmann, Richard 41
Engels, Friedrich 151
Emerson, Ralph Waldo 18
Empson, William:
  'Doctrinal Point' 18
Everest, Kelvin 16n

Fisher, A. S. T. 84n
Fisher, Roy 10, 14, 165, 183–91
  'Barnadine's Reply' 191
  A Furnace 184
  'If I Didn't' 188–90
  'Of the Empirical Self and for Me' 186–7
  'The Memorial Fountain' 185–6
  'The Thing about Joe Sullivan' 184
Fitzgerald-Hoyt, Mary 134n
Forbes, Deborah 12n
Foster, Roy 37
Franklin, George 68n
Frost, Robert:
  'The Most of It' 5
Frye, Northrop 12n
Fuller, Loie 20

Garratt, Robert F. 122n
Gelpi, Albert 10–11, 142
Gerrard, Nicci 112
Ginsberg, Allen 1
Gordon, Lyndall 61
Gregson, Ian 188, 189
Griffiths, Eric 35, 167

Hart, Henry 169, 177n, 180, 181
Hartman, Geoffrey H. 179n
Haughton, Hugh 132n, 177
Hazlitt, William 122
Heaney, Seamus 10, 14, 25–6, 121, 131–3, 135–42, 165–6, 167
  Beowulf 135
  'Blackberry Picking' 134
  'Crediting Poetry' 139
  'Door into the Dark' 134, 146
  'Exposure' 136
  'From Monaghan to the Grand Canal: The Poetry of Patrick Kavanagh' 141
  'Frontiers of Writing' 140

'Glanmore Sonnets' 132, 139
The Government of the Tongue 138
'The Interesting Case of Nero, Chekhov's Cognac and a Knocker' 139
'The Making of Music' 137
'Oysters' 139
'The Peninsula' 131
'Personal Helicon' 137, 138
'Place and Displacement' 140
Seeing Things 140
'Singing School' 136–7
'Squarings' 140
'Thatcher' 131
'Tollund' 140–1
'The Tollund Man' 140–1
'The Unacknowledged Legislator's Dream' 139
'Vision' 152
'Voices from Lemnos' 140
'Wordsworth's Skates' 141–2
Hecht, Anthony 85n, 90, 91n
'Hill, A' 8–9
Hemans, Felicia:
'Casabianca' 28
Herbert, George 179
Herd, David 10n
Hill, Geoffrey 6, 10, 14, 165–83
'An Apology for the Revival of Christian Architecture in England' 180
Canaan 181–2
'Churchill's Funeral' 181
'The Conscious Mind's Intelligible Structure—A Debate' 178
'The Death of Shelley' 169, 180
'Elegiac Stanzas, On a Visit to Dove Cottage' 177–8
The Enemy's County 170
'Funeral Music' 172, 180
'Genesis' 174
'History as Poetry' 106
'Holy Thursday' 179
'In Ipsley Church Lane 2, 183
'Of Commerce and Society' 169–70
'Of Coming into Being and Passing Away' 168
The Orchards of Syon 175
'Our Word is Our Bond' 179
'Ovid in the Third Reich' 106, 179
'Poetry and Value' 165
'Poetry as "Menace" and "Atonement"' 170–1, 178, 180
'Redeeming the Time' 166, 172–3, 175
Rhetorics of Value 165, 173
Scenes from Comus 174–5
Style and Faith 166
'To John Constable: In Absentia' 182
The Triumph of Love 170–2, 174, 176–7
Without Title 183
Hogle, Jerrold E. 116
Hopkins, Gerard Manley 166, 179, 183
'Spring and Fall' 175
Horton, Patricia 132n
Hughes, Ted 4n:
'Skylarks' 2–5

Jaccottet, Philippe 19
Joyce, James 121

Kavanagh, Patrick 10, 14, 121, 123–31, 145, 147
'Auden and the Creative Mind' 126
'Canal Bank Walk' 124, 127
'A Christmas Childhood' 129–30
Come Dance with Kitty Stobling 123
'Epic' 126, 130, 136
'Inniskeen Road: July Evening' 125, 141
'Lines Written on a Seat on the Grand Canal, Dublin' 130
'The One' 123–8
'Question to Life' 127
'Self-Portrait' 123–4
'Violence and Literature' 129–30
'Winter' 128–31
Keats, John 1, 22, 39, 41–2, 60, 73, 82, 90, 118, 121, 125
Endymion 68n
The Fall of Hyperion 55, 74, 97, 99, 106–7
Hyperion 97
Isabella 89
'La Belle Dame Sans Merci' 79, 180
Lamia 19, 62
'Ode on a Grecian Urn' 21, 30, 58, 59, 81, 128, 138, 143, 168, 181
'Ode on Melancholy' 101
'Ode to a Nightingale' 1, 28, 70, 73, 133, 143, 168, 178–9, 180
'Ode to Psyche' 19, 130
'On the Grasshopper and Cricket' 14
'To Autumn' 117, 134
Keller, Lynn 145, 147n, 148
Kelsall, Malcolm 157
Kendall, Tim 145, 152n, 154, 162
Kermode, Frank 6, 55
Keyes, Sidney:
'William Wordsworth' 8

Larkin, Philip:
'Dockery and Son' 185
'High Windows' 20, 175

Larrissy, Edward 12n
Levertov, Denis:
   'O Taste and See' 8
Longenbach, James 31
Lovejoy, A. O. 7–8
Lowe, Peter 68n
Lowell, Robert 10, 26, 66
   'Second Shelley' 14
Lowes, John Livingston 153

McDonald, Peter 75n, 168, 172
McGann, Jerome 5, 89, 95, 157, 158
McKendrick, Jamie 25n
MacNeice, Louis 97
   'Eliot and the Adolescent' 96–7
Mahon, Derek 10, 14, 19, 121, 134–5, 142–4
   'The Apotheosis of Tins' 143
   The Hudson Letter 143–4
   'A Lighthouse in Maine' 135
   'Sappho in "Judith's Room"' 144
Mallarmé, Stephane:
   'L'Azur' 19–20
Marvell, Andrew 119, 124
Mason, Emma 28n
Milton, John 179
   Comus 175
   Paradise Lost 114
Molino, Michael R. 132n
Montague, John:
   The Rough Field 121–3
Moody, David A. 67, 68, 73–4
Moore, Thomas:
   'Epistle VII, To Thomas Hume Esq., M. D., from the City of Washington' 158–9
Montale, Eugenio:
   'L'anguilla' 152
Muldoon, Paul 5, 10, 125
   'The Briefcase' 150, 152
   'I Remember Sir Alfred' 146
   'Madoc: A Mystery' 14, 133, 145–64
   To Ireland, I 126, 147, 148

O'Brien, Conor Cruise 37
O'Leary, John 34
Olson, Charles 190
Owen, Wilfred:
   'Exposure' 1
   'Strange Meeting' 1

Parker, Michael 132n
Paulin, Tom 122
Payley, Morton D. 72
Perloff, Marjorie 184, 190
Perry, Seamus 53n, 115

Peterfreund, Stuart 13
Plath, Sylvia:
   'Lady Lazarus' 13, 28
Phillips, Carl 179n
Pinksy, Robert 26n
Pound, Ezra 183, 184
   Cantos 33, 48n, 122
   'The Return' 78

Quinn, Antoinette 125, 126, 127
Quinney, Laura 22

Rader, Melvin M. 113n
Rainey, Lawrence 68n
Read, Herbert 101
Reeves, Gareth 70, 93
Rich, Adrienne 13
   'A Long Conversation' 23–4
Ricks, Christopher 12n, 26n, 62, 64n, 65, 70, 76n, 176
Rimbaud, Arthur 73, 102
Roberts, Andrew Michael 165, 176n
Roe, Nicholas 163
Ruoff, Gene 8
Rzepka, Charles 26n

Said, Edward 94
Schlegel, Friedrich 2
Shakespeare, William 125
   Antony and Cleopatra 69
   Hamlet 60
   Macbeth 50, 115
   Measure for Measure 174
   The Tempest 71
Shackleton, Sir Ernest 68n
Shelley, Percy Bysshe 22, 29, 34, 35, 46, 60, 61, 73, 74–6, 78, 83, 110, 184
   Adonais 13, 14, 18, 40, 43, 48, 57, 64, 65, 75, 76, 89–90, 112, 125, 135, 164, 168, 171, 182
   Alastor 17, 20, 51, 52, 63, 75, 99, 117, 121, 148, 153, 183
   The Cenci 76, 112
   'The Cloud' 27
   The Daemon of the World 61
   A Defence of Poetry 15, 16, 27, 77, 91, 99, 119, 120, 135, 139, 167, 172, 183
   Epipsychidion 55, 63–4, 69
   Hellas 56, 115
   'Hymn to Intellectual Beauty' 7, 48, 80, 92, 181
   'Julian and Maddalo' 35, 46, 75, 111, 122
   Laon and Cythna 1, 38, 139, 171
   'Lift not the painted veil' 62
   'Mont Blanc' 43, 117, 152

Index

'Ode to the West Wind' 5, 14, 31, 32, 48, 54, 68, 76–7, 79, 90, 100, 137
'On Life' 61
'On the Medusa of Leonardo da Vinci' 52
Prometheus Unbound 2, 12, 16, 20, 21, 44, 54, 58, 62, 65, 69, 73, 79, 82, 90, 100, 111–14, 117, 128, 140, 181
Queen Mab 61, 139
'The Sensitive Plant' 31, 43
'Stanzas Written in Dejection, near Naples—December 1818' 132
'To a Skylark' 2–4, 69, 108
'To Jane: "The keen stars were twinkling"' 64
The Triumph of Life 31, 34, 40, 41, 43–5, 77, 79, 81, 104, 174, 181
'With a Guitar. To Jane' 71
Sissman, L. E.:
  'Upon Finding *Dying: An Introduction*, by L. E. Sissman, Remaindered at Is' 6
Smith, Christopher J. 149
Smith, Grover 82
Smith, Stan 140
Southey, Robert 133, 146, 147, 148, 149, 156, 157
  Madoc 149
  Thalaba 159, 164
Spender, Stephen 10, 13, 83, 97–104
  'Beethoven's Death Mask' 103
  'Dolphins' 101–2
  Eliot 97
  'In railway halls, on pavements near the traffic' 101
  'I think continually of those who were truly great' 103–4
  'The Landscape near an Aerodrome' 99
  'Not palaces, an era's crown' 99–101
  'One More New Botched Beginning' 102
  Poems for Spain 1
  'Poetry and Revolution' 99
  'The Pylons' 99
  'Rejoice in the Abyss' 103
  'Rolled over on Europe' 97
  'Without that once clear aim, the path of flight' 99
  'Worldsworth' 102–3
  World Within World 83, 99
Spiegelman, Willard 26n
Stabler, Jane 158n
Stafford, Fiona 12n
Stallworthy, Jon 1
Stead, C. K. 60
Steiner, George 105
Steinman, Lisa M. 5
Stevens, Wallace 10, 13, 22, 143, 184
  Adagia 21, 31
  'Anecdote of the Jar' 30
  'Clear Day and No Memories' 18
  'The Course of a Particular' 32, 176
  'Esthétique du Mal' 13–14, 17, 19, 41, 105–20
  'Evening without Angels' 19
  'Final Soliloquy of the Interior Paramour' 33
  'Long and Sluggish Lines' 22
  'Mozart 1935' 31
  'The Noble Rider and the Sound of Words' 32
  Notes toward a Supreme Fiction 17, 19, 30
  'Of Modern Poetry' 23
  'The Plain Sense of Things' 131
  'Poem with Rhythms' 31
  'A Poet that Matters' 33
  'The Snow Man' 32, 131
  'Tea at the Palaz of Hoon' 131
  'Two or Three Ideas' 18
Synge, John Millington 42

Taylor, Charles 72
Tennyson, Alfred, Lord 108
  In Memoriam 78
  'Tears, Idle Tears' 58
Turley, Richard Marggraf 12n

Vassallo, Peter 41n, 45
Vaughan, Henry 179
Vendler, Helen 23, 26n, 109, 117, 132n, 184

Wainwright, Jeffrey 174
Wasserman, Earl R. 13
Weinfeld, Henry 20
Whitman, Walt 108
  Song of Myself 187
Williams, William Carlos 163
  'Spring and All' 14
Wills, Clair 159n, 161–2
Wolfson, Susan J. 73
Wootten, William 184
Wordsworth, Jonathan 48n
Wordsworth, William 5, 8, 14, 18, 24, 34, 46, 60, 71, 73, 76, 80, 86, 102, 115, 122, 123, 125, 136, 140, 166, 180
  'Composed upon Westminster Bridge, 3 September 1802' 33
  'Elegiac Stanzas, Suggested by a Picture of Peele Castle' 108, 177
  The Excursion 95
  Home at Grasmere 173–4
  'I Wandered Lonely as a Cloud' 6
  'Lines Written in Early Spring' 17

Lyrical Ballads 123
'Michael' 179
'Ode: Intimations of Immortality' 21, 27–8, 51, 63, 103, 108, 122, 169–70, 175, 181, 182
'Ode to Duty' 8
Peter Bell 126
'Preface to *Lyrical Ballads*' 24, 74, 121, 173, 176
'Preface to Poems (1815)' 74
The Prelude 2, 5, 9, 11, 23, 25, 52, 67, 81, 83–4, 85, 87, 91, 92, 103 108–11, 127, 128, 132, 135, 136–9, 142, 167, 171, 173
'Resolution and Independence' 74, 168, 177, 179
'The Ruined Cottage' 48
'The Solitary Reaper' 1
'Tintern Abbey' 3, 17, 25, 57, 84, 85, 92, 108, 118, 141
'The world is too much with us' 8

Yeats, William Butler 5, 6, 13, 34–59, 46, 136, 137
'Among School Children' 23, 56
'Ancestral Houses' 126
'Anima Hominis' 21
'Are You Content?' 42
'Blood and the Moon' 21
'Byzantium' 21, 58–9
'The Circus Animals' Desertion' 7, 37, 42, 71–2, 123, 127
'Coole and Ballylee, 1931' 20, 47, 50, 51–2
'Cuchulain Comforted' 45–6
'Dialogue of Self and Soul, A' 36–7
'Easter, 1916' 48, 52–3
'Ego Dominus Tuus' 13, 35–7, 39, 42, 43
'Fallen Majesty' 55
'The Fisherman' 9–10
'A General Introduction for my Work' 53
'The Gyres' 56, 57–8
Later Essays 46
'Leda and the Swan' 20, 41
'Long-legged Fly' 138
'Meditations in Time of Civil War' 21, 55, 140
'Nineteen Hundred and Nineteen' 20, 41, 54, 140
'The Nineteenth Century and After' 15
'The Philosophy of Shelley's Poetry' 20, 43, 49, 53
Per Amica Silentia Lunae 36–7, 40, 42, 46, 173
'The Poet and the Actress' 42, 43
'Prometheus Unbound' 44
Purgatory 78
'The Second Coming' 1, 56–7, 88
'The Secret Rose' 54
'September 1913' 34
'Two Songs from a Play' 7
A Vision 36, 40, 46, 47, 113

Zambon, Francesco 152